Mentoring, as my good friend Howar : of
the most powerful yet under-utilized life
would not have taken the course it di. nen
along the way. As a coach, I saw firsthand the difference between players
who had trusted mentors, and those who unfortunately did not. This
straightforward book will inspire and motivate you in a profound way. I
highly recommend it.

Tom Landry
NFL Hall of Fame, Dallas Cowboys

Howard and Bill Hendricks have produced a book much-needed in
America today. *As Iron Sharpens Iron* is a classic Hendricks approach to life.
Insightful, inspiring, and encouraging. No one will put the book down
unchanged. Great information.

Zig Ziglar
Author and Speaker

Dr. Howard Hendricks is one of my favorite people. He combines a great
wit and keen intellect in his teaching. Both Howard and Bill have provided
a much-needed message for Christians today: We all need mentors along
life's path. Their book also helps us to understand that we need to mentor
others. I highly recommend it.

Larry Burkett
Founder and President
Christian Financial Concepts

This book is a balanced combination of solid biblical principles and fascinating personal experiences. It grips you, instructs you, and excites you
about doing what God wants you to do. It makes mentoring an adventure
that leads to maturity and service.

Warren W. Wiersbe
Author and Conference Speaker

I have admired, respected, and loved Howard Hendricks for more than
forty years. As a speaker and writer on leadership and mentoring, he is
without equal. Mentoring and being mentored are among the most important but often missed relationships in life. Howard Hendricks' wisdom and
insights are a treasure, and I recommend his book with enthusiasm. This
book can change your life—and that of another.

Bill Bright
Campus Crusade for Christ International

I can think of no one in the Christian world better qualified to speak on mentoring than Howie Hendricks. I am a product of his mentoring and can honestly say that few have shaped my life as he has. In this book, Howard and Bill do a phenomenal job of challenging those who need to be mentored, as well as those who need to mentor: This is a significant book.

Ronald W. Blue
Founder and Managing Partner
Ronald Blue and Co.

An outstandingly helpful book on the powerful concept of mentoring—something every Christian needs to be involved in. A great resource.

Lorne C. Sanny
The Navigators

Howard and Bill Hendricks' book could not come at a more important time in the history of the church and our nation. There is such a need, especially in the urban community, for mentors—people who can encourage and challenge our youth and be personal examples of how to live. I strongly recommend this book.

John Perkins
Publisher
Urban Family Magazine

The process of mentoring means duplicating and even multiplying. Howie and Bill Hendricks present great insight into the entire process of mentoring. It is a book worth reading, and then doing.

Norm Sonju
COO and General Manager
The Dallas Mavericks

Anytime I can sit at Howard Hendricks' feet to learn, I'll do it. Reading this book is no exception! I cannot think of an individual more qualified by experience and insight to address effective spiritual mentoring than Howard. Here's a graphic manual, eminently practical and applicable, by one who speaks out of his experience in the fine art of mentoring. Don't miss his insights!

Ted W. Engstrom
President Emeritus
World Vision

There's a long line of men in front of me with whom I share one thing in common: Howard Hendricks is our spiritual mentor. Every Timothy has a Paul. Dr. Hendricks is a Paul to us. His iron has sharpened our ax. Lay yours upon the grinder and watch the sparks fly!

Joe White
President
Kanakuk–Kanakomo Kamps, Inc.

Bravo! Howard and Bill offer refreshing, straight talk about men's needs, our tendency to avoid them, and some down-to-earth help. I felt invited to break out of some bad habits and ruts and to form some partnerships with other men of faith. Thank you!

Pete Hammond
Director
Marketplace–InterVarsity Christian Fellowship

Mentoring is not an option, it is a necessity. Dr. Hendricks and Bill give profound yet practical insight on the priority, process, and practice of this vital need in every man's life.

Tony Evans
Author, Speaker, Senior Pastor

Howard Hendricks addresses a critical issue in today's issue in today's world with a clarity and directness that reaches both the mind and the heart.

Jerry Bridges
The Navigators

I can think of no one more qualified than Howard Hendricks to tackle this much-needed subject of men mentoring men. With his son Bill's help, Prof. Hendricks has produced a masterpiece. Men, buy and read this book! You will never be the same.

Joseph Stowell
President
Moody Bible Institute

Howard Hendricks is a mentor of mentors! Christian leaders around the world have been marked by this man. As teacher, coach, guide, and patriarch, he has mentored thousands in a ministry of multiplication. May his tribe increase! Together with his son Bill, they have captured these transferable secrets.

> John Van Diest
> President
> Vision House Publishing

This book challenges us to build into the life of another person as well as be responsive to having our life enhanced by another. It effectively convinces us that our physical, mental, and spiritual journeys of life urgently need a "Paul," a "Barnabas," and a "Timothy" relationship. You will find this book encouraging, inspiring, convicting, and enjoyable. We need it!

> Jack A. Turpin
> Founder and Chairman
> Hall-Mark Electronic Co.

As you read this book, you will learn more about the importance of relationships in the process of becoming what God wants you to be. Howard and Bill help us to understand the importance of others in the process of becoming.

> C. William Pollard
> Chairman
> The ServiceMaster Co.

For more than 35 years I have known, loved, and admired Howie Hendricks. I am not alone, He has left his mark on thousands of lives. In a real sense, only he knows the mentoring secrets that have marked men for a lifetime. I'm grateful he has decided to put into print his mentoring guidelines and techniques. They are threads drawn from the fabric of God's timeless tapestry. *As Iron Sharpens Iron* will be the classic on mentoring, I commend Howie and his son Bill for this contribution to our lives.

> Chuck Swindoll
> President, Dallas Theological Seminary
> Radio Bible Teacher, Insight for Living

Howard Hendricks is always worth listening to. Having benefited in a life-changing way from being mentored by a man thirty years my senior, I can recommend mentoring enthusiastically. *As Iron Sharpens Iron* gives you a valuable "how to" guide to the process.

> Bob Buford
> Author of Halftime: Changing Your Game
> Plan from Success to Significance

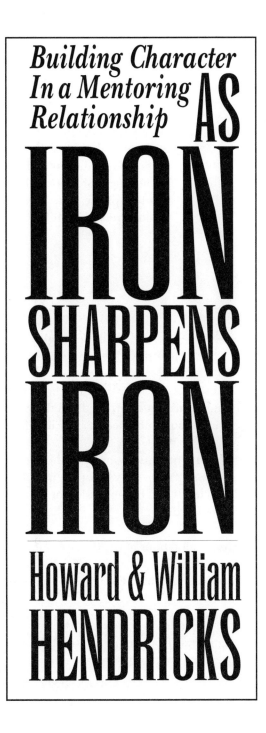

Building Character In a Mentoring Relationship **AS**

IRON SHARPENS IRON

Howard & William HENDRICKS

Moody Press, a ministry of the Moody Bible
Institute, is designed for education, evange-
lization, and edification. If we may assist you
in knowing more about Christ and the Christian life, please write us without obligation:
Moody Press, c/o MLM, Chicago 60610

ISBN: 0-8024-5631-6

Printed in the United States of America
4 6 8 10 9 7 5

Contents

Features

About the Authors

HOWARD HENDRICKS (Th.M., Dallas Theological Seminary: D.D., Wheaton College) is a distinguished professor and lecturer at Dallas Theological Seminary. He is also chairman of the Center for Christian Leadership. Dr. Hendricks has written or edited numerous books, including *Heaven Help the Home, Teaching to Change Lives, Husbands and Wives,* and the best-selling *Living by the Book.* He and his wife, Jeanne, have four grown children.

WILLIAM HENDRICKS (B.A., Harvard University; M.A., Boston University; M.A., Dallas Theological Seminary) is president of the Hendricks Group, a communications development group in Dallas. He has written or co-written many books, including *Exit Interviews, Your Work Matters to God, I Ain't Goin' Back,* and *Living by the Book.* He and his wife Nancy, have two daughters.

Introduction

A book is essentially a conversation between an author and a reader. So as we begin this conversation, we as authors feel that it will help to share some important information up front, so that you'll gain the most as you read what follows.

First, you'll notice that this book is presented in two parts. That's because mentoring is a relationship between two people, the mentor and the person being mentored (often referred to as a protégé). In our experience, there are far more men looking for mentors than there are willing to serve as mentors. So Part 1 addresses this majority group of prospective protégés. We describe the benefits of having a mentor, how to find such a guide, how to get the relationship going, and how to make the most of your interaction.

Part 2 looks at this same relationship from the mentor's point of view. In some ways, the mentor is the key to the relationship. So we explain what a mentor is and does, and then challenge men to take on that role. As in Part 1, we talk about how to get mentoring relationships established, but we spend the bulk of our time on how mentors can "structure" their time with protégés for maximum growth and benefit.

Feel free to start reading whichever part of the book seems to pertain to your immediate needs. However, be sure to read the other part of the book so that you'll have some appreciation for the other side of the relationship.

Also be sure to read "A Mentoring Action Plan" that follows the main text. Prepared by Jim Bell, our good friend at Moody Press, this workbook will help you evaluate and meet your goals in starting a developing a mentoring relationship.

In *As Iron Sharpens Iron*, we have tried to emphasize the practical rather than the theoretical, the *how* rather than the *why*. That's because our objective in writing this book, which is really just a primer on the subject, is *to get men involved in the mentoring process.* Our goal is to see hundreds and even thousands of readers develop mentoring relationships as a result of reading this material. We recognize that the theoretical foundations and the empirical research related to mentoring are important; in fact we are already at work on another book that will consider some of those things. But here the point is to get men actually involved in vital relationships with each other.

That brings us to another point: *As Iron Sharpens Iron* is addressed specifically to men. That is largely because the book was prepared to coincide with the 1995 schedule of Promise Keepers conferences, which are devoted to the needs and issues of men. Of course, mentoring is a process that can benefit women as well as men, so by targeting this discussion toward men we do not mean to exclude women. All of the concepts and principles described here probably apply equally to women as well as men, and except for a few obvious cases, female readers can probably substitute the words "woman" or "women" for the words "man" or "men," without changing the substance of what we have to say. (Our next book on mentoring will discuss the issues of mentoring for both women and men.)

Some readers—particularly those who have been Christians for a while—may assume that "mentoring" is just a fancy word for discipleship. There's no question that the two are related and overlap somewhat. But they are not exactly the same (see page 182). Nor is mentoring limited to a person's spiritual life—prayer, Bible reading, church involvement, and other religious activities. As we'll see, the influence of mentors tends to affect areas of life far beyond the personal and the religious.

In order to make this material as transferable as possible, we have included numerous illustrations of real-life people. Most of these stories have come from the literature of mentoring and from our personal experience. In a few cases, we have changed names and identifying circumstances in order to protect the privacy of the people involved.

Finally, from here on you will notice that the writing is in the first person singular ("I," "me," "my," etc.), as if only one person were speaking. The voice you hear is Howard's. This is partly because it is is much easier to write in the singular than in the plural and also because Howard has been teaching and practicing this subject for more than forty-five years. However, keep in mind that there are two authors—who happen to be father and son—working together to enlist you into our shared belief in the value of mentoring.

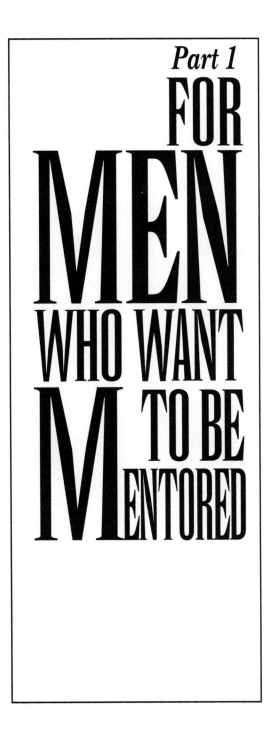

Part 1

FOR MEN WHO WANT TO BE MENTORED

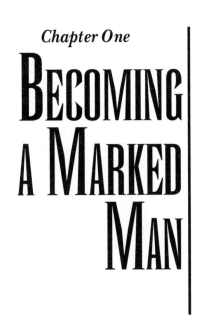

Chapter One

BECOMING A MARKED MAN

Let's begin with a question: *Who are the people who have helped to make you who you are today?*

I'm referring to the people who have *marked* you, who have made a significant impact, a lasting impression on your life. The individuals who, at a critical moment, redirected your path such that today you look back and say, "I never would have become who I am were it not for that person's influence."

Obviously, one or both of your parents may jump to mind. You may have been blessed with a father who consistently guided you with words of wisdom and modeled the qualities of love and sacrifice. Or perhaps your mother paved the way by responding to tough times with even tougher faith and character.

But I'm thinking primarily of individuals outside your family—a teacher, a youth pastor, an adult in your neighborhood, a man in your church—persons who have had little if any vested interest in your welfare, who nonetheless have invited you into their lives in a way that has indelibly marked your own life.

If you can remember someone who fits that description, then you know by experience what a deep and lasting difference a relationship like that can make. If not, I assure you that the benefits are without parallel (as we'll see shortly).

In my own life, I can recall several of these profoundly influential figures who were strategically used by God to change the course of my life. The first was a man named Walt. Had it not been for Walt, I seriously doubt whether I would have ever become a follower of Jesus Christ.

I came from a broken home. My parents were separated before I was born, and neither one paid much attention to my spiritual condition. To put it bluntly, I could have lived, died, and gone to hell without anyone even bothering to care.

But Walt cared. He was part of a tiny church in my neighborhood that developed a passion to affect its community for Christ.

"Would You Like to Play Marbles?"

Walt's passion was to reach nine- and ten-year-old boys like me with the gospel. I'll never forget the Saturday morning I met him. I was sprawled out on a Philadelphia sidewalk playing marbles. Suddenly someone was standing beside me. I looked up to see this gangly guy towering over me— all six feet, four inches of him. My mouth sort of dropped open.

"Hey, son, how would you like to go to Sunday school?" he asked.

That was an unfortunate question. To my mind, anything that had the word "school" in it had to be bad news. So I shook my head no.

But Walt was just getting started. "How would you like to play marbles?" he asked, squatting down.

Now he was talking my language!

"Sure!" I replied, and quickly set up the game. As the best marble player on the block, I felt supremely confident that I could whip this challenger fairly easily.

Would you believe he beat me in *every single game!* In fact, he captured every marble I had. In the process, he captured my heart. I may have lost a game and a bit of pride that day, but I gained something infinitely more important—the friendship of a man who cared. A big man, an older man, a man who literally came down to my level by kneeling to play a game of marbles. From then on, wherever Walt was, that's where I wanted to be.

A Ph.D. in Caring

Walt built into my life over the next several years in a way that marked me forever. He used to take me and the other boys in his Sunday school class hiking. I'll never forget those times. He had a bad heart, and I'm sure we didn't do it any good, running him all over the woods the way we did. But he didn't seem to mind, because he cared. In fact, he was probably the first person to show me unconditional love.

He was also a model of faithfulness. I can't remember a time that he ever showed up to his Sunday school class unprepared. Not that he was the most scintillating teacher in the world. In fact, he had almost no training for that. Vocationally, he worked in the tool and die trade. But he was for real, and he was also creative. He found ways to involve us boys in the learning process—an approach that made a lasting contribution to my own style of teaching.

Overall, Walt incarnated Christ for me. And not only for me, but for thirteen other boys in my neighborhood, nine of whom also came from broken homes. Remarkably, eleven of us went on to pursue careers as vocational Christian workers—which is ironic, given that Walt himself completed school only through the sixth grade. It just goes to show that a man doesn't need a Ph.D. for God to use him to shape another man.

The Preacher and His Protégé

On the other hand, God sometimes gifts a person such that every time he opens his mouth, someone somewhere seems to profit by it. Donald Grey Barnhouse had that kind of impact on me, particularly when I was just starting out in the ministry.

Dr. Barnhouse was for many years pastor of the Tenth Presbyterian Church in Philadelphia. He was a brilliant preacher and a profound interpreter of Scripture. He often said that "the size of your God determines the size of your faith." He himself had an enormous view of God, and as far as I could tell, a humongous faith. Perhaps that was his greatest legacy to me—his lofty vision of the Savior.

But he also taught me the value of clear communication. He was a master of the illustration, able to draw the most amazing analogies from the simplest of everyday experience to portray the deepest spiritual truths. I longed to do that as well as he did. So one day I asked him to show me how. His response was typically terse: "You wouldn't be willing to pay the price!"

"Of course I would," I insisted.

"Well, then, take anything on this desk in front of you and find an application in it." With that, he turned on his heel and left. For the next several hours, I sat there determined to find a useful principle in the mundane objects before me. To this day, I still engage in that discipline.

Another of his strengths was the question-and-answer session. He would give a lecture and then invite anyone in the room to fire questions at him—the more difficult, the better. I was amazed—and delighted—to watch him handle each one. The response of his listeners showed me the value of that method of teaching. In fact, I find myself gravitating toward that format in my own work as a communicator.

Would I ever have learned these lessons in another way? Who can say? What matters is that God sent Dr. Barnhouse into my life at a critical moment, just at the time when I was forming my basic approach to ministry. In a very real sense, I can say that he helped to make me who I am and that, apart from his tutelage, my life might have taken a very different direction.

Searching for a Guide

What is it that causes certain people to have such a profound influence on our lives? Is it something in them or in us—or in both of us? Do these relationships just happen—an accident of being in the right place at the right time—or can we intentionally take steps to make them happen?

Wherever I go today, I hear men, young and old, asking these kinds of questions—if not out loud, at least to themselves. They wonder, "Where can I find someone with a little more wisdom and experience than I have who would be willing to help me as I navigate my way through life?"

For example:

- An adolescent in Buffalo is trying to resist mounting pressure to join a gang in his neighborhood. His father is long gone; his older brother is in jail; his mother supports the family. This kid is as sharp as they come, and he wants to do the right thing. But he's scared. He wishes he had an older male to give him courage and practical advice.

- A college student in Boston is going after a double major in business and finance. Eventually he expects to work in corporate America.

But he also wants his life to make a difference for the cause of Christ. He's looking for a businessman who not only knows the ropes and can give him career advice and contacts but also can show him how to integrate faith with day-to-day work in a distinctive, practical way.

• In Atlanta, a young leader named Daryl Heald leads The Capital Group, an association of more than four hundred guys in their twenties and thirties who have expressed a commitment to learn how to honor God in every area of their lives. Twice within the last three years, Daryl has polled the entire group to find out how many meet on a regular basis with an older man for advice, encouragement, accountability, or prayer. In the most recent poll, only 2 percent said they did. But *the other 98 percent were unanimous* in saying they would welcome such a relationship.

• The massive demographic bulge known as the Baby Boomers starts moving into its fifties during this decade. That means that hundreds of thousands, and ultimately millions, of men will begin to ponder a series of predictable questions: *What have I accomplished? What does my life amount to? How much success is enough? What have I done that is significant? What do I care about? What am I going to do when I quit my present career? How is my life going to turn out? What will I be remembered for?*

Given the traditional way that men tend to process deeply personal matters like these, it's a fair guess that most male Boomers will try to answer these questions all by themselves. However, if given a choice, a vast number would give anything for the help of an older man.

The Very First Mentor

Wherever you turn today, you will find men looking for a guide, a coach, a model, an advisor. They are looking for someone who knows about life.

In essence, they are looking for a *mentor.* When the Greek warrior

Odysseus went off to fight in the Trojan War, he left his young son, Telemachus, in the care of a trusted guardian named Mentor. The siege of Troy lasted ten years, and it took Odysseus another ten years to make his way home. When he arrived, he found that the boy Telemachus had grown into a man—thanks to Mentor's wise tutelage.

Based on this story, we now speak of a mentor as someone who functions to some extent as a father figure (in the best sense of the term), a man who fundamentally affects and influences the development of another, usually younger, man. Later we'll define the term *mentor* more comprehensively.

For now, I invite you to return to my earlier question: *Who are the people who have helped to make you who you are today?* In other words, who have been *your* mentors? What was their contribution to your life? How much less of a man would you be right now if you had never known these people?

Mentoring Is a Must!

As you think about these individuals and the determinative impact they have had, you can quickly see why relationships with mentors are not an option for men today, but an essential. Mentors look inside us and find the man we long to be. Then they help to bring that man to life.

At their best, mentors nurture our souls. They shape our character. They call us to become complete men, whole men, and, by the grace of God, holy men. The Bible puts it this way: "As iron sharpens iron, so one man sharpens another" (Proverbs. 27:17). Have you been sharpened against the whetstone of another man's wisdom and character?

Of course, it's possible that you are among the growing number of men who say (usually with great regret), "I've never had any mentors. I can't recall anyone who took much interest in my development."

If that's true, it reflects more on the generations ahead of you than it does on you. It also bears evidence to the sad fact that people of different generations are not coming alongside each other now the way they once did. Even so, let me assure you that it's never too late to let someone influence your life. Mentoring knows no limits in terms of age or experience. If you are willing to be directed as you take responsibility for your personal growth, then you are a prime candidate for mentoring.

A Primer to Help You Get Started

This book was written to help you get started in that process. My son Bill and I will explain what a mentor is, where to find one, and how to cultivate the relationship. We'll give you practical suggestions for gleaning from another man's expertise and provide lots of real-life examples to demonstrate what we're talking about.

In Part 2, we'll turn our attention to the mentor, the man who is willing to set the pace for other men. You might be surprised to learn that the mentor stands to gain as much if not more from the relationship than the person he mentors—and even more surprised that sooner or later someone out there will probably look to *you* as a mentor in his life. Does that make you feel uneasy? Stay tuned—you may be more qualified than you think!

Our objective is straightforward: to steer as many men as we can into vital relationships that produce and reproduce men of God.

But before launching into that process, I want to show why these relationships are indeed *vital*—that is, why you can't afford to do without them as a husband, a father, a son, a grandfather, a friend, a worker, a citizen, a child of God. Mentoring relationships are vital because the world can be vicious, indeed perilous.

Miami Herald columnist Leonard Pitts, Jr., describes "the unforgiving wilderness that stretches from boys to men." I'm afraid too many of us are trying to cross that wilderness by ourselves, trying to reach personal and spiritual maturity solely on our own resources. We'll never make it that way.

Fortunately, God has provided a better way. Let's consider the benefits of mentoring in the next chapter.

Chapter Two

"I BELIEVE IN YOU"

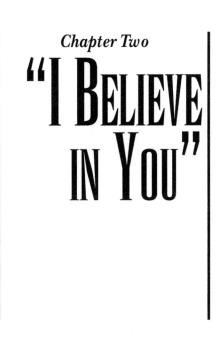

The value of mentoring derives from the value of relationships. Show me a man's closest companions and I can make a fairly accurate guess as to what sort of man he is, as well as what sort of man he is likely to become. You see, people tend to rub off on each other—again, "as iron sharpens iron."

Julius learned the truth of this principle during his teen years. Born into a single-parent family in a rough neighborhood in Denver, Julius was headed for deep trouble by the time he reached adolescence. Like many kids in those circumstances, he was aimless, angry, and, as much as anything, bored.

During one of Julius' frequent trips through the juvenile justice system for offenses such as shoplifting, vandalism, and car theft, a detention officer took him aside. "Julius, I've gotten to know you a lot more than I care to," he told him. "You have no business being in here. You could make something of your life—but not the way you're going. If I introduced you to someone who could help you stay out of trouble, would you be willing to go with him and do what he tells you?"

The Gentle Bear

In this way, Julius met Jerry, a bear of a man who had a relatively simple view of life: "Jesus said to love your brother. My brother was shot and killed during a robbery attempt when he was sixteen. So since I've got no brother of my own anymore, I've got to love somebody else's brother."

Following this approach, Jerry combed the streets of Denver, searching for teenage boys headed for trouble. Jerry had three things going for him in relating to these young men: his enormous size, which was dominating, if not intimidating; his background as a college football player, until injuries forced him from the game; and his loyalty. It was this latter quality that made a particular impression on Julius.

"He stuck with me every step of the way—and I wasn't the easiest kid to stick with," Julius recalls, looking back on his youth from the vantage of a stable marriage and family life, and a job in sales. "The first thing he did when he bailed me out of the house [the detention center] was to make me memorize his phone number. We spent an hour doing that, right there in the car, before we even went anywhere.

"I thought he was crazy. But later, I saw he was just letting me know he cared. He would be there for me. All I had to do was call. Anytime, day or night, for any reason, he said to call him.

"I remember this one time, I fell asleep on the bus. I had been up all night because one of my sisters got sick while Momma was off working. After school I went to this job that Jerry got for me, and then on the way home I dozed off. When I woke up, it was real quiet. I sat up and looked around. The bus was dark and cold, and the engine was turned off. I looked out the window, and there were all these other buses around. That's when I realized, I was in the bus pound! The driver had parked his bus and gone off without waking me up.

"So I went to the front of the bus and got the door open. Just as I stepped off, these flashlights hit me, and somebody yelled, 'Hold it right there, punk!'

"Next thing I know, four guys had me up against the bus, patting me down. It was the security guards for the pound and the transit police.

"'What's going on?' I'm asking. 'You don't understand! I fell asleep!'

"'Shut up!' they kept saying. 'We know what you've been doing.'

"It turns out that some guys had broken into the pound that night and sprayed paint all over the buses—even mine. I guess the transit police thought I was one of them, and they were going to take me in. I kept trying to explain what happened, but they kept telling me to be quiet."

Loyalty Like a Pit Bull

"Finally, while we were waiting for a car to take me downtown, I turned to one of the officers and said, 'Call Jerry Pomeroy. He'll tell you

I'm clean.'

"I guess that guy had heard of Jerry, because he sort of nodded and muttered something like, 'We'll see.' Anyway, he went off to use the phone, and I started praying that Jerry would show up.

"Pretty soon, he did. The officers started telling him their story, and then he asked me what was going on. I told him what I knew, and when I got to the part about waking up and getting off the bus, one of the policemen goes, 'C'mon! What do you take us for, kid? A parking lot full of spray painted rigs, and you're the only one running around in it! And you expect us to believe you were *asleep*?'

"'Let me see the bus,' Jerry said, and we walked over to the one I had been riding in.

"'When did you actually find him, officer?' Jerry asked.

"'Just as he was getting off. He was probably hiding inside, but we saw him stand up and walk to the front. Then he opened the door and stepped down. That's when we nailed him.'

"'Well, if he was inside the bus, how do you explain the paint on the *outside* of the doors?' Jerry asked, pointing to some lines of paint there.

"That got them to back down. And because I was with Jerry, and he was vouching for me, they let me go. After that, I had no doubts that he believed in me. Not that I didn't ever let him down. But he always believed that I didn't *have* to do wrong. He'd always say, 'Julius, God didn't make you to be bad. That's something you choose. He made you to be good. You got to live the way He planned it, man. You got to live the way *He* wants you to live.'

"You know, the more I got to know Jerry, the more I realized that things *could* be different, that I didn't *have* to get wild and do stuff that hurt other people. Jerry was like this older brother who wouldn't let me mess up my life. He *made* me go to church—which is a good thing, or I wouldn't have found the Lord. He also *made* me stay in school, and that's how I got a job.

"He used to take me and other guys up to the mountains to go fishing and camping. I can see now that one of the main reasons I stayed out of jail was because I was out of town every weekend! He knew I would just get in trouble if I stayed home, and he wouldn't allow that. He expected more of me than that. He was like a pit bull that bites down on your leg and won't let go—I mean, in a good way. Once he decided he was going to love you, man, he wouldn't let go! He just wouldn't let go!"

The Longing for Male Affirmation

Can you see the extraordinary power of a relationship? It can transform a man's life. That's why Jesus, after spending a night in prayer, chose twelve men to be "with Him" (Mark 3:13–14: Luke 6:12–13). He knew that His greatest impact would come from living side by side with hand-picked men day after day.

There is no substitute for knowing and being known by another human being. There is no other way to experience what deep down we really want as people—to be heard, to be understood, to be affirmed, to be valued. God has put into each of us a longing to be significant, to feel that our life counts. Yet countless men feel inadequate and insecure, no matter how much talent they may possess.

One of the greatest spokesmen for the cause of Christ today is Chuck Swindoll, host of the national radio broadcast "Insight for Living," for many years a pastor and now president of his alma mater, Dallas Theological Seminary, where I happen to teach. I remember when Chuck was a student. From the moment I met him, I felt, "This guy's a winner!" He was a go-getter. He always sat in the front row. His questions were extraordinarily perceptive. After class he would be up front, plying me with even more questions. It was abundantly clear that this man had a bright future ahead of him.

At least it was clear to me. For his own part, Chuck will tell you that for years he struggled with self-doubt. In fact, at times he even thought of quitting the ministry. One factor (among many) that helped him hang in there was our relationship. As Chuck puts it, "Hendricks believed in me when I didn't believe in myself!"

What a profound testimony to the fact that men today are starving for male affirmation. They need it no matter how much talent they may possess. Was there ever any doubt about Chuck's God-given pastoral gifts? Of course not. They were outstanding. Nevertheless, he still needed someone to come alongside and affirm him as a person.

That's the role of a mentor. Every man needs another man—one whom he respects—to cheer him on, to insist, "You can do it!" He needs that because of the ceaseless onslaught of negative messages telling him, "You're not smart enough," "You're not wealthy enough," "You're not strong enough," "You don't have what it takes."

Is that how you've come to feel about yourself—that you don't really have what it takes to be, say, a follower of Christ, a husband, a father, a competent worker, a man? If so, I suggest you look for a mentor, someone who can see past your fears and failures to the person God intends you to be.

Benefits of Having a Mentor

In this chapter I want to suggest five reasons why finding a mentor to influence your life will be one of the wisest moves you'll ever make. To be honest, I've known a handful of men for whom a mentoring relationship didn't work out quite the way they hoped; but I've never met anyone who regretted giving the process an honest effort. Here's why: A mentor (1) promotes genuine growth, (2) is a model to follow, (3) helps you efficiently reach your goals, (4) plays a key role in God's pattern for your growth, and (5) benefits other people in your life. Let's look at each of these benefits in turn.

A Mentor Promotes Genuine Growth and Change

The goal of every mentor should be the emotional, social, and spiritual growth of his protégé, the person he mentors. In fact, the simplest definition I know of a mentor is a person committed to two things: helping you grow and keeping you growing, and helping you realize your life goals.

Now what does it take to accomplish those two objectives? If it were merely a matter of writing down a few principles and publishing them in a book, we could transform the world in short order.

But life doesn't work that way. Only people can act and make choices and change and grow. However, for most people, growth and change simply won't happen apart from a *relationship* with someone perceived as significant who will influence their development and provide motivation and accountability.

Consider the case of Public School 121 in East Harlem, New York. If you were a sixth grader in that school in the late 1970s, the chances of your ever graduating from high school were less than 50 percent, due to the usual problems associated with poverty and life in a ghetto community—high crime, drugs, unwed pregnancies, a low value placed on education, absentee fathers, and working mothers. I'm sure that all the usual methods to keep kids in school were tried. But for the most part they failed. It became a foregone conclusion that if you attended P.S. 121, you stood a good chance of not making it.

Then in the spring of 1981, a businessman named Eugene Lang was invited to speak at commencement. Lang had graduated from P.S. 121 years before and went on to become the president of a highly successful venture capital firm. Now he faced a room of sixty-one kids who basically had no future. What could he possibly have to say to them?

Lang pocketed the stuffy speech he had prepared and threw out a simple but powerful proposition: for any kid who stayed in school and graduated, Lang would pick up the tab for a college education.

The offer stunned and then galvanized those kids. According to the statistics, only thirty of them could be expected to make it to their senior year of high school. In fact, fifty-two of them did. Thirty-four of those went on to college, and the rest graduated from high school or received equivalency degrees and became productive citizens holding down steady jobs.

What made the difference? Was it the money? Not really. As a *New York Times* editorial later explained, "[Lang's] gift of money is less important than his gift of himself—a hands-on philanthropy. . . .

"As he relates it, he realized soon after making the commitment that putting up money was the easy part. More difficult, but every bit as important was to invest time [in] personal attention to the students, whose ghetto backgrounds fit them precisely for the description, 'disadvantaged.' Mr. Lang . . . welcomed the students in his corporate offices and became their true patron."[1]

Can you see how Lang created a *personal* bond between himself and those kids? He said, in effect, "I'll believe in you," and then backed up that pledge by placing himself on the line to see that they had a chance to succeed. While everyone else was telling them, "You'll never make it!"

Lang told them, "You *can* make it—and I'll help."

That's the power of a mentoring relationship. If you know someone really cares, you are much more likely to give your best effort rather than disappoint. But if you're swimming against the tide all by yourself, chances are you'll just give up.

A Mentor Provides a Model to Follow

Several summers ago our family held a reunion of sorts at Lost Valley Ranch in Colorado. During our week-long stay, my older son, his wife, and my son-in-law signed up for a class in fly-fishing. Taught by one of the country's premier guides, the instruction culminated in an all-day fishing expedition on a world-class trout stream in the Rockies.

My three fishermen will tell you that that outing was an unforgettable experience. But as you might guess, they didn't start out on that stream. In fact, their guide kept them away from water of any kind until the third session.

You see, fly-fishing is an art. It's not something a person is born knowing how to do. It takes an experienced angler to initiate the novice into the sport. The most important part of the process is watching while the guide demonstrates the graceful rhythm of the cast, from the 10 o'clock position to the 2 o'clock, back and forth, back and forth. Then after a while he hands the rig to the novice and says, "You try it."

This is the principle of modeling, and learning almost any complex skill requires it. In fact, Albert Bandura, the renowned psychologist who taught for many years at Stanford University, claims that most human behavior is learned observationally through modeling. His pioneering work in this field has shown that modeling is the greatest form of unconscious learning there is.

For example, scores of books have been written in recent years on fathering. But none of them has made or can make anywhere near the impression that a real, live father makes on his children. Whatever patterns your father established, whether good or bad, healthy or unhealthy, those are the basic patterns you are going to repeat with your own children, at least initially. Your experience of your own father is what "father" means to you.

Of course, the reality is that more and more men today need to find a different model of a father. Their own fathers painted a flawed portrait of how a man should relate to his family—often because they, in turn, lacked a suitable model to follow. If this describes your situation, I challenge you to seek out, among other mentors, a man who demonstrates at least something of Christlikeness in regard to his family. Otherwise you will almost certainly repeat with your own children the very things that you hated about your own background.

The principle of modeling is underscored by the doctrine of the Incarnation, the truth that God became flesh. Of the infinity of ways that an infinite God could have revealed Himself to humanity, His primary means was through a human being, Jesus Christ. Jesus was God in the flesh, as well as the perfect model of godliness.

This incarnational truth is woven into the fabric of the New Testament. For example, Philip asked Jesus, "Show us the Father," to which He replied, "Anyone who has seen me has seen the Father" (John 14:8–9). Later, Peter pointed out that Jesus left us an example of godly endurance, "that you should follow in his steps" (1 Peter 2:21).

Likewise, Paul urged the Corinthians, "Follow my example, as I follow the example of Christ" (1 Corinthians 11:1). And he and his companions intentionally declined any remuneration from the Thessalonians but instead worked hard to earn their own living, "in order to make ourselves a model for you to follow" (2 Thessalonians 3:7, 9).

God always wraps His truth in a person. That's the value of a godly mentor. He shows what biblical truth looks like with skin on it.

A Mentor Helps You to Reach Your Goals More Efficiently

Have you ever walked through an airport terminal and stepped onto a moving sidewalk? Suddenly you are whizzing along at two or three times your normal pace, even though you are keeping the same stride. It's an amazing feeling.

That's a good analogy for how a mentor can help you pick up the pace of your personal development. He can save you time and energy in reaching your goals. He can accelerate your progress because he knows things you don't know. He has friends and acquaintances that you don't have. Often he can open doors that you couldn't budge. Most important, he asks questions that you never considered. You may be making good progress already as you walk along through life. But when he joins you, your pace can quicken, and your progress can seem a lot easier.

A student I'll call Jay was recently invited by an extremely successful company president to fly with him in his corporate jet from Dallas to Chicago. This man is so respected in the business world that any junior executive in town would give his right arm just to get time with him.

Imagine Jay's surprise, then, when during the trip this industry leader turned to him and said, "I want to make a deal with you. I'll teach you everything I know about business if you'll teach me everything you know about the Bible."

What an opportunity! Jay has often told me of his desire to know more about the business world so that he can have a more relevant ministry to laymen. If he pursues that relationship, he's going to learn more about business in three months than any MBA program could teach him in three years. In turn, the business executive will make tremendous strides in his understanding of the Bible.

A Mentor Plays a Key Role in God's Pattern for Your Growth

Earlier I mentioned how God used a man named Walt to bring me to faith in Christ. Actually, Walt was only one of many factors. It would be a mistake to overlook the people in Walt's church who were praying for their community. Likewise, my grandmother was also praying for me. And let's not forget the person who shared the gospel with Walt himself.

God always uses a matrix of influences to carry out the process of conversion. In the same way, he always uses a matrix of influences to help believers mature in Christ: the Word, the home, the local church, experiences in ministry, crises and conflicts, books, tapes, and conferences, to name just a few.

A mentor can play a vital role in this maturity matrix—by no means the only role, but a vital one. For example, think of the strategic role that Barnabas played in Paul's life just after his conversion. None of the Christians at Jerusalem wanted to associate with Paul (then known as Saul). They didn't trust their former enemy. No matter how hard he tried, he could not break into their circle. "But Barnabas took him and brought him to the apostles" (Acts 9:27). That broke the ice and essentially launched Paul's spiritual formation.

God intends that you develop under the helpful influence of seasoned believers. Hebrews 13:7 says, "Remember your leaders, who spoke the word of God to you. Consider the outcome of their way of life and imitate their faith." That's a mandate for modeling and mentoring.

By the way, notice that the passage speaks in terms of *leaders* (plural). Ideally, you should seek out a variety of influencers during your life, not just one. That way you get a broad perspective.

A Mentor's Influence Benefits Others in Your life

The final reason why you need to pursue mentoring relationships is that the benefits go far beyond your own personal needs. Your spouse, your family, your church, your community, your coworkers and others where you work—everyone you touch stands to gain by whatever strides you make as a result of the growth process.

Recall Eugene Lang's influence on the students of P.S. 121. The postscript to that story is that Lang himself was the product of a mentoring relationship. After graduating from high school, he worked at a menial, dead-end job until an older friend recognized his potential and offered to pay for his college education. In other words, someone believed in Eugene Lang and made a personal commitment to further his development. Do you think that person's timely contribution had anything to do with Lang's offer to those kids?

Just imagine the return on that initial investment. It blessed Lang with an education. In turn, that made it possible for Lang to eventually run a productive business that not only employed his own people but, as a venture capital firm, created jobs for countless other people.

Imagine, in turn, the return on Lang's investment in the fifty-two kids who made it through high school. Instead of ending up on the streets in gangs or on drugs or in jail, fifty-two kids became contributing members of society.

Can you see the beauty of allowing someone to rub off on you in a positive, significant way? Even as you are blessed, you become a channel through which God blesses others. That's why Paul instructed Timothy not only to emulate him but to pass on the things he had learned "to reliable men who will also be qualified to teach others" (2 Timothy 2:2). The apostle was describing a process of spiritual reproduction.

Mentors—An Invaluable Lifeline

Do we need that process today? More than ever! Too many men are trying to go it alone in terms of their marriage and family life, their personal life, their work, or their spiritual commitments. They are trying to scale mountains of Himalayan proportions solely on the strength of rugged independence.

It won't work. Men need mentors, seasoned guides to help them along the way. Bobb Biehl of Masterplanning Group International has pointed out that mentoring is like a group of men scaling a mountain. If a guy is linked to another guy above him, and that man in turn is linked to other men farther up the cliff, then together they have safety, stability, and strength. If a man slips and begins to fall, fifteen or twenty climbers absorb the impact and pull him back from disaster.

But imagine a man climbing alone, with no support system. He may achieve great heights. But one wrong move and he can fall thousands of feet to his death, without so much as anyone hearing his cry. That's why Scripture says, "Two are better than one because they have a good return for their labor. For if either of them falls, the one will lift up his companion. But woe to the one who falls when there is not another to lift him up" (Ecclesiastes 4:9–10, NASB).

The tragedy is that more and more people in our society are traveling through life as Lone Rangers. They are placing less and less value on their relationships, with the result that each succeeding generation experiences greater isolation, loneliness, and even despair.

Do you want to change that? It starts with you. Decide right now to begin looking for a mentor, someone who is committed to helping you grow and keeping you growing, and to helping you realize your life goals. Refuse to believe the lie of the devil that says only weak men need help. The truth is, it is men who seek help who become strong.

How do you find a mentor? I'll give you some pointers in the next chapter.

PEER MENTORING

Mentoring relationships take many different forms. Perhaps the one familiar to most people is when an older person (the mentor) guides, tutors, coaches, or otherwise influences a younger person (the protégé) in a profound, lasting way. This is the sort of relationship that Mentor had with Telemachus and that Paul had with Timothy. In this book, when we talk about "mentoring," we generally are referring to this sort of mentor/protégé relationship.

However, the more one investigates the practice of mentoring in our society, the more one finds an interesting phenomenon: many of the characteristics that define mentor/protégé relationships are also taking place among people who are basically the same age—within five or six years of each other. At first one is tempted to describe these simply as friendships, but they are actually peers mentoring each other. Peer mentoring has enormous benefits, and I strongly encourage you to pursue these kinds of relationships.

Illustrations of Peer Mentoring

Two examples from Scripture of peer mentoring are Jonathan and David, and Barnabas and Paul. An outstanding contemporary example is the long-term relationship that has existed between Jerry White, president of The Navigators, and Fred Hignell III, president of a real estate development and management company. Here's how Jerry describes their relationship: "Fred and I met more than ten years ago through a mutual friend. . . .

"We had several common traits: an engineering background, a strong choleric personality, a commitment to reach our friends for Christ, and a deep desire to be godly men, husbands, and fathers.

"Early on in our friendship we began by discussing our goals for our family, personal lives, and jobs. We traded specific prayer requests. We had no verbal commitment of our accountability. Yet accountability was implicit. And as we became more frank with each other, we developed a trust that fostered additional openness. Accountability was the result, not the initial intent."[1]

Encourage, Enhance, and Motivate

Now compare Fred's journey up the other side of the mountain: "As I began to grow in my spiritual walk, and as God brought men with spiritual depth into my life, being a 'lone ranger' became less attractive.

"I began to realize that to remain teachable as I got older, and to end well in my Christian walk, I needed to develop one or more relationships that would require me to be open and vulnerable.

"When my friendship with Jerry began, I was not looking for an accountability relationship. But as we spent time together, I saw he was a man with whom I could be transparent, who would keep a confidence, with whom I could share my 'paddle.'

"Jerry and I are goal-oriented, so our accountability began with discussing our annual goals and then following up to track our progress. After we attended a conference where the speaker advocated developing significant accountability relationships, we defined a clear purpose for our relationship: 'to encourage, enhance, and motivate each other to love Jesus with all our heart, soul, and mind, and to finish life without dishonoring God's name.'"[2]

Indispensable Help in Deep Waters

Jerry and Fred can tell you about numerous times when their lives have definitely been "sharpened" against each other's wisdom. They have seen each other through career changes, major life decisions, and family troubles. One of the most gripping moments in their friendship, and one that reveals the incredible worth and power of peer mentoring, was the tragic murder of Jerry's thirty-year-old son Steve, who was shot to death while driving a cab in Colorado Springs.

"[My wife Mary and I] sped home in shock to find Fred already there to help," Jerry recalls, "sharing our desperation and grief. . . . We lived numbly through the days of memorial services, over-whelmed by the complications of this terrible event.

"Fred, his wife, Kaylinn, and [two other couples] literally guided our lives during those days. But I especially needed someone to look to and pray with. Fred was there; he helped me think things through and even suggested decisions.

"Most of my life I had been the strong one, self-sufficient, helping others through hard times. Now I really needed others. I was weak and unsure where my emotions would be from day to day— guilt, sorrow, fear, or just weariness. Fred sensed my mood and shared Scripture or just prayed.

"Even after Fred returned to Chico, he called almost daily to check on me. He kept me accountable on cutting back my travel schedule. He warned me that I could not carry on with 'business as usual.'. . .He kept me accountable on several aspects of my recovery from grief. He would ask how much sleep I was getting and if I was beginning to exercise again.

"Fred did a lot of listening, and at times, he gave strong counsel. His help was indispensable."[3]

Can you feel the depth of that relationship? That's what can happen when men of similar ages pursue vital relationships with one another.

Chapter Three

KNOW WHAT YOU NEED

It's a documented fact in the retailing industry that men and women approach shopping in fundamentally different ways. Women tend to "shop around," visiting store after store, comparing values, prices, and personnel. When they finally find just the right combination of factors, they *may* make a purchase—but not necessarily. They are just as likely to say, "I think I'll look around."

Men, on the other hand, tend to shop in a highly targeted way. They decide on what they want. They decide on the store that has what they want. They go to the store. They find the item. They pay their money. And the shopping "event" is over. Get in and get out. That's the male pattern.

This is especially true at Christmas. A guy will wait until December 22, 23, or maybe even the afternoon of the 24th before he rouses himself to go buy his presents. He walks into a store, grabs a few items, plunks down his credit card, and goes home. (As a result, a man will tend to spend considerably more on Christmas gifts than his wife.) As one retailer described it, men don't see Christmas shopping as fun unless they are racing the clock. "It's crisis management!" she says.

I'm not going to debate the wisdom or folly of that approach. But I would point out that its success lies in a man knowing what he intends to buy. If he is clear on that, half the battle is won. He can go shopping just days (or even hours) before Christmas, confident that things will work out because he knows exactly what he's looking for. All that remains is to go out and find it.

The same is true with finding a mentor. The key is knowing what you need. In the last chapter I offered five reasons why mentoring relationships are vital to personal and spiritual growth. But it is unlikely that you will seek out a mentor until you have identified ways in which a mentor would be vital to *your* growth. You see, the issue is not whether I think mentoring is a good idea; that's self-evident. What matters is whether *you* are convinced of your need for the process.

I'm suggesting that your search for a mentor begins, not out in the world shopping the "marketplace of mentors," but with you. You must assess your own needs to determine what sort of mentor you should look for.

"Know Thyself"—Easier Said Than Done

Unfortunately, many men find self-assessment to be a difficult, if not a dead-end, process. In the first place, people often lack insight into themselves. Jesus was aware of this tendency, because he asked His followers, "Why do you look at the speck of sawdust in your brother's eye and pay no attention to the plank in your own eye?" (Matthew 7:3). We can all point out where others need help. We tend to be blind to—or unwilling to recognize—our own liabilities.

In other words, we lack objectivity. We often can't distinguish between our perceptions and reality. I've had men in my office declare with absolute certainty that their marriages were solid as a rock, only to watch them return a week later falling apart at the seams because their wives had walked out on them. They were blind to how bad the relationship had actually become.

Or take the case of Michael Ovitz, a well-known and highly successful agent in the entertainment industry, who was recently mentioned in the "Intelligencer" column of *New York* magazine. The columnist was passing on the gossip that Ovitz was now working from his Brentwood Park, California, home rather than his Beverly Hills office. For whatever reason, the item referred to this decision as "more evidence that everybody is getting into the spend-quality-time-with-the-family trend."

To everyone's surprise, the following letter soon arrived at *New York* magazine, signed by Ovitz's three kids:

We are avid readers of *New York* magazine, and so we were most interested in the December 12 edition of your "Intelligencer" column

["Ovitz In; Shapiro Out"] revealing the newly acquired nesting habits of our father, Michael Ovitz.

As it has been years since we have seen him at home on a weekday, we would be most grateful if you could reveal to us the exact vantage point from which our neighbors achieved these reported sightings. Indeed, catching a look at Dad in daylight, at home, on the odd Tuesday or Wednesday, would be well worth the few hours of surveillance necessary to record this historic event.

We thank you very much for consideration of our request and again please know how much we are looking forward to reading about Dad's comings and goings in your fine publication.[1]

Do you need a wake-up call like that? As men, we tend to get so focused on our various pursuits that we develop tunnel vision. We can become experts in our vocations and avocations but ignorant about ourselves—especially our weaknesses.

And even when we do gain greater self-knowledge, many of us don't know what to do with it. This is the Achilles' heel of the self-help movement. People will go through all sorts of inventories and assessments to help them identify various traits and tendencies. (Some of these can be quite useful.) Yet when all is said and done, participants are liable to respond, "OK, I now know XYZ about myself. Great! How can I use that to get a job . . . find a mate . . . succeed in life?" The information may be accurate, but rather than using it to mature in their character or work on bad habits, many men tend to use it pragmatically to accomplish a task at hand. And even those men who seek emotional or spiritual growth often do not know how.

In short, it's easier said than done to follow through on the ancient dictum, "Know thyself." We can become so focused on using self-evaluation to accomplish a task—getting a job, finding a wife, achieving professional success—that we forget to apply it to maturing as men.

That's another reason why it helps to have a mentor. Not only can he guide you into greater insight, he can help you translate that insight into action. Furthermore, he can motivate you to action, and, equally important, hold you accountable for what you do or do not do.

Discovering Your Needs

Yet that presents a Catch-22: I've suggested that you need to assess your needs in order to find a mentor, yet you need a mentor to help you assess your real needs.

Let me help you out of that quandary by serving as something of a mentor to you (through this book) by posing five fundamental questions designed to bring to the surface your areas of need. These are the kinds of questions I usually put to men who come my way looking for help and guidance. How would you answer each of them?

1. What do you want?

The purpose for asking yourself "What do I want?" is to discover your objectives. What are you trying to accomplish? In seeking a mentor, you are essentially asking a man to make a lasting difference in your life. So the question is, In what way do you want him to make a difference? What tangible outcome would you like to see from the relationship?

One way to clarify your objectives is to ask, "Where do I want my life to be in ten years?" Describe what you would like to see yourself become. Then ask, "What will it take to achieve that?" Follow that question with another important one, "What stands between me and that outcome?"

For example, Peter, age twenty-six, decided that in ten years he wanted to be holding down a stable job, supporting a family. At the time, he was in an entry-level position in his company, and he was unmarried and dating no one seriously. Peter's objectives may sound simple, but they helped him identify people in his company

> ### A.W. TOZER'S RULES OF SELF-DISCOVERY
>
> The late A.W. Tozer, an imminent theologian who for years challenged and prodded the body of Christ to action, suggested seven areas that reveal our values and our true commitments:
>
> 1. What we want most.
> 2. What we think about most.
> 3. How we use our money.
> 4. What we do with our leisure time.
> 5. The company we enjoy.
> 6. Whom and what we admire.
> 7. What we laugh at.

who could guide him in a career path there, as well as network him to others outside the organization. His objectives also helped him reflect on the qualities he desired in a wife, which became useful not only in his dating relationships but also in discussions about women and marriage with an older, married man at his church.

Another man, named George, took stock of his life at age forty. He realized that he had achieved most of his business goals and in ten years would probably be retired. The prospect that he might spend the rest of his life on a golf course scared him so badly that he literally sat down and wrote up a different vision of what he wanted to be doing at age fifty, based on his resources, values, and commitments. He determined to make his expertise in business and management available to pastors, because he often found these to be major problem areas for them. That gave him a blueprint for structuring his time and for seeking out men who could help him achieve his vision.

Another way to uncover your objectives is to take an inventory of the basic categories of your life: your work, your marriage and family, your spiritual life, your relationship to your church, and your involvement in the community at large. How would you evaluate yourself in each of those areas? What "grade" or "score" might you receive in each of them? Be honest, and list the chronic problem areas. Then ask the hard questions: "Where do I feel inadequate?" and "Where do I experience repeated failure?" If you keep digging to answer those questions, you should be able to surface some places in your life where you need to grow.

A third way to identify your objectives is to think in terms of four levels of human competency: knowledge, attitudes, habits and behaviors, and skills. In other words, what knowledge or information do you wish to acquire that you don't currently possess? What attitudes or values do you feel you must cultivate? What habits and behaviors are you trying to establish or break? What practical skills do you wish to develop?

Here are some examples of what I'm talking about. If you are making statements like these, it suggests areas where you want to develop.

Knowledge
- "I don't know how to go about buying a house."

- "I don't have an overall grasp of the Bible. I want someone to teach me what the Bible is all about."

Attitudes
- "I want to become more generous. I have so much, but I find myself holding onto everything with a tight grip."
- "I struggle with racial prejudice. I need help to change my attitudes."

Habits and Behaviors
- "I tend to 'mouth off' at people, and I want to break that habit."
- "I feel I need to pray more."

Skills
- "I need to learn to use a computer."
- "I need to know how to interview prospective employees."

As you think about your needs and objectives, it helps to distinguish between immediate crises and ongoing concerns. For example, if someone has filed a lawsuit after slipping on your walkway, your immediate need is for a lawyer, not a mentor. Later, as you prepare to defend yourself, you might seek the counsel of a man who has been through a similar courtroom case, finding out how he handled the situation.

Likewise, if your wife has just informed you that she is involved with another man, your immediate need is for a marriage counselor, not a mentor. Later, after the situation has stabilized, you would benefit from the wisdom of a man who understands something of what you have been through. (Of course, if you already have a mentor, that's an ideal time to turn to him for insight, support, and advice.)

The point is that the best use of a mentor is for fundamental, long-term growth and development. If you already have a mentor, he can be invaluable when you are facing a crisis. But a crisis is not the best time to look for a mentor, because your focus is on fixing an immediate problem, not addressing long-term objectives or core issues.

2. What price are you willing to pay?

Once you have clarified what you want to accomplish, you need to establish those objectives as priorities. It does no good to state what you need if you have no intention of doing what it takes to meet that need. That may require some sacrifice on your part.

I remember standing out on the practice field of the Dallas Cowboys several years ago with the head coach, Tom Landry. It was dusk. The team had worked hard. Now they were in the clubhouse, showering up from the day's practice.

I asked Coach Landry, "How many of these guys really have the potential to be All Pro?"

"We don't take any guys that don't," he replied, much to my amazement. Then he continued, "The deeper question is, how many will actually *become* All Pro? The answer is, only the ones who are willing to pay the price."

Then he pointed out on the field. "There's an All Pro tight end."

Sure enough, Jackie Smith was out there catching passes from one of the assistant coaches. It was now almost dark, but this guy was purposely running the routes so that he could literally catch balls he couldn't see.

Coach Landry taught me that there is no magic about a ball player earning enough respect from his peers to be voted All Pro. It's a matter of hard work. Doing what it takes. In a similar way, if you've set realistic, achievable goals for your life, don't look for some sort of magic to enable you to reach them. It's a matter of hard work—focused, directed work under your mentor's tutelage.

The question is not just what do you want, but how badly do you want it? Wendell, a busy graduate student, sought out a man in his church to meet with him regularly and hold him accountable for his prayer life.

"Fine, when do you want to meet?" the man asked.

"Well, I've got a pretty hectic schedule," Wendell replied.

"That's OK. Let's do it early in the morning, before your day stacks up. Say, 6:30."

"Six-thirty!" the student gasped.

"Is that too late?" the man asked, sincerely assuming that the fellow was already booked at 6:30. "We can do it at 6:00 if that's more workable. Or even earlier."

Finally Wendell admitted that he usually didn't get out of bed until 7:45 at the earliest.

"Are you sure you want to get together?" the man responded with doubt in his voice.

It was a fair question—the sort of question you need to ask yourself before you invite someone else to give you his time. Suppose he takes you seriously and offers to do *whatever* it takes to help you accomplish your objectives. Are you prepared to pay the same price?

3. How do you plan to accomplish your objectives?

Most of us don't plan to fail, we fail to plan. As you prepare to approach someone for help with your needs, I suggest that you come up with at least a rough idea of the means you plan to use to accomplish your objectives. This involves thinking through the details such as *who* else you feel might need to be involved in the process, *what* you might need to pursue your efforts, *when* you intend to execute your plans, and *where* this is all going to take place.

Your prospective mentor may modify these plans, but don't ask him to do all your thinking for you. Show up with a proposal, not a blank piece of paper. I'm not suggesting a formal, tightly scripted document (though that might not be a bad idea in some cases). Just show that you have thought things through. It's OK not to have all the final details. It is not OK to approach someone and say, "Hi, I'm looking for a mentor," and expect him to take it from there.

Bill was recently approached by a friend who said she wanted to work on her writing. She knew that Bill has expertise in this area, so she asked if he would critique some samples of her work. He agreed, and she sent him three essays that she had written, one of which had been published in her church's newsletter. In a note accompanying the essays, she said that she was aware that Bill was under a tight deadline on a project, and there was no rush for him to read through her material.

Now that was a good plan—a simple plan, to be sure, but clear and effective nonetheless. The woman told Bill what she wanted, what he could do, and what her expectations were in regard to the time frame involved.

(The interesting punch line to this story is that eventually Bill sent her back some comments on her writing, and an invitation to send more, which she did. At the end of the year, she alluded to Bill in her Christmas letter to family and friends as a "mentor" in regard to her writing. Bill was initially taken aback by the use of this term. But the more he thought about it, the more he realized that he was acting in the role of a mentor. By his willingness to participate in this person's plan, he was having a marked influence on her motivation and technique as a writer.)

4. What is your personal dynamic?

Knowing yourself means just that—knowing *yourself*. It means recognizing and affirming your personality and temperament, your natural bent, and the instinctive ways in which you relate to others. Your relationship with a mentor will be a deeply personal experience, so your personal traits ought to weigh heavily as you search for a prospective mentor. You'll want to carefully consider how those traits fit (or clash) with the traits of someone with whom you may be spending a great deal of time.

Looking for a mentor is a bit like looking for love. There's a chemistry involved. It's not just a mechanical pairing of an older man with a younger man. That's one reason why formal mentoring programs in corporations and other organizations sometimes founder. They throw two strangers together and then wonder why communication, trust, and respect don't happen.

The key is knowing your personal dynamic. For instance, do you focus primarily on tasks or relationships? Do you tend to be outgoing or introverted? Are you more fascinated by ideas or by people? Are you characterized by high energy or low? Do you arrive at conclusions by investigating and analyzing all the facts, or more by intuition? Are you willing to play your role, whether it's the quarterback (in charge), or a lineman (dedicated player)? Are you motivated by gaining recognition or by meeting a challenge (or some other drive)? Are you a morning dove or a night owl?

There are dozens of questions like these that might be considered in evaluating your personal style. There is also a growing number of assessments available to measure some of these things (see pp. 177–178).

But don't get hung up on psychological instruments or introspective navel-gazing. You are going to learn far more about yourself through your relationship with a mentor than through any personality test or profile.

Still, it helps to have some idea of who you are as you try to establish that relationship.

Let me illustrate why. My late friend, Trevor Mabery, was a brilliant surgeon. He was also an invaluable mentor to countless doctors practicing medicine today. Occasionally I would tag along as he took a group of medical students on his rounds at the hospital. His bedside manner was a work of art. He would take time with the patient to explain the surgical procedures, answer any questions, and even pray. Then outside the room he would turn to his students and explain his methods. He took their questions, and then posed a few of his own. He had a relational style of mentoring that worked well with young doctors who needed explanation, encouragement, and a reminder that medicine is about treating people, not just "cases."

Contrast that to Dr. Donald Barnhouse, whom I mentioned earlier. He was without peer in helping young ministers grasp a concept of the Almighty. But he could be severe and brusque in relating to people. I remember one time he asked me to drive him to a speaking engagement at the First Presbyterian Church of Tyler, Texas. As he prepared to give his message, he invited the congregation to bow with him in prayer. At that point, the organist began to play. Dr. Barnhouse stopped right in the middle of his prayer, turned to the organist, and said, "Hold it, lady! I love music. I love prayer. I hate music and prayer!" Needless to say, she let him continue a cappella.

Then there was the time he introduced a mainline denominational official, with whom he sharply disagreed, as "a first-class promoter, a second-class psychologist, and no preacher of the gospel at all!" On another occasion, he was asked to give the charge at the installation service of a new Presbyterian pastor. "*Never* become a moderator of the presbytery," he warned the man, "because then you will *have* to compromise." The remark might have been overlooked had not the moderator of the presbytery been sitting right there on the platform!

Barnhouse always said what he thought, whether it was politically correct or not. So at least you always knew where you stood. But if you were the sort of person who needed a lot of empathy, patience, and handholding, he was not your man.

As you begin to scout out potential mentors, pay attention to your personal dynamic. You need not find someone exactly like you. In fact, you will benefit more from someone who complements your personality and has strengths in areas where you don't. But unless you can flex and roll with the punches, you may be asking for trouble if you latch onto someone who is your polar opposite in terms of temperament, relational style, and natural bent.

5. How do you learn?

In some ways, the question of learning style may be the most important of all. Mentoring is a developmental process, which means that you are constantly going to be on a learning curve. You'll surmount that curve a great deal faster if you know how you learn best.

Unfortunately for most of us, our educational system has not been of much help in this regard. It tends to define "learning" as the ability to regurgitate a set of notes on an exam. In fact, somewhere along the way, you may have had an experience like this one: You show up to an exam and find the question, "Discuss such-and-such." So you discuss it. Then at the next class you get your exam back, and there's a big, fat "C" on it!

Now, to be honest, you weren't really expecting an "A." But you certainly didn't expect a "C," either. Furthermore, as you read over your essay and check it with your class notes, you start thinking, "How in the world could I have gotten a 'C'? I wrote exactly what he told us in class!"

So you make an appointment to see the professor. You explain your problem, and he looks back over what you have written.

"Well, is it wrong?" you finally ask.

And he says, "No, it's not really *wrong*. But your problem is, you didn't state it in the words which I gave in class."

Does that make you crawl the walls the way it does me? That's intellectual dishonesty! You see, what that professor really wants—and should say so on the exam—is a restatement of his own words. The question should read, "Please state, *in my words only* (PLEASE NOTE: NO OTHER WORDS WILL BE ACCEPTABLE)..."

As a seminary professor, I'm not the least bit interested in whether my students can parrot back to me what I've said in class. I want to know whether they can produce in the area to which God has called them. If all they've got is a set of class notes, they'll run out of gas in short order. But if I've helped them *learn how to learn,* they can essentially keep going forever.

In what way do you learn best? Some people are readers. To them, a library card is the key to the kingdom. Other people learn by doing. They have to have a hands-on experience before they grasp the subject. Others can learn only in a group setting. They thrive on stimulation from other people and by being part of a team. Other people learn primarily by watching someone else demonstrate the activity, and then they try it themselves. There are all manner of learning styles. Knowing yours is the best thing you can do for your personal growth and development.

Here's an exercise to help you identify your unique approach to learning. Imagine that you have received some new piece of equipment that you have never used before—a bicycle, a pair of skis, a computer, whatever. How would you go about learning to use that equipment? Would you open up the owner's manual and read it cover to cover? Or would you be more likely to ignore the manual and figure it out by trial and error? Would you call up a friend and ask him to show you how the thing works? Or would you enroll in a class for instruction?

There is no "right" or "wrong" way to learn. The question is, How do *you* learn? What works best for you? If you think through your history, you should be able to identify the times when you really got hold of some new body of information, or some new skill—as well as the times when you learned the least. Your ideal learning style is a clue as to what sort of person can best help you obtain your objectives, and under what circumstances.

Objectives. Priorities. Means. Personal dynamic. Learning style. The more you know about yourself in these areas, the more successful you'll tend to be at finding, recruiting, and benefiting from a suitable mentor. Answering these questions will help you know whether you are ready for a mentor, and if so, what sort of person you should look for. It will also help you evaluate whether you are the sort of person a mentor is looking for—a question I'll discuss in the next chapter.

Chapter Four

WHAT MENTORS LOOK FOR

One of the annual rites of spring is the National Football League's draft of college players. Other professional sports have drafts, but whether any of them quite compares to the NFL's in either size or excitement is debatable. In my city, Dallas, the NFL draft has become such a big deal that one radio station broadcasts the entire selection process live from first round to last, with color commentary in between the picks.

The point of a draft is to give all the teams in a league a reasonably fair shot at acquiring the athletes they believe will work best in their systems, based upon their respective draft positions. Of course, with such developments as free agency and salary caps, selecting the right players has become a sophisticated art. Yet when you think about it, professional drafts are really no different from boys on a sandlot or a basketball court choosing up sides for a game. In both cases, the point is to get the best players.

A Selection Process

I'm afraid a similar situation prevails in the "mentoring draft." I don't want to overstate anything, but I do want to be frank. Far more men are looking for a mentor today than there are mentors looking for men to influence. I wish that were not the case, and my prayer is that books like this one and other efforts will turn that around. But for now, it's a fact of life that for every man willing to serve as a mentor, there may be a hundred men looking to be mentored.

That means that there is an inevitable selection process taking place. Men who are worthy of assuming a mentoring role tend to be oversubscribed. As a result, they have to pick and choose where they are going to invest their time.

They cannot take all comers. (By the way, if this sounds unfair, perhaps it is. But remember that Jesus Himself *chose* twelve men out of the hundreds who followed Him.)

This puts the job of finding a mentor in an entirely different light. Up until now, I've been speaking of this search as if you go out, interview a bunch of candidates, and then make your selection. But the truth of the matter is that the mentor is more likely to do the selecting. Therefore, the question is, how can you avoid being dealt out of the "draft"? What sort of person is a mentor looking for—and are you that person?

The Profile of a Protégé

To be fair, different mentors look for different things when they evaluate men who ask for their time, energy, wisdom, and affection. In a moment, I'll tell you what matters most to me, given who I am and my particular style. But let me suggest a few things that any mentor would want to see before he commits to such an important relationship. Here are five questions that reveal the profile of a protégé. As you read them, ask yourself, "How do I stack up?"

1. Is he goal-oriented?

One of the unfortunate things about my line of work is that I have to travel extensively to do it. That may not sound so bad to you. In fact, people often say to me, "Boy, Howie, it must be great to travel to all these glamorous places around the world and speak to groups of people!" The people and the ministry I love, and I do enjoy seeing new places. But getting there and back is anything but glamorous.

At any rate, in all my travels this has never happened to me, and I hope it never happens to you: Imagine that I board a plane leaving Dallas-Fort Worth International Airport for Chicago. Twenty minutes into our flight the pilot comes on the speaker and says, "Well, folks, we're leveling off at our cruising altitude of thirty-six thousand feet. By the way, I know this flight is booked for Chicago, but I thought we would just fly around instead and see the countryside. We'll land whenever we're low on fuel. I really can't say where we'll end up. We'll just see what happens."

Imagine such an announcement! A flight plan like that not only would be ridiculous—it could be perilous! Yet a lot of guys are no different in terms of life: just flying along. Where are they headed? There's no telling. Certainly *they* don't know! Worst of all, they don't seem to care. They sort of have the attitude, "Wherever I end up, that's fine by me."

Now few guys would dream of doing that in their jobs. But the amazing thing is, they'll do it in their marriages, with their kids, in their spiritual and personal lives, and so on. They have no direction or aim. They just drift.

That's why earlier I pointed out the importance of establishing objectives, and then translating those objectives into priorities. I was describing the process of goal-setting. Show me a man with a set of well-defined goals, and I'll show you a man on his way to achieving results. Conversely, show me a man with fuzzy goals—or worse, no goals—and I'll show you a man with both feet planted firmly in midair, on his way to nowhere, just flying around until he runs out of gas.

No prospective mentor wants to work with a man who looks like he is headed nowhere. Why bother? You see, if a person has no interest in arriving at a destination—*any* destination—then there is really no way to help him. I could go up to the cockpit of that wayward aircraft and say to the pilot, "Look, you need to turn this plane due north and get to Chicago!" But if he doesn't care where he ends up, I'm wasting my time. He may temporarily set a course for O'Hare just to humor me, but as soon as I turn my back, he'll drift off course.

Are you wandering your way through life or heading toward a destination? You may not have identified a precise destination, and that's OK; a mentor can help you do that. Likewise, you may be off-course; a mentor can set you straight. But if you have no intention of getting anywhere, there can be no wrong heading. There can also be no progress.

2. Is he actively seeking a challenging assignment and greater responsibilities?

Mentoring is all about personal growth and development. So it stands to reason that the best person to mentor is the one who wants to increase his capacities. He's the man who refuses to accept that he has gone about as far as he can go. He always wants to push out beyond his comfort zone, to conquer new mountains, to acquire greater expertise.

Walt, the man who befriended me when I was a boy, was like that. In fact, that's how he found me. I mentioned that he was a member of a brand-new church in my neighborhood. One day he went to the Sunday school superintendent and said, "I want to start a Sunday school class."

Now that's impressive for a guy who had never made it past the sixth grade. If I had been that superintendent, you know what I might have been inclined to say? "Ha, ha! Yeah, Walt, sure, a Sunday school class. Uh, how much education did you say you've had? I'll tell you what, why don't we put you in the nursery. You can change diapers or something. I really think that's more suitable, don't you? I mean, after all, you obviously don't realize what it takes to teach a Sunday school class."

I don't know whether Walt's superintendent was thinking that. I do know that he said, "We don't have any openings for you."

Most guys would have walked away at that point. In fact, a lot of men would have breathed a sigh of relief. "Whew! I dodged that bullet!" would have been their attitude. But Walt was a breed apart. He kept insisting that he wanted to teach a Sunday school class, so finally the superintendent said, "Good. Go out and get a class. Anybody you find is yours." So that's what Walt did.

What an incredible example that set for me! Walt was modeling the invaluable quality of seeking the next frontier. Are you bound and determined to grow like that, to step up to the next level in terms of personal challenge? That's what it's going to take for you to mature as a follower of Christ. Paul said that he was constantly reaching forward, constantly pressing ahead, to attain the "prize for which God has called me heavenward in Christ Jesus (Philippians 3:13–14). He was describing the process of personal and spiritual growth. To grow, we have to push ourselves, to get beyond being too comfortable, too complacent, or too contented.

Yet I'm afraid too many of us are like cats by the fireside—comfy, cozy, and half asleep. I'm meeting too many men who have a V-8 engine under their hood but are only firing on about four cylinders. Instead of tearing up the track, they are coasting along. God has given them incredible gifts and abilities, and unbelievable opportunities. Yet they are wasting most of these resources by settling for lives of comfort and convenience.

Do you aspire to more than that? Are you eager to get off the playground and onto the battleground, where the real victories are won? If so, you are far more likely to attract the attention of a potential mentor. He's looking for future champions, not spectators.

3. Is he an initiator?

The McDonald's restaurant chain once promoted the advertising slogan, "We do it all for you." That brilliantly captures the mind-set of a world where the customer is king. But when it comes to your mentor, you *don't* want him to do it all for you. Indeed, he can't do it all. You have to take some initiative. You have to be something of a self-starter. That's who a mentor is looking for—someone who is making plans and taking action.

I once tried to help a guy who was entirely too passive in terms of his self-development. He was expecting me to do all the work. So one day I tested him. "Last time we met, we talked about four items for you to work on," I said. "Do you recall what those four things were?"

He hemmed and hawed, and finally managed to name three of them. But he hadn't followed through on a single one. "Why don't you come back when you're ready," I told him as I saw him to the door.

He never did come back, and to be honest, I had mixed feelings about that. On the one hand, I thought it was tragic that a guy who actually had tremendous ability suffered from the crippling liability of passivity in the relationship. On the other hand, I was somewhat relieved to be rid of him, because a passive protégé is nothing but a drain on one's time and energy. I have limited amounts of both, so I prefer to invest them in people who essentially burn on their own once the match has ignited their kindling. Your prospective mentor is likely to feel the same way.

Joseph Stowell was a person burning with initiative. Now president of Moody Bible Institute, Joe was a student of mine at the seminary. Like Chuck Swindoll, he was already a man on a mission by the time I encountered him. He was an extraordinarily proactive learner, engaged in the process, keen on acquiring information, and intent on making use of it. After classes, he would ply me with questions as if he couldn't get enough.

The fact is, Joe's growth was largely the product of Joe's initiative. He was already looking for a developmental plan. I just happened to be there at a strategic moment to help him along the way—*his* way, the way that God intended for him.

A self-starter like that makes an ideal protégé, because a mentor has to put very little energy into the guy in order to see enormous amounts of energy coming back out. In fact, the self-starter almost doesn't need a mentor; he seems to develop on his own. Yet ironically, he makes it on his own precisely because he finds people who hold the secrets to his development.

Michael Zey, a sociologist who conducted a two-year study of mentoring in the corporate world under a grant from the National Institute of Mental Health, heard a corporate vice president put it this way: "You can flounder and take what fate brings to your door, or you can go about your career in a more conscious way."

That's a challenge to take initiative. Don't sit on the sidelines! Don't let fickle fate determine your destiny! As the Roman poet said, *Seize the day!*

How do you seize the day? A young executive explained to Zey, "I made myself available. I made it very clear [to my mentor] that I was at his beck and call. The time schedules around here often get very cramped, and it's necessary to work for short periods of time very long hours and weekends, and I let him know at the outset, 'Here's my phone number. If we have to work, if you have any problems, I'm available. Don't hesitate to call.'"

If that spirit of initiative applies in the business world, how much more in the realm of personal and spiritual development? Wherever it is displayed, it is almost irresistible to a prospective mentor. It says, "I'm in this heart and soul. I'm going for broke. You're going to invest your time somewhere. Why not in me? I'm a thoroughbred. I'm worth your time."

4. Is he eager to learn?

My passion is teaching. That means I have given my life to motivating students to learn. If you attend one of my classes, I will go out of my way to engage you in the learning process.

However, I can tell you from personal experience that in most educational settings today—including mentoring relationships—the burden of motivation rests on you as a learner. If you're not eager to learn, there are very few people who are willing to teach you. They just won't invest the energy that it takes to light a fire under your curiosity and imagination.

On the other hand, if you show up with fire in your eyes, ready to absorb everything that a knowledgeable individual has to offer, you will have little trouble attracting and holding that person's interest.

Douglas Hyde was a major leader in the Communist Party in England during the 1930s and 1940s. However, in 1948 he converted to Christianity. Later he wrote a fascinating little book, *Dedication and Leadership*, in which he pointed out that the means of developing leaders among the communists were not all that different from the means of developing leaders among Christians. The only real difference, Hyde observed, was that the communists had actually employed those means.

Hyde devoted an entire chapter to a young man named Jim. Jim had approached Hyde after a lecture in which Hyde boldly asserted that the Communist Party could take anyone who was willing to be trained in leadership and turn him into a leader. Sizing him up, Hyde took Jim to be a man who "was almost pathetically anxious to be turned into a leader." In fact, "as I looked at him I thought that I had never seen anyone who looked less like a leader in my life."

According to Hyde, Jim was extremely short and fat, with a pale complexion, a slightly crossed eye, and worst of all, a most debilitating handicap: "Quite literally he came to me and said: 'C-c-c-comrade, I w-w-w-want you to t-t-t-take me and t-t-t-turn me into a l-l-leader of m-m-m-men.' I looked at Jim and I wondered how I was going to do it. Then I thought to myself: 'Well, I told the class that we could take anyone who was willing to be trained in leadership and turn him into a leader, and here is Jim pathetically anxious for me to do it. This is a challenge.' So I set about the job."

Then Hyde writes: "It will be observed that I had made only one qualification. This was that the would-be leader must be willing to be trained. This presupposes a certain attitude of mind, which Jim already had. It was, so far as I could see at that moment, almost the only thing I had to build on."

What was that one qualification, that one attitude? An eagerness to learn, a willingness to be trained. It was indeed all that Jim had—but it was enough to get started.

Jim spent many months showing up to lectures and classes, listening to the leaders discuss communist philosophy, history, and strategy. Then they put a man under Jim for him to tutor. From there they sent him into his workplace to build relationships with other men and gradually infect them with the seeds of communist thought. Eventually they even enrolled him in a public speaking course.

"[Jim] was appalled at the thought," Hyde wrote. "But he knew, nonetheless, on the basis of his experience in tutorial work that he had unsuspected potentialities. So he went. We did not turn him into a great orator, we did not even entirely cure him of his stutter, although, as he gained confidence in himself this became modified and finished up as a noticeable but not entirely unhelpful impediment in his speech."

Jim eventually assumed leadership in his industry's local trade union and from there went on to become a national leader and a key agent of the Communist Party. As Hyde put it, "Jim, the most unpromising-looking piece of human material that ever came my way had become a leader of men."[1]

What a tragedy that this man's life and energy were not captured for the kingdom! What an even greater tragedy that countless men like Jim today are also being passed over because they look unpromising on the outside. If only we could pay attention to the man on the inside who cries out, "Turn me into a leader of men!"

But keep in mind, the key to Jim's development was his insatiable commitment to learn to be a communist. He *demanded* to be taught. He was not to be denied. No wonder his limitations became irrelevant. What difference did a speech impediment make to laborers in England in the 1930s and 1940s? Their world was turning upside down, and even on the brink of disaster. A man who could speak with authority was a man who could gain a hearing, no matter how poor his enunciation. Jim kept showing up, learning what he needed to learn, so that he earned the right to lead men.

Are you as eager to learn as Jim was? There is no stopping a man who is curious and teachable. Those who have something to teach you will invariably find a way to let you drink from their wealth of knowledge if you convince them that you are genuinely interested. You will appeal to such men, because they instinctively respond to someone who has an insatiable desire to learn.

5. Is he willing to assume responsibility for his own growth and development?

Recently Bill wrote a book entitled *Exit Interviews: Revealing Stories of Why People Are Leaving the Church*. He interviewed about two dozen "disillusioned Christians," people who for one reason or other have decided to part company with the organized church or parachurch.

At the tail end of the book, Bill reminds every reader—whether inside or outside the church—that ultimately each one of us must take responsibility for our own spiritual growth. Ideally, churches can be of real help in that process, but the final responsibility always lies with the individual.

As a result of our mobile, transient culture, "you can no longer rely on a church or any other institution to supply cradle-to-grave support," Bill observes. "In all likelihood, no one is going to track with you over the course of your spiritual pilgrimage. I'm not saying no one cares. I'm just pointing out that long-term responsibility for spiritual development has shifted from the church to you as an individual believer."[2]

So the question is, What are you doing to manage that responsibility? Or are you expecting someone else to pick you up, tell you what to do, and manage your life for you? If so, you will be sorely disappointed, because no one will. Or worse, someone *will* take over your life—and almost certainly lead you to ruin.

One time I was visiting the headquarters of ServiceMaster, a multibillion-dollar conglomerate whose objectives are: "To honor God in all we do; to help people develop; to pursue excellence; and to grow profitably." This company, which has businesses in health care management, residential and commercial cleaning, pest control, lawn care, and many other service industries, has a reputation for outstanding commitment to its employees and, conversely, for outstanding loyalty from its employees.

So I asked the late Ken Hanson, the chairman of the board, "How do you motivate your people?"

His answer was simple: "They motivate themselves." Then he went on to explain, "In our performance appraisals, we assume that the person knows his field. Otherwise we wouldn't have hired him in the first place. That's why we don't set his goals for him. Instead, we ask, 'What do *you* think is a realistic goal?' We let him set it—and usually he sets it much higher than we probably would have. But whatever he determines, *that's* the goal we hold him accountable for when it comes time for his annual review."

What a brilliant illustration of helping people take responsibility for their own growth and development. As a mentor, the last thing I have time to do is to set someone's agenda for him. I'm more than happy to hold his feet to the fire for the agenda *he* sets. But I will not be responsible for dictating what he should do with his life, nor will I do it for him. Nor will I make his decisions for him, because I cannot be responsible. It's his life. He's got to live it. Ultimately, he is responsible for it.

Too many men today are walking around holding an emotional umbilical cord in their hand, looking for a place to attach it. I suppose they intend to feed off someone else's strength so that they'll never have to learn how to find food on their own. But what a terribly unhealthy way to live!

Paul told young Timothy to "fight the good fight" of faith (1 Timothy 1:18). That was a mandate for Timothy to take charge of his life. Paul had his own spiritual battles to wage, and having fought them well, he was in a good position to mentor Timothy in the process. But Timothy's battles were Timothy's to win or lose. Paul could not fight them for him. Timothy had to earn his spurs on his own.

Are you willing to accept responsibility for living your life? The kind of man you want as a mentor has a sixth sense to warn him against spiritual and emotional deadbeats who want to sponge off his strength and character. He's not about to give his best time and energy to such people. But when he recognizes a fellow who has made some basic decisions, who is really committed to the growth process and just needs some direction and help, then he is much more inclined to say, "Let's get together."

My Selection Process

When I think of the men over the years on whom I feel I've had a substantial impact, almost every one of them checks out in all five of these areas. Some have been unusually strong in one or more of the five. But to one degree or another, every one of them has been goal-oriented, looking for bigger and better things, an initiator, eager to learn, and responsible in terms of his own development.

I find that these traits are common throughout the world of mentoring relationships. However, every mentor has certain things that are particularly important to him, things that he especially looks for in a potential protégé. For me, initiative is the key. I invariably pay attention to initiative to qualify my prospects.

I remember one student who excelled in this area. He dogged my steps to find opportune moments to spend time with me. "Can I walk you to your car? Can I have lunch with you? Can I grade papers for you?" He wasn't a pest about asking these things. He just took the initiative to let me know that he was available—which was important, because my schedule is usually booked up weeks and months in advance. The squeaky wheel always gets the grease, and, needless to say, we ended up spending some significant time together. I think the key to making that happen was his enthusiasm and persistence, which were highly motivating for me.

Another thing I look for is a guy who follows up on suggestions. As a professor, I get asked a lot of "where can I find" questions. Students are looking for information. So I'm constantly referring them to books and other resources that have it all laid out, in a far better way than I could explain it.

Imagine, then, how I feel when I put a guy onto a book that has exactly what he says he needs, and then later find out he never read it—never even consulted it! The next time he comes asking for a lead, do you suppose I'm inclined to spend much time helping him solve his problem?

Or take the guy who promises much but delivers little. I'm afraid my Dutch and German ancestry predisposes me to impatience with people who don't follow through on their commitments. It would be better not to have promised anything than to have promised and not followed through.

I just lose all confidence in that sort of person. My instinct says that he's going to waste my time.

Jesus told a parable about this very thing (Matthew 21:28–31). A man had two sons. He asked both of them to go to work in the family vineyard. One said he would, but didn't. The other said he wouldn't, but did. As Jesus asked His disciples, which son did the will of his father? It was not the one who promised to go, but rather the one who actually went. That's the kind of man I'd prefer to work with.

I'm now speaking about certain things that go on at a subconscious level in the mind of a mentor. They are subtle things, intuitive things: Do I have confidence in this guy? Is he on the ball? Is he going somewhere? Is he going to pan out? Is he going to be fair with me, or take advantage of me?

These are subjective judgments, to be sure, and more than once I've been proven wrong in my reading of an individual. But I would be lying if I didn't tell you that these are the kinds of questions that a man ponders when you signal to him that you're looking for a mentor. So you might as well ask them of yourself.

What About You?

How do you stack up? I suggest that you go back through the five questions right now and do some honest self-assessment. But let me reassure you if you feel somewhat discouraged or overwhelmed at this point. Most men who want to be mentored feel that they are less than ideal material for anyone to work with. It goes back to what I was saying in chapter 2: Most men have been beaten down with the lie that they don't have what it takes to be significant. In fact, most of the men I've mentioned as examples of the mentoring process felt that way early on. It is only in retrospect, looking back on where they have come from, that they now realize how much they had going for them.

So take heart! Even in the NFL draft, some of the early-round picks, presumed to be destined for super-stardom, turn out to be busts. Meanwhile, other guys selected at the bottom of the pile—and even a few walk-ons—turn out to be the All Pros and Hall-of-Famers.

Mark it well, then: if you are committed to growing, there are men out there who will help you. In the next chapter, I will help you find those men.

Chapter Five

THE MARKS OF A MENTOR

"Looking for a mentor is a bit like looking for love." Do you recall that statement from chapter 3? It's an intriguing idea, because in our culture, most men think of love as something that "just happens." A young man meets a girl and suddenly "falls" in love with her. He claims she "stole" or "captured" his heart. It's as if love were a big yellow bus: one day the guy steps into the street without looking, and—*Wham!*—love knocks him flat.

That may or may not be an accurate perception of how a man meets the love of his life, but I can assure you that finding a mentor rarely "just happens." To be sure, there's a chemistry involved. But there are definitely ways to help all the "chemicals" react.

We know this from sports, particularly at the college level. Think about some of the legendary coaches over the years: Bear Bryant, Woody Hayes, Joe Paterno, Eddie Robinson, or Bill McCartney in football; John Wooden, Adolph Rupp, Dean Smith, or John Thompson in basketball. If you were to poll athletes who played under these men, you would find a substantial number saying words to the effect, "I wanted to play for Coach So-and-So since I was a boy." To that end, they went out of their way to draw that coach's attention and hopefully earn a spot on his team.

In fact, there are even cases of parents moving to the state where the coach's school was located, in order to get their son noticed, and hopefully, recruited. Naturally, there were no guarantees. But these athletes and their families were intentional about placing themselves in the path of opportunity.

Being Intentional

In a similar way, you must be intentional about looking for a mentor. You must be proactive. You must deliberately and strategically place yourself in the path of opportunity, where you can increase your chances of linking up with a person who can influence you.

In this chapter and the next, I'll show you some ways to do that. The place to start is by clarifying what sort of person you are looking for. I've already challenged you to take a long, hard look at yourself, and in the previous chapter I painted a picture of how a prospective mentor will tend to look at you. Now let's consider how to find that prospective mentor.

Marks of a Mentor

Here are ten characteristics, ten marks of a mentor I would suggest.

1. A Mentor Seems to Have What You Personally Need

In chapter 3, I encouraged you to identify your objectives in terms of four categories of human competency: knowledge, attitudes, habits and behaviors, and skills. Did you come up with some items of developmental need? Whatever those objectives are, the only person who can help you achieve them is the one who has already developed those capacities himself.

This should be self-evident, but for many people, I'm afraid it's not. I'm appalled at how often a person who knows little about a subject is placed in a position where he has to teach that subject. For example, when my older son was in junior high school, he was placed in an algebra class taught by a football coach. Naturally, the students assumed that this man must be something of an expert in algebra. In fact, he had a master's degree, so no one thought twice about it.

Then one day my son and his friends began to notice discrepancies between the textbook and what this coach was teaching in class. When challenged, however, the man just brushed it off. No one wanted to insist that he was wrong, so they let it go. Eventually the end of the year came, and most of the students passed algebra—though few really understood the subject—and went on to the next grade. Later, however, my son came home with the news that this coach's master's degree was in physical education! He was completely unqualified to teach algebra, and in attempting to do so had done more harm than good.

When you go looking for a mentor, find someone who really knows something about the area in which you want to grow. If you want to develop a prayer life, look for someone who demonstrates a consistent prayer life. If you want to become more generous and responsible with your money, look for someone who has money and is strategic and faithful about how he disburses it. If you want to work on your marriage, find someone whose marriage is solid.

It's a basic principle of spiritual nurturing: you cannot impart what you do not possess. So look for men who actually have the goods, not just men who look good.

2. A Mentor Cultivates Relationships

An effective mentor has to be willing to give of himself to another human being. He must be capable of establishing and maintaining a relationship. Otherwise, he will have difficulty attracting anybody, despite the considerable value of what he may have to offer.

This is often what limits certain scholars and artists from making much of an impact on others in a relational way. They may be a gold mine of resources, but they have trouble cultivating relationships. It would take a younger man far too much effort to try and extract the riches of their expertise.

Please don't misunderstand. I am not saying that a man who is by nature private, somewhat introverted, or even reclusive cannot function as a mentor. He very well may. Indeed, some people who operate with a low-key relational style have far more to offer than most people realize.

The key question is, Can the man initiate and sustain a productive, give-and-take relationship with another human being? Remember, a mentor is someone who is committed to your growth, and to helping you realize your life goals. How effectively can a man help you if he is consumed with his own interests, needs, and agenda? It's not that you can gain nothing from him; but he is hardly an ideal prospect for a mentor.

3. A Mentor Is Willing to Take a Chance on You

A mentor is going to make a certain investment in you—an investment of time, energy, emotion, trust, and other resources. He may even invest cash.

We saw that in the case of Eugene Lang, where someone made a financial investment in his education, and later Lang put aside some money for the kids at P.S. 121.

Investments always involve a measure of risk. This is as true in mentoring as anywhere else, because there are no guaranteed outcomes to the mentoring process. Not every protégé pans out. I've worked with guys who later "shipwrecked their faith," as Paul put it, perhaps describing two of his own younger followers (see 1 Timothy 1:19–20). Even Jesus had a Judas.

So there are no guarantees. Hopefully, you will prove yourself worthy of someone's investment. But as you seek an "investor," you have to ask yourself: Is this person willing to run the risk with me? Or is he so risk-averse that he'll never give me a chance?

This is a very personal point for me, because it takes me back to my fifth grade class. I've already mentioned my troubled home background. By the fifth grade, I was bearing all the fruit of a kid who feels insecure, unloved, and pretty angry at life. In other words, I was tearing the place apart. However, my teacher Miss Simon apparently thought that I was blind to this problem, because she regularly reminded me, "Howard, you are the worst behaved child in this school!"

So tell me something I don't already know! I thought to myself, as I proceeded to live up (or down) to her opinion of me.

One time I got so out of hand that she physically grabbed me, shoved me into my desk, tied me to my seat with a rope, and wrapped tape around my mouth. "Now you will sit still and be quiet!" she announced triumphantly. So what else could I do?

Needless to say, the fifth grade was probably the worst year of my life. Finally I was graduated—for obvious reasons. But I left with Miss Simon's words ringing in my ears: "Howard, you are the worst behaved child in this school!"

You can imagine, then, my expectations upon entering the sixth grade, where my teacher was Miss Noé. The first day of class she went down the roll, and it wasn't long before she came to my name. "Howard Hendricks," she called out, glancing from her list to where I was sitting with my arms folded, just waiting to go into action. She looked me over for a moment, and then said, "I've heard a lot about you." Then she smiled and added, "But I don't believe a word of it!"

I tell you, that moment was a fundamental turning point, not only in my education, but in my life. Suddenly, unexpectedly, someone believed in me. For the first time in my life, someone saw potential in me. Miss Noé put me on special assignments. She gave me little jobs to do. She invited me to come in after school to work on my reading and arithmetic. She challenged me with higher standards.

TEN MARKS OF A MENTOR

The ideal mentor is a person who . . .

1. Seems to have what you personally need.
2. Cultivates relationships.
3. Is willing to take a chance on you.
4. Is respected by other Christians.
5. Has a network of resources.
6. Is consulted by others.
7. Both talks and listens.
8. Is consistent in his lifestyle.
9. Is able to diagnose your needs.
10. Is concerned with your interests.

I had a hard time letting her down. In fact, one time I got so involved in one of her homework assignments that I stayed up until 1:30 in the morning working on it! Eventually my father came down the hall and said, "What's the matter, son, are you sick?"

"No, I'm doing my homework," I replied.

He kind of blinked and rubbed his eyes, not quite sure whether he was awake. He'd never heard me say anything like that before. Finally he shook his head and said, "You're sick!"

What made the difference between fifth grade and sixth? The fact that someone was willing to give me a chance. Someone was willing to believe in me while challenging me with higher expectations. That was risky, because there was no guarantee that I would honor Miss Noé's trust.

Everyone likes the end product of mentoring, especially when it yields a peak performer—the star athlete, the successful businessperson, the brilliant lawyer, the impressive communicator. But how many of us want to deal with the person at the front end of the process? Remember Jim, in the last chapter? Douglas Hyde called him "the most unpromising-looking piece of human material that ever came my way." Yet Hyde gambled on Jim's willingness to be trained, and the investment paid off handsomely.

As you look for a mentor, consider whether your prospect seems willing to put himself on the line to help you become the man God created you to be.

4. A Mentor Is Respected by Other Christians

Paul urged Timothy to find "reliable men who will also be qualified to teach others" (2 Timothy 2:2). How does one determine whether a man is "reliable"? One important way is by the testimony of other men, particularly those who are seasoned in the faith. A mentor should be respected by other effective Christians. In fact, among the qualifications for leaders in the church are that a man be "above reproach" and "respectable" (1 Timothy 3:2). (It is worth noting that men of maturity also should have a good reputation among those outside the church, 3:7.)

Paul was not describing a popularity contest but an assessment of character. The issue is whether the man in question actually lives out the faith he professes.

As you consider a potential mentor, you need to conduct something of a background check on the prospect, particularly if you do not know him personally or have not known him for very long. Ask around to find people who have known him well over time—perhaps a pastor, a friend, a coworker. Generally speaking, what is their opinion of this individual? Do they speak highly of him? Or do you get the sense that they have reservations? How much do they trust and respect him?

I'm not suggesting that you go digging for dirt. The point is quality control. Just as your mentor is taking a risk with you, so you are taking a risk with him. Allow other people's opinions, particularly those of mature believers, to indicate whether he is worth the risk. And even if he does not turn out to be perfect (and none of us is), you will at least be aware of his limitations up front.

5. A Mentor Has a Network of Resources

The more extensive a network your mentor has, the better. Linda Phillips-Jones, a leading expert on mentoring in the corporate world, points out that mentors can help you reach your life goals because of *who* they know and *what* they know. This knowledge base gives them tremendous power to promote your welfare.

For example, Bill has a friend named Chris who wanted to develop in the area of fund-raising for nonprofit work, especially projects related to evangelism and overseas missions. Chris himself has control over certain funds, and he also is being asked more and more to help raise money for others. He realized that fund-raising can be a sophisticated art, and he needed help in learning that art from the standpoint of both the fund-raiser and the donor.

So Chris did a very smart thing. He nosed around until he identified a man who has raised millions of dollars for Christian ministries over the years and is regarded by many as a genius in this area. The two linked up, and today Chris is being tutored by one of the preeminent fund-raisers in the country.

Consider the resources that this man can make available. He has a Rolodex of names and phone numbers that Chris does not. He knows people by their first names whom Chris would otherwise have to address by title and last name. He knows where the people of means hang out and how to access their exclusive domains. He knows who gives, how much they give, why they give, and to what sorts of causes they give.

No amount of schooling, reading, research, or hard work on Chris's part could ever equal what he has through his connection to his mentor. One phone call, one letter of introduction, one important piece of information from this man, and Chris is already miles down the road.

What is your prospective mentor's network of resources? Can he help you because of who and what he knows? Consider carefully whether he can guide you beyond himself to other resources, such as people, organizations, and information. Remember Julius, the teenager in Denver? It was because of his connection with Jerry, who was highly regarded by the authorities, that he was able to avoid being charged for the vandalism in the bus pound. It was also through Jerry that Lavon found a church and, indirectly, a job.

In a similar way, your mentor can help you with your needs and objectives by introducing you to people, books and seminars, programs, and other resources that can encourage you in your development. In fact, the better his network, the more help he will be.

6. A Mentor Is Consulted by Others

One of the best indicators that a man would serve well as a guide is if he is already serving as a guide to others. This goes hand in hand with the matter of respect mentioned earlier.

In the business world, it doesn't take long for new hires to discover which senior-level people are open to promoting younger associates and which ones have little interest in helping. The prime candidates are the ones who already have a reputation as mentors.

Likewise, in the church, good advisors tend to develop a word-of-mouth reputation. In fact, they often develop a following of sorts. People start seeking them out on a regular basis for advice, encouragement, perspective, and prayer. The word on the grapevine becomes, "So-and-So knows what he's talking about. He can really help."

This ability to offer counsel is crucial. It is not wisdom alone that qualifies a man to coach another man, but his ability to communicate effectively and apply his wisdom to the other man's need. So as you evaluate your prospects, ask yourself: Does it look like this guy has something to offer? If so, will he be able to use what he knows to give me insight and advice? Has anyone else ever found him to be a source of counsel and wisdom? If not, you may be setting yourself up for disappointment by trying to force him into a mentoring role.

7. A Mentor Both Talks and Listens

The issue is communication. As someone who has devoted his life to trying to practice and teach this art, I've learned that most people think of communication as being all about speaking. But the truth of the matter is that you become an effective communicator by becoming an effective listener.

Therefore, one of the keys to good mentoring is good listening. This is a fundamental truth, often misunderstood by would-be mentors. I run into men all the time who think they are unqualified to serve as mentors because they aren't polished speakers. "Who, me?" they reply when I suggest that they build into the life of a younger man. "Howie, you don't understand. I wouldn't know what to say."

"Can you invite a guy to lunch and let him do the talking?" I ask.

"Yeah, sure," they say.

"Then start there. That's what a young man needs anyway. He's looking for someone who will let him spill his guts about his background from a broken home, his struggling marriage, his disappointments on the job, his hopes and fears for the future. If you draw him out on what really matters to him, you won't be worried about speaking; you may be trying to get a word in edgewise."

Without question, communication is a two-way street, involving both speaking and listening. But of the two, listening is by far the harder to learn. You see, it's a documented fact that people can hear four to ten times as fast as a speaker can speak—which means that listeners have a lot of time in which to be distracted. It takes work to stay focused on what is being said, and to listen beneath the external content of the message to its underlying meaning and implications.

But if a man learns to listen, then he is more likely to be listened to when he speaks. You probably know this from personal experience. Have you ever been in a group of people where some windbag drones on and on, giving you far more of his opinions than anyone cared to know? Every time someone makes a comment, he's got to say something in response.

Meanwhile, off to the side is a quiet individual who has been taking it all in. Suddenly, at a key moment, he pipes up and begins to say something. Everyone is glued to his words, because they have learned by experience that this person knows what he is talking about. He doesn't waste words. Neither does he waste anyone's time.

This sort of man tends to make a good mentor, because he has mastered the discipline of effective listening. A good mentor is always a good listener. If you bring him a problem, a question, a comment, an idea, he will more than likely help *you* figure it out and run with it, rather than regale you with his own polished presentation. In the end, that's what matters. Mentoring is not about your mentor displaying his brilliance. It is about you as a protégé learning to step up to the next level, so that you develop *your* competencies.

8. A Mentor Is Consistent in His Lifestyle

It is self-evident that a hypocrite is unqualified to guide other men to attaining higher character. No one respects a man who talks a good game but fails to play by the rules.

Yet I wonder whether we take the issue of lifestyle seriously enough, particularly in light of what I mentioned earlier about modeling. If, as Bandura claims, modeling is the most powerful form of unconscious learning there is, then what your mentor does and how he lives will have a far greater impact on you than anything he says. In fact, you may forget 90 percent of what he says, but you'll never forget how he lived.

Bill encountered an interesting illustration of this principle during the go-go real estate market of the 1980s. He met a developer we'll call Rip, whose business of setting up investment partnerships was booming. Rip was signing up so many wealthy professionals that he couldn't get new projects going fast enough. Part of his salesmanship was that he had woven what he called "biblical principles of business" into his deals. He became a darling of the Christian radio and lecture circuit and even set up a consulting practice to advise other businesses in the area of management. Rip seemed to have found the keys to running a business "God's way." Why, wasn't that evident from his incredible success?

Then the real estate market crashed. Suddenly, no one wanted Rip's hot properties. Deals started coming apart. Lenders began asking for money. Lawsuits began to be filed. Then one day Rip dropped out of sight. Naturally, his investors and partners began investigating. They discovered that Rip had skipped town, leaving them to pick up the pieces of the financial mess he had left behind.

Contrast that to another acquaintance of Bill's named Kip. Kip was also a developer. He too talked about integrating biblical principles into his business. He too signed up wealthy professionals to finance his deals. And when the market crashed, he too found himself in desperate straits, owing a lot of money to a lot of people.

But unlike Rip, Kip felt that, as a matter of conscience, he needed to work out payback plans with his investors. He believed that he had an obligation as a Christian to do whatever it might take to make good on the commitments he had signed. If it meant taking his kids out of private schools, moving to a smaller house, living a simpler lifestyle, working second and third jobs—so be it. Whatever and however long it might take, Kip pledged to honor his word.

Today, Rip has moved to another state and set up shop all over again.

Meanwhile, Kip lives in a modest home, managing the handful of properties that he was able to hang onto. Now that the market has turned around, he is gradually working his way out of debt.

Now which of these two men would you want to mentor you in terms of integrity in the marketplace? Which one has something to say about following through on one's commitments? Which one has earned the right to speak on how faith might apply to the work world? The answer is obvious, isn't it? There is no substitute for a man of consistent Christlike character. He doesn't have to try and snow you with words. His life is the most eloquent sermon there is.

Of course, you'll never find a perfect man, so don't bother looking for one. In fact, the New Testament does not call for models of perfection, but rather models of *progress* in the faith. Paul instructed Timothy to be diligent in following godly teachings. "Give yourself wholly to them," he wrote, "so that everyone may see your progress" (1 Timothy 4:15). Thus you want a mentor who is progressing toward maturity. That means a man who is authentic—as honest about his failures and weaknesses as he is realistic about the things he has going for him.

9. A Mentor Is Able to Diagnose Your Needs

Earlier I said that you should look for a mentor whom you believe has what you personally need (point #1). However, since you may not be fully aware of what you need, it helps to find someone who can help you evaluate and identify what you need. All of us have blind spots, areas of which we are unaware. That's why we need people who can diagnose our developmental and spiritual needs.

My mechanic is Bob Smith of Auto Maintenance in Garland, Texas. Since I don't know the front end from the back end of a car, Bob seems like a genius to me. I'll drive my car in and say, "Bob, I've got this noise in the motor. I don't know if it's serious or not, but I thought I better have you check it out."

So he raises the hood, turns the engine over, listens here, listens there, gets out a screwdriver, tightens this screw, adjusts that one. Next thing I know, the engine is running as smoothly as the day I bought the car.

"Howie, you're all set," he says, and I pay him the bill. Now Bob would be more than happy to explain to me what was wrong with my car. But usually I just take his word for it. In the first place, I know I can trust him. But beyond that, I wouldn't know what he was talking about anyway. That's why I take my car to him, rather than trying to work on it myself. I don't know cars. He does. He faithfully and accurately diagnoses my car's ills and remedies them.

But suppose I take my car down the street to Mr. Rip U. Off's repair shop. I pull in and say, "Rip, I've got an oil leak. Is it serious?"

He crawls under the car for two-and-a-half hours and then comes at me with the bill. "We've got it taken care of, Mr. Hendricks," he says. Curiously, I notice that he's no longer chewing the gum he had when he started the job. Anyway, I shell out a couple of hundred bucks and leave.

But five miles down the road, my engine seizes and the car grinds to a halt. Later I go back to Rip and say, "What gives here? The dealer says I've thrown a rod, and my engine is shot. How come you didn't fix that?"

"You told me you wanted me to fix the oil leak," Rip replies, "so that's what I did. You didn't say anything about checking for other problems."

I don't know about you, but when I'm out of my depth, I need a competent person who not only can see that something is wrong but can figure out what it is and how to fix it. I need someone who can distinguish between nagging symptoms and underlying diseases. A good mentor has that sort of analytical ability.

And the more time I spend with my mentor, the better he will be able to spot critical problems. At the end of my first semester at Wheaton College, I was flunking three subjects. As if that were not humiliating enough, one of the courses I was failing was English. Can you believe, I had won the English Award at my high school the previous year! I was thoroughly discouraged, because, despite my best efforts and long hours of "study," I wasn't making the grade.

Finally, I went to visit my English professor—a wise old man whom I fully expected to confirm that I was not college material. He had instructed me now for about three months. To my surprise, he said, "Howie, your problem is that you don't know how to read." He then put me onto some resources that taught me the real skills of reading and, in the process, transformed my education.

Now I could have taken a course in learning how to study, or hired a tutor, or learned to type, or done a hundred other things to try and beef up my academic standing. But none of them would have made much difference, because they all would have been dealing with something other than the fact that I didn't know how to read. By contrast, my professor, who had observed me over time, put his finger on the fundamental problem, and gave me a way to address it. In so doing, he enabled me to function at a higher level than I ever thought possible.

10. A Mentor Is Concerned with Your Interests

By now you may have realized that looking for a mentor requires a moderate dose of healthy self-interest. We're talking about *your* life and *your* development. Therefore, you are looking for someone who will champion *your* best interests.

Unfortunately, many men of great competence also have great egos that preclude them from serving anyone else. They are more likely to try and build their kingdoms on top of your shoulders than to place the resources of their kingdoms at your disposal. I suggest that you avoid trying to recruit such men as your mentors. You will do most of the giving and have very little to show for it in the end.

Instead, you ideally want a man whose greatest joy is to see you succeed. If you succeed, he succeeds, and if you fail . . . well, he's there to pick you up, dust you off, and get you back on your horse.

Earlier I said that mentoring involves a risk for the mentor, but the risk has to do with what happens to the protégé, not what happens to the mentor. If your mentor has such a vested interest in the outcome of things that he cannot afford to allow you to fail, then both of you need to rethink the relationship. Clearly, the man has something to prove, and he is using you to prove it.

I'll say more about this to the mentors in Part 2. But as you consider prospects for a mentoring relationship, ask yourself: Will this man be committed to *my* development? Has he shown a capacity for serving as a stepping stone with anybody else? Where does the center of gravity seem to be in his relationships? Is there a dynamic balance between his needs and the needs of others, or does everything revolve around him and his agenda?

The Perfect Mentor?

As you evaluate men according to the ten marks of a mentor listed in this chapter, be realistic: you are going to find that almost every man falls short in some way. In other words, *you'll never find the perfect mentor.* Even if you think you have, sooner or later you'll uncover some flaws. But the point of this list is not to disqualify as many men as possible, but to urge you to aim high. A mentor can have a profound influence on your life, so it's worth finding the most qualified person you can.

Have you got a few prospects in mind? If not, let me show you where you can find some.

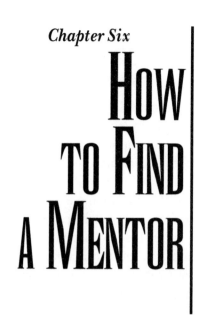

Chapter Six

How to Find a Mentor

When my boys were young, we used to go fishing in Colorado. Our accommodations provided access to a small pond known as Presbyterian Lake—which made a lot of sense to me and my boys, because for us hooking a trout tended to be a matter of predestination (or lack thereof). You could have summed up many of our outings with Jesus' words, "Many are called, but few are chosen."

The crazy thing is that while we sat by the hour, waiting for even a nibble, just down the shoreline were usually two old duffers who each had a couple of poles, and they couldn't reel the fish in fast enough. One of them would be landing a fish, and his other line would be twitching like a lightning rod! Meanwhile, his partner would be dozing, while his two lines danced back and forth.

This happened time after time until one day I asked them how they caught so many fish.

"You using the right bait?" they asked me.

I showed them my expensive lures, and they just grinned. "Those won't catch you anything. You've got to use these Balls O' Fire," they said, reaching for a jar of small, red, bead-like bait. "Put three of 'em on a hook, like this, and throw it in. Drives the fish crazy."

So we drove to town and bought some Balls O' Fire. That afternoon, we caught a couple of fish.

However, the next day we were back to square one. We spent all morning casting our entire jar of Balls O' Fire into Presbyterian Lake, to no avail. Not a single bite! Yet there were those two codgers again, cleaning out the lake.

Finally I walked down the shoreline for more advice. "I don't understand," I said. "We're using Balls O' Fire like you said, but we're not having any luck."

Once again they grinned and pulled out their bait. "They're bitin' on cheese marshmallows today," they said, showing us some orange, spongy puffs.

Back to town we went to buy a jar of cheese marshmallows. That afternoon we caught a couple of fish.

But the next day was the same old story. New bait, no bites. Yet as usual, the old-timers were reeling them in. This time I didn't wait to pay a visit. "Looks like you've almost caught your limit already," I said as I approached them.

"Yep."

"What bait are you using?" I asked, fully expecting yet another product of which I'd never heard. But all they did was point to their jar of cheese marshmallows.

"That's funny," I said, "we're using the exact same thing, and we haven't caught a one."

"Well, that's cause you're fishing in the shallow part of the lake," one of them told me. "See out there where my line is? There's a pretty good drop-off there, and trout like to gather in that hole when it's hot like today." Then he turned away to pull in yet another sizable fish.

About this time it finally dawned on me that fishing takes more than throwing a hook in the water. *It takes knowing the fish.* The more you know about the species you are trying to catch, the more likely you are to catch them.

The same applies to hooking up with a mentor. You've got to study the species. In the last chapter I described ten characteristics to look for. In this and the next chapter, I want to discuss where you are likely to find these people, and what it takes to attract their attention and establish a mentoring relationship.

Places to Look for a Mentor

The *where* of finding a mentor is deceptively obvious: potential mentors are all around you. Yet this is deceptive because we tend to overlook people who have real promise in this regard. "You mean Harry, the guy down the street?" we say to ourselves. "Why, he's just a . . . a guy! He's a good guy, but he's not like a Tom Landry, or a Dawson Trotman (founder of the Navigators), or the apostle Paul."

Yet that attitude betrays a fundamental misperception about mentors. We tend to assume that mentors have to be unusually successful, or prominent, or brilliant, or outstanding in some other way. But the truth of the matter is, many of the best mentors are not spectacular—just solid. They may not stand out in a crowd. Indeed, some of them are virtually camouflaged by their surroundings. But they're out there, and to notice them, we have to be like a hunter in the woods—knowing *what* to look for, and *where* to look.

For example, say you're a college or university student. The most obvious place to look for a mentor is among the faculty. Is there a particular professor who draws your attention, a person who, the more you look at him, the more he resembles the pattern presented in chapter 5?

What about your church? Check out the pastoral staff and some of the more mature laymen to see if they display some of the marks of a mentor.

And how about your workplace—probably the dominant arena for most men's relationships? Think through your coworkers, your supervisors, your vendors, and others in your field or industry. Think through your union, your professional associations, the names in your Rolodex, your alumni directory. Anybody strike you as at least a possibility?

Or suppose you really need help in terms of your family or marriage. Where can you find a mentor for that department? The obvious choice is your church. (And may I say, in passing, that with or without a mentor, it's going to be very difficult for you to grow very far in your faith unless you are an active participant in a solid, biblically based body of believers. That's not an option; it's an essential.)

However, you may not be in a church that has many families in it. If so, consider whether you, your wife, and your children might not be well served to attend a church that does have families. Or, if that isn't possible, at least sign up for a week at a family camp or a Bible conference, where you'll meet some couples who have raised their kids and survived to tell about it.

Another potential source is the families of your children's schoolmates.

We hear a lot today about the breakdown of the family, but let's not forget that there are still many homes where couples are managing to keep a fire lit in the rain. And even if you are unaware of who your children go to school with, your wife is not. Mothers of school-age children tend to have extensive networks. In fact, other families may know more about what's going on with your family than you do! I would check it out.

What About Non-Christians?

Now let me digress for a moment to answer what may be a question in your mind at this point. I've suggested several "pools" in which to go fishing for a mentor. Some of them, such as the business world or the public schools, will have non-Christians as well as Christians. Am I suggesting that you be mentored by an unbeliever?

Let's think about that. Ideally, you want to look for mentors who are solid men of faith. Remember, that was one of the marks of a mentor that we looked at in the last chapter. But our definition of a mentor—a man committed to helping you grow and realize your life goals—does not necessarily exclude people who have not yet come to Christ.

It's a mistake to think that only believers can make a substantial, positive impact on your life. Some non-Christian men live generally moral lives by following basic Judeo-Christian codes, such as the Ten Commandments and the Golden Rule. As a result, they can instruct us about positive traits, character, and professional growth.

In fact, some of the greatest lessons I've ever learned, I learned from unbelievers. My father, for example. He was a career Army man for whom punctuality was more than virtue—it was a way of life. He used to say to me, "Son, if you show up late, I'll send flowers to your funeral." To this day, I don't know how to be late.

Or take the guy Bill came across as a teenager, when our 1967 metallic-green Ford Mustang broke down in traffic. Bill pushed the car into a filling station and asked for help. The owner was a crusty, crude old bird who puffed on a fat cigar while he looked under the hood. The shop walls were adorned with girlie calendars, and it was pretty evident that this was no shrine of faith. The man poked and prodded, spat and swore, until finally he said, "Here's your problem," and held up a spark plug wire. "Sometimes they get a short in 'em, and it sure knocks the [expletive] out of the engine."

After the wire was replaced, Bill went into the office to pay up. He had two dollars and change. The bill came to a little more than five dollars. "Can I write you a check?" Bill asked.

The station owner nodded, and Bill made out the check. After handing it over, he reached for his license. But the owner told him, "I don't need to see that. If you're gonna stiff me on a five-dollar check, then you're really not worth a [expletive]!"

It was a basic lesson in honesty, and from a most unexpected source. But it was a lesson that Bill never forgot. That non-Christian knew the meaning of the words *trust* and *honesty*.

Whenever possible, your first choice for a mentor should be a vibrant Christian who can challenge you from a biblical foundation. But when a qualified non-Christian appears, don't automatically rule him out just because he's not a follower of Christ. He may actually invigorate your faith—and you may find that your relationship causes him to consider his own spiritual needs.

The caution is, just be aware of the stream from which you are drinking. As Paul wrote, "Test everything. Hold on to the good. Avoid every kind of evil" (1 Thessalonians 5:21–22).

Pray for a Mentor

May I give you three practical suggestions for finding a mentor? First, pray for one. You may not take prayer seriously, but God does. The New Testament says that a man who was no different than you or I prayed earnestly that it would not rain, and for three and a half years no rain fell. Then, when his people were finally convinced that the Lord is indeed God, he prayed again, and the skies came apart in a downpour (James 5:17–18).

Let me point out that when Elijah started praying for rain, there was not a cloud on the horizon. Six times he sent his servant to see if any storms were brewing, but the man saw nothing but blue sky. Only on the seventh time did the servant spy a cloud. Yet even then, the cloud was so far away that he dismissed it as inconsequential, only "as small as a man's hand." But Elijah knew that his prayers were about to be answered (1 Kings 18:41–46).

As you pray for a mentor, you've got to trust God, even though you cannot see any prospects on the horizon. Searching for a mentor is one of those times when, as Scripture says, you have to walk by faith, not by sight (2 Corinthians 5:7). I assure you, where prayer focuses, power falls.

I feel so extremely confident about this because I've seen it happen time and again. In 1993 I spoke on the subject of mentoring at the Boulder, Colorado, gathering of the Promise Keepers. More than 50,000 men had filled the University of Colorado football stadium. I stated a truth that has not changed: "Every man here should seek to have three individuals in his life. You need a Paul. You need a Barnabas. And you need a Timothy."

As I explained, these are three kinds of mentoring relationships that a man desperately needs to pursue: a Paul, an older man who can build into his life; a Barnabas, a peer, a soul brother to whom he can be accountable; and a Timothy, a younger man into whose life he is building. At the end of the time, I asked every man present to bow his head and pray that God would lead him to a Paul, a Barnabas, and a Timothy.

Ever since that gathering, I've had guys all over the country give testimonies similar to the one a fellow shared with me just recently: "Prof, I was there when you spoke at Boulder. I prayed that God would lead me to a Paul, a Barnabas, and a Timothy. Well, I've now got a Paul. I've now got a Barnabas. And it looks like I've got a Timothy. God is answering my prayer!"*

Are you on your knees before God, imploring Him to lead you to a man who will fundamentally affect the course of your life? "Ask and it will be given to you; seek and you will find; knock and the door will be opened to you. For everyone who asks receives; he who seeks finds; and to him who knocks, the door will be opened" (Matthew 7:7–8).

---

* This book primarily discusses how to be a Paul (mentor) and a Timothy (protégé) in your mentoring relationships. However, there are valuable benefits in becoming a Barnabas, too—having a peer relationship with another man in which you challenge each other to personal growth and remain accountable to one another (see Peer Mentoring, pp. 32–34).

Start Looking

A second piece of advice is to get your antennae up. In other words, start looking for these people. Open your eyes. See what's out there.

Sometimes I visit the single men's dorm at Dallas Seminary, and we get into a discussion. The topic of conversation invariably starts out with something theological, like predestination, but it always ends up with women. One time we were talking about the qualities a man values in a woman, and one guy finally asked, "So Prof, how do I find this girl?"

"Well, are you dating?" I asked him.

"Oh, no! I'm way too busy for that."

I said, "Well, how do you expect to find the right one? You think God's going to let her down on a sheet out of heaven?"

If you intend to catch fish, you've got to go where the fish are. But you know, a guy will spend hundreds of dollars for a bass finder and spend all day trolling around a lake to find a school of fish, yet he won't even take five minutes to open his address book and see if somebody in there looks like a potential coach for his life. And he wonders why God doesn't seem to be answering his prayers!

By all means, pray. But then, *open your eyes!*

Make Contact

Finally, start to experiment with the process. Get into circulation. Ask a man out for breakfast or lunch. Talk with him. Pray with him. See if the relationship takes hold. Find out if there's a chemistry there. Mentoring develops out of that kind of initial contact.

And here's a pointer on how to stimulate some interaction: most of us respond to people who respond to us, particularly in the area of our expertise. We feel more comfortable talking about that. So starting there can help to break the ice in the relationship.

For instance, my late friend, Jimmy Squires, made a hobby of studying the Civil War. He knew all of the dates, all of the battles, all of the generals, and so on. He had studied maps of troop movements and visited the battlefields. He could entertain you for hours with fascinating stories and little known facts about that conflict. He even had a collection of artifacts from that era.

Jimmy also had a very large heart for younger men. But if a guy wanted to cultivate a relationship with Jimmy, the best place to start would not be with his own needs and concerns; the time would come to discuss those issues. My advice would have been to draw out Jimmy on his expertise as a Civil War buff. Remember what I said in the last chapter? The key to effective communication is listening. By listening to a man like Jimmy Squires—whatever his topic—a young man earns the right to be heard when it's his turn to speak.

Study the fish. Know the species. Ask yourself: What turns this guy on? What's his hot button? Then gear your moves in that direction. The point is not to try and manipulate your man into a relationship he doesn't want, but rather to be informed about what matters to him. If it matters to him, it ought to matter to you. After all, isn't that what you're going to be asking him to do—to care about the things you care about? Relationships grow out of mutual interests and concerns.

The Deer Hunt

Return with me to Presbyterian Lake. My boys and I learned the hard way that the reason we weren't catching many fish was that we really didn't know a lot about fish. We were sincere. We were dedicated. We were patient. However, none of that made much difference, because the angler's art is not a matter of inner resolve, but of knowing and responding to the behavior and feeding habits of fish. In a similar way, hooking up with a mentor requires that you know something about mentors.

One reason I knew so little about fish was that I was not raised in the outdoors. But my close friend Trevor Mabery was. I don't know that any man was ever happier than Trevor to be tramping about in the woods, or crouching down in a duck blind. He was at home out in the wild. It was just something in his blood. On one occasion, Trevor took Bill hunting and repeated the lesson that we learned at Presbyterian Lake: The key to success is knowing the species.

In the late 1960s, Trevor was a surgeon in the Air Force. One summer, our family visited his family when he was stationed at Vandenberg Air

Force Base near Lompoc, California. On the evening before the last day of our stay, Trevor invited Bill to go bow hunting for deer. Bill, about eleven at the time, had only one question: "What time do we start?"

So at 4:30 the next morning, Trevor and Bill set out in Trevor's VW Beetle. As they drove out to the area designated for hunting, Trevor pointed out the different spots where he had seen deer in previous years. "There must be thousands of them out here," he said. "We'll see if we can get you one."

Bill looked out into the blackness, straining to glimpse a pair of eyes or a flash of white. "I don't see anything," he said.

"They see you."

The two drove on in silence, until Bill asked, "How're we gonna get close enough?"

"You have to think like a deer," Trevor replied.

Bill was pondering the meaning of that statement when Trevor pulled the car off the road, turned off the engine, and killed the lights. He rolled down his window, and the chilly morning air wafted into the car. Bill rolled down his window too. After his eyes adjusted, he could just make out a stand of scrub trees that had rooted themselves to the sandy, solitary coastal plain.

For what seemed to Bill like an eternity, Trevor sat without saying a word. He was listening. Finally he leaned over and spoke in a low monotone. "It's foggy out. That's good. I think there's a deer off to your right. It'll be over here in a minute.

Sure enough, about five minutes later, Bill saw a doe come walking out of the trees, not twenty yards in front of the car. Thrilled out of his mind, he leaned over to Trevor and asked, "What should we do?"

"Nothing. She'll be a mile away before you even get the door open."

The deer had stopped and turned her face to the car. A moment later, she turned tail and trotted away.

After another ten minutes had passed, and a sooty gray half-light revealed more of the woodlands, Trevor slowly opened his door and stepped out of the car. Bill followed suit. They lifted their bows and arrows from the backseat and buckled themselves into their gear. Then Trevor led the way down a rutty cut through the terrain.

About a mile in, Trevor stopped and held up his hand. Bill listened intently, but the fog shrouded everything in muffled silence. Trevor studied the dirt in front of them. Then he leaned over and mumbled in Bill's ear.

"I'm going to walk on down this road. Give me about five minutes. There may be a deer just over that ridge in front of you. If you're careful, you'll be able to get up on him and get off a shot. If you don't get him, he'll run over my way, and I'll have a try. You ready?"

Bill nodded, wondering how Trevor knew what was on the other side of the ridge. He kept his eyes glued to the terrain in front of him as Trevor slipped away.

Bill counted to sixty five times, then he started off toward the ridge. As he came up on it, he slowed down and began gingerly taking footsteps, trying to sneak over the crest of the hill. As the other side came into view, he saw nothing but a little dip and then another rise. He paused to listen, then started down into the ravine.

Halfway down he saw it. The deer had lifted its head—crowned by a small rack of antlers. It was standing in the depression on the other side of the second ridge. Suddenly it looked the other way, and Bill made his move. Crouching down in the hollow, he drew an arrow and fitted it to the bowstring. Then he began inching up the hill. If he could only get an angle, he just knew he could hit it. Finally he stood up to take his shot. He looked straight ahead to where the deer should have been. But the animal was gone.

Three hours later, Bill and Trevor headed home. Neither one saw another deer.

"I was so close!" Bill kept saying as they warmed up the car. "I mean, he was right there!"

"You'll get him next time, Billy."

"Yeah, but who knows when that'll be!"

"Well, you'll just have to come back out here. They'll be waiting for you."

"Maybe so. But he was so close! He was right there! I bet I'll never get that chance again."

"You will. You will. You just have to think like a deer."

Trevor knew how to think like a deer. That explained his moves throughout the hunt, as Bill later realized. The pauses of silence. The intense listening. The low monotone in the ear. The observation of dirt and wind and terrain. Trevor's behavior was determined by the behavior of the deer. Who knows, if Bill had not been along, perhaps Trevor would have brought home a trophy. (On the other hand, I think Trevor got a bigger kick out of teaching Bill about hunting than bagging another buck.)

If you want to find a mentor, I suggest that you think like a mentor. He is not a particularly exotic species, nor is he difficult to track down. But as we'll see, he is easily spooked by men who are careless or ignorant of his habits.

Chapter Seven

FIRST STEPS

Richard Bolles, the career planning guru widely known for his best-selling book *What Color Is Your Parachute,* says that the average job hunt takes between six and eighteen weeks, depending on the state of the economy. Since there is a lot of similarity between finding a mentor and finding a job, it is not unreasonable to figure that it may take you between six and eighteen weeks to find someone who can serve in a mentoring capacity. It may take even longer.

I point this out for two reasons. First, to help you adjust your expectations. Second, to underscore the fact that you've got to put some time and effort into the process. *It won't just happen.*

Now some men, on hearing that, will want to drop out right here. If that's how you feel, let me make one request before you quit. In chapter 2, I discussed five ways in which a mentor can transform your life. Would you be willing to reread that chapter and reconsider the valuable benefits that you'll be missing out on if you decline to hook up with a mentor?

I make no apology for trying to talk you into sticking with this process. After more than forty-five years of working with men in terms of mentoring relationships, I can tell you without reservation that the men who are making the greatest impact for God in this generation are men who have placed themselves under the tutelage of other godly men. There's no comparison! If you care about making any kind of difference with your life—in your work, with your family, in your community, in your faith—then find someone who can help you grow and realize your life goals.

How do you enlist a man in that effort? Sooner or later you've got to approach him and recruit him to your team. For many men, this first step is the hardest to take and where the process most often starts to break down. So let's examine what's involved.

The Approach

I've mentioned that there are any number of places where you can look for someone who might qualify as a mentor. Let's suppose you've identified a candidate. What do you do next? The answer is, it all depends on your relationship to this individual. How well you know him determines your next step.

As you'll notice in the diagram below, there are three possibilities: (1) you already know the man, and he knows you; (2) you do not know each other personally, only by name; or (3) you have no relationship whatsoever. (I've presented these options on a continuum, because obviously there is a range of possibilities.)

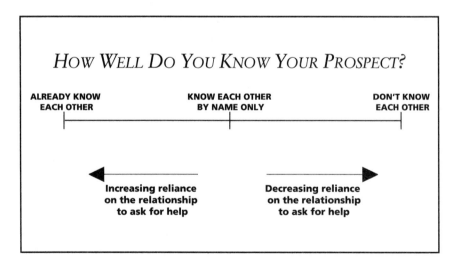

HOW WELL DO YOU KNOW YOUR PROSPECT?

ALREADY KNOW EACH OTHER	KNOW EACH OTHER BY NAME ONLY	DON'T KNOW EACH OTHER

Increasing reliance on the relationship to ask for help

Decreasing reliance on the relationship to ask for help

There are many variables that affect any individual case, so we need to be cautious about this. But generally speaking, the better you already know the man you are considering as a mentor (that is, the farther to the left you are on the diagram), the more you can rely on the relationship in order to ask for the man's help. Conversely, the less known you are to the man in question (that is, the farther to the right you are), the more you must base a request for help on something other than the relationship. Let's consider the three possibilities in turn:

1. You Already Know the Man

If you already know the man, and he knows you, then asking for his help is not that difficult. It's part of the nature of relationships. Of course, just because you ask for a man's input doesn't automatically make him your mentor. But at least you know that the next time you've got an issue, you can probably turn to him again. And he knows that you are serious about your life. That's the sort of positive, productive interaction that can turn into a mentoring relationship.

2. You Know Each Other by Name Only

Let's change the scenario a bit, to reflect the middle position on the diagram, where you only know each other by name. Say you've got a serious problem with one of your children—perhaps a life-threatening illness. It's quite possible that you would want to talk with another parent who has been down this road. But who? You ask your pastor for a referral, and he mentions Pete, a guy who attends another church and whose daughter was diagnosed with the exact same condition as your child's.

Now suppose you had met Pete one time at a convention, in passing. That sort of name-only acquaintance might make it awkward for you to just call up Pete and ask him for help, as if you were old friends. But there are several other ways to go. For example, you could have your pastor call first and feel Pete out about talking to you.

Another possibility is to go ahead and call Pete yourself, remind him of your brief encounter at the convention, briefly describe your situation, and then ask him if he knows of any resources that would help. Presenting the matter in those terms allows Pete to choose how much or how little he wants to get involved. But there is a strong possibility that he will talk about his own experience with his daughter's illness. At the very least, he will have been offered a chance to help—and people usually like to help, to the extent that they can.

Is this a mentoring relationship? It doesn't start out there, but it could turn into that. The point is that your initial approach would be determined more by the problem at hand than by the relationship. Quite possibly, a deeper relationship would grow out of this first conversation. In fact, you might want to ask Pete if you could call him again from time to time, which leaves the door open to future possibilities.

3. You Are Strangers to Each Other

Consider the third position in the diagram: You have no relationship at all with the person whose help you want. In that case, your approach will probably focus on the man's expertise, at least until a relationship is established. After all, you wouldn't want to presume on a relationship that doesn't exist.

Ted Engstrom tells of the time Pastor Harold Warner of Tucson, Arizona, received a card from a young man in his congregation. The card had one of Gary Larson's "The Far Side" cartoons on the front, in which a goofy-looking little kid is sitting between two rough and tough cowboys in a Western saloon. The boy has just spilled a glass of milk, and one of the cowboys has turned to him, saying, "So . . . you must be the one they call 'The Kid.'" Underneath the cartoon, the young man who sent the card had handwritten, "Yes, and I want to be discipled." Inside the card was the note, "I would like to express my desire to be discipled, counselled, and formed by you and the men of your like-mindedness."

This young man was making it crystal clear to Pastor Warner that he was looking for a mentor. And as his pastor it was appropriate that Warner either serve as his mentor himself, or find a man in his church who could. But suppose Warner had never even met this young man. Suppose the fellow didn't even go to Warner's church. In fact, suppose you received a card like that from a total stranger. How would you react? You probably would feel it to be a bit forward, wouldn't you? You might applaud the desire for growth, but it would only be natural to feel hesitant about volunteering your help. That's what could happen between you and your prospective mentor if you lead off with a highly personal request.

On the other hand, if you approach him about matters that he normally deals with anyway, you are much more likely to gain a hearing. Years ago, when I was still active in my radio ministry, The Art of Family

Living, I sometimes received mail from people who expressed an interest in vocational ministry. Because my passion is to train people for that very thing, I was more than happy to write them back with answers to their questions and suggestions for how to get started. In fact, I recruited some of them to attend Dallas Seminary, where they became my students, and we developed a closer association.

The point is, consider carefully how well you know a person before you approach him for help. There is no one, "right" way to solicit that help; the approach varies with the relationship. With someone you know well, you can ask for help as a friend. But with a stranger, you have to consider how to attract the man's interest, win his trust, and persuade him to give you what you want.

Twenty Ideas for Initiating a Mentoring Relationship

There are endless possibilities for how to make that initial contact with someone you'd like to recruit as a mentor. This is an area where creativity and initiative count for a lot. Obviously, some people will be better than others at initiating relationships. But here's a list of twenty ideas to get you started—and also to stimulate your own creative juices! Remember, we're talking here about attracting the attention of a prospective mentor and encouraging him to get to know you better. You'll still need to cultivate the relationship once it is established (more on that in the next chapter).

1. *Call him up and ask for an appointment to see him about a specific issue.* This is the front-door approach. Sometimes it works. Sometimes it doesn't. The more well-defined your topic or question is, *or* the better you know the man, the more successful you are likely to be. For example, Mark is struggling with his boss, who has a vicious temper. So he calls Neil, a man about ten years older, who is is in a similar line of work and goes to the same church, and asks to have breakfast with him to discuss his situation.

2. *Use a go-between to set up a meeting.* This is the strategy of "piggybacking" on someone else's relationship to the individual. For example, your Bible study leader might arrange for you to have lunch with him and Larry, who is someone you'd like you talk with about changing careers.

3. Get a referral. This is what the business world calls "networking." By using the name of a mutual acquaintance ("So-and-So suggested that I call you . . ."), you establish a measure of trust. Just be sure that your prospect has a positive opinion of So-and-So. Also, realize that dropping a name *at best* only opens the door. You have to take it from there. So for example: "Hi, my name is Howard Hendricks. I'm new to the city, but I know John Doe, who I understand goes to your church. John gave me your name as someone who knows a lot about father-son activities in the area. I have a boy who is growing up fast, and I need to start spending a lot more time with him. Could you give me some ideas for activities that he and I can do together with other fathers and sons?"

4. Praise the person on his expertise, then ask him to use it to help you develop yours. In her book *The New Mentors and Protégés,* Linda Phillips-Jones tells of a young man named Andy who wanted to meet an expert in a particular field. The expert had written numerous journal and magazine articles and had received quite a bit of criticism for his views. Andy wrote a letter defending the expert's position and sent it to the editor of one critical newspaper. "The letter was printed, and Andy sent a copy of it to the man, accompanied by a request for a personal interview. The prospective mentor could hardly say no."

You could use the same principle to approach your prospect. For example: "Ted, that was an excellent lesson you gave to the men's group yesterday. Could I buy you lunch to find out how you go about putting something like that together?" "Andrew, thanks for your prayer at the meeting. You really seem to have an intimacy with God. Do you think I could learn to pray like that?"

5. Offer to join the man's team or project. Making yourself useful to him affords him a better position to be useful to you. For example, a man named Jerry wanted to get to know Earl, an older man in his church whom he regarded highly. One Sunday Jerry noticed in the bulletin that Earl had been appointed to head a service project sponsored by the church. As soon as the worship service was over, Jerry found Earl and signed up as a volunteer on the project. That experience led to others, and the two men became good friends.

6. Offer to solve a problem for him. Mentors tend to be like the rest of us—they don't want people to bring them problems nearly as much as they want them to bring solutions. That's certainly true for me. I had a student once who insisted on waxing my car, which had a dull and splotchy finish. Afterward, the automobile looked like new. When he asked to have lunch a few weeks later, I was more than happy to oblige.

7. *Bring him an interesting opportunity that you have.* By an "interesting opportunity," I mean interesting *to him*. It needs to be worthy of his attention. For instance, Bill has a very high regard for a man in our community who is a creative genius in the display of information. In fact, Bill has studied this man's work to gain clues for his own approach to communication. Recently Bill was asked to serve on the board of a museum which is just getting started. Guess who he immediately contacted about participating in this project? The man is now keenly interested and heavily involved, and Bill gets to observe him up close.

8. *Bring him information in which he might be interested.* This principle is illustrated time and again in the job market. A man will research an industry to identify trends and determine the company he wants to work for. Then he approaches the president of the company and lays out a convincing case for how he could help it become more competitive. More often than not, an industrious man like that gets hired. The same approach can work in securing a mentor. Don't bore him with what he already knows. Tell him something he needs to know, and you will have his ear.

For example, suppose your prospect is interested in a particular cause, such as helping troubled youth. You come across a write-up of a novel and successful approach to that problem being tried in another community. Why not clip it and send it to him with a note: "Al, I saw this and thought of your concern for kids. I'd like to discuss that with you sometime. I'll give you a call."

9. *Ask him to read and react to something that you have written.* An essay, a report, a proposal, an article, a story, or a poem. If you happen to write, and you think that something you've written might interest him, send him a copy for his review and feedback. As a professor, I get this all the time. But I have friends who are doctors, lawyers, real estate people, camp directors, contractors, and even dude ranch operators who tell me

about something some young man has sent them because he wants their input as seasoned people of faith.

A variation on this theme is to invite your prospect to come see something that you have done and give you an evaluation. Examples: a home or building that you are working on; a display that you have created; a play that you are directing or performing in; a project in which you have responsibility.

10. Respond to something that he has done. This is the flip side of the previous suggestion. For example, write your prospect a letter or note that shows you have carefully thought about a book or article he has written, or a speech he has given.

11. Ask the man to tell you about his *mentors.* This works especially well if you already know the man reasonably well. By telling you about the men who have built into his life, your prospect will be building a closer bond with you. He will also tend to enjoy recalling these people, and he will recognize that you are personally interested in mentoring. Don't be surprised if he asks you about that!

12. Interview him in connection with a project that you are working on—or one that he is working on. This is particularly useful if you've never met the man before. The interview format provides a specific reason for getting together. And the project can be almost anything: setting up a committee at church, installing drywall in your home, teaching your son to dribble a basketball, planning a project at work. By approaching him about a project, you avoid the tension that naturally arises when relating to a stranger, but you still make initial contact. Later you may be able to pursue a deeper friendship based on that experience.

13. Send him something that you have produced—a book, a product, a photograph—with a note thanking him for his inspiration. Flattery? Sure it is. And as they say—it can get you everywhere (if used appropriately). The point is that every man needs affirmation. You may well make your prospect's day with a sincerely written note, and it offers an opportunity for follow-up later.

14. Honor him publicly. In speeches, in your writings, in reports, even in casual conversation. Let people know that you think highly of your prospect, and why. If you win an award, honor him in your acceptance speech. Sooner or later, you may have the opportunity to meet him, in which case you can legitimately say, "You've been such an inspiration to me. I really think of you as a mentor."

A man named Hunter was quite fond of quoting a particular Christian leader to the people at his church. He loved the man's writings and audiotapes, which he found to be a great source of inspiration and insight. Of course, Hunter never imagined that he would ever get to meet this individual in person.

Then one day the pastor called to say that this leader was coming to speak at the church. Would Hunter's family be willing to host the man in his home during his stay? Naturally, Hunter was more than glad to oblige. "I'm his biggest fan," he told him.

"I know," the pastor replied. "That's why we asked you."

The speaker had a wonderful time staying in Hunter's home, and the two struck up a friendship that lasted many years.

15. *Take advantage of any structured opportunities for interaction that he offers.* This is especially true if your prospect teaches in any form. For example, if he leads an adult Sunday school class, be sure to attend. If he holds seminars, enroll in one. If he offers training classes, sign up. These are golden opportunities, because the whole point of these venues is to allow the man to influence people—including you—with his ideas and presence.

16. *If he has ever told you to look him up sometime, take him up on his offer.* Have you ever had someone close a conversation or letter with the words, "Let's get together sometime"? If the man with whom you are trying to get together has ever used that line, follow up on it. Contact him and remind him of his offer, and ask when you can come by. Let him know you are genuinely interested in getting with him, and try to set a definite day, time, and place for a meeting.

17. *Enlist the man's support even before you need it.* They say that the best time to look for a job is when you already have one. Likewise, the best time to raise money is when you don't need it. A similar principle applies to finding a mentor: as odd as it sounds, the best time to approach a potential mentor is when you don't need his help. Why? Because you're more relaxed, and the situation is less threatening when you don't need to ask for any favors.

So, if you're still in high school, vocational school, college, or graduate school; if you are still dating, but getting serious about marriage; if you are just starting a family; if you are new to a church—while you are still in relatively "low stress" circumstances like these, anticipate the man whose help you may need someday. Then make yourself known to him. Let him know that you are aware of who he is and why he attracts your attention—perhaps because he is in the same career that you are pursuing, or you admire his marriage and family life, or you recognize that he is a leader in the congregation.

If he lives some distance from you, ask if you can correspond with him occasionally about issues and trends in your field, or about what it means to be an effective husband or father. Let him know that you value his opinion. During holidays or vacations, see if you can drop in for a half-hour to update him on your progress.

18. Give him periodic updates on yourself. Mentoring relationships often take a long time to develop—sometimes years. One way that happens is when the prospective protégé stays in touch with a man whose input he values, just to let him know what he is up to. An occasional phone call or a note with a Christmas card can signal to the prospective mentor, "I'm still out here. I'm still growing. I'm still interested in staying in touch." When the time is right (see the next point, #19), the relationship may blossom.

I have guys who drop me a note every time they change jobs. Others drop me a line every time they launch a new project. I like that, because it keeps me informed. It also leaves the door open to future contact.

19. Wait for the right timing. Have you ever stopped to consider that a number of your future mentors (and you're going to need several mentors—*plural*—during your life) may already be within your circle of acquaintances? They can't help you right now. Maybe they are not ready, you are not ready, or both. Still, by cultivating your relationships, you store up personal capital that can pay off later when the time is right. One day you'll say, "I need help in this or that area—and I know just the man to contact."

20. Pray for a mentor. Again, where prayer focuses, power falls. In the end, you've got to trust God to supply you with men who can influence your life. To be sure, you've got to stay on the lookout, but you've also got to stay on your knees. Ask God to bring men into your life who can take you to higher levels of personal and spiritual maturity.

One Thing Not to Do

I've been describing different ways that you can approach a prospective mentor and enlist him in your development. In the next chapter, I'll have more to say about defining and cultivating the relationship. But I need to warn you about one thing that is liable to shut the relationship down even before it gets started. If I were you, I would *avoid using the terms "mentor" or "mentoring," unless your prospect uses those terms first.* Otherwise, you may scare him off.

This caution may surprise you in light of the fact that I've been using the terms "mentor" and "mentoring" over and over in this book. But think about it from the prospective mentor's standpoint. Imagine that you show up in front of a guy, and after some casual conversation to break the ice, he asks you why you wanted to get together. So you clear your throat and say, "Well, the truth of the matter is, I'm looking for a mentor. Will you mentor me?"

You are liable to get one of two reactions. On the one hand, he may look at you sideways and say, "Huh? What's a mentor? I don't know what you're talking about!" I doubt that will instill confidence in you.

However, a more likely scenario is that he will give you that deer-in-the-headlights look and turn fifteen shades of pale before he holds up his hands and says, "Oh, buddy, you've got the wrong guy! I mean, I'm not—I can't—I-I-I wouldn't know the first thing about that. A mentor? No way!" Somehow, I don't think you want that reaction, either.

But why would an otherwise calm, competent, and compassionate individual react this way? Because the truth of the matter is, *most men do not see themselves as potential mentors.* It doesn't matter whether or not they actually have that capacity (and most do); they don't see themselves that way. And that's determinative.

For some, it's the feelings of inadequacy that our culture seems to reinforce: "You're not smart enough," "You don't have enough training," (and often in the church) "You're not spiritual enough."

Others are afraid of sounding pretentious. You see, in our society, it's OK for someone to perceive me as his mentor; it's not OK for me to see myself as his mentor. This is nonsense, of course, but it's also reality. So you have to consider it.

An additional problem is that many men have false or unrealistic expectations of what a mentor is and does. They hear the word "mentor," and they think of some holy man or guru who has God's infallible word from on high for every question he's asked. It's like Moses on Mount Sinai, with the trumpets blaring and the smoke billowing, and the Shekinah glory coming down. Or they think in terms of heavy-duty responsibility, as if they have to check out every move you make, and every time you run into trouble they've got to bail you out.

Frankly, I don't know whether books like this one help or hurt these perceptions. My hope is that *As Iron Sharpens Iron* can correct them (see Part 2). But you've got to start with where your man is. I warn you that with many men, use of the word "mentor" will spook them.

Fortunately, you don't need to use the terms "mentor" or "mentoring" to establish the relationship you want. In the end, it doesn't matter how you describe or define it; what matters is that you *develop* it. So don't get hung up on whether the interaction you've got going with another man is or is not a so-called "mentoring relationship." Just pay attention to the relationship.

Are you willing to glean from another man's wisdom, experience, and expertise? Are you willing to seek him out for advice? Are you willing, when it is appropriate, to bare your soul and let him see and feel what is inside you? Are you willing to ask him for help in troubleshooting problems, recommending resources, introducing you to people, and otherwise opening doors to the world and windows to the mind? That's "all" we're talking about.

Chapter Eight

STRATEGIES FOR GROWTH

In the late 1970s, a group of psychiatrists and other scientists was fascinated by an intriguing new computer program called DOCTOR. By all outward appearances, DOCTOR seemed to be capable of taking the place of a psychotherapist conducting an interview with a patient. As the patient keyed his troubles into the computer, DOCTOR responded with remarkably accurate observations and surprisingly sympathetic comments.

The scientists hailed this as a breakthrough. Someday, they predicted, therapy would be handled by computer. No more trouble making diagnoses. No more malpractice premiums. No more patients on the couch. (Apparently the prospect that a machine might put them all out of work never occurred to anybody!)

Imagine the scientists' surprise, then, when the author of DOCTOR revealed that the program was merely analyzing the patient's language and responding with various scripts, all of which had been prepared beforehand. There was no real interaction taking place. The machine did not "understand" the patient. The program could not replace a psychiatrist (though, on the other hand . . .).

Relationships with a Purpose

We need to keep the lessons of DOCTOR in mind as we talk about mentoring relationships. I've been describing the process whereby you can link up with a mentor. But as we've seen, there is no patented way for doing that. Much as I might like to give you a computerized, systematized, fail-safe, tried-and-true method, that is unrealistic. There is no one-size-fits-all approach. Each relationship is unique.

We saw something of this in the last chapter, where I pointed out that you have to gear your moves on the basis of the relationship. If you know your prospective mentor well, it's easier to ask for his time and help. But if you don't know him at all, you have to find something other than the relationship to carry the initial contact.

In this chapter I want to talk about the agenda that you establish with your mentor once you've broken the ice and established something of a bond. By *agenda*, I mean your purpose in getting together. Your agenda is comprised of the things you intend to work on—your goals, your issues, your problems, your needs. Defining an agenda is key, because it forms a basis for everybody's expectations. It also determines what you actually do in the interaction. "What are we going to be doing when we get together?" your mentor may be asking. (You may be wondering the same thing.) An agenda answers that question.

However, in order to come up with an agenda that works for both of you, you need to consider a couple of variables.

Formal Versus Informal Mentoring

There are two basic kinds of mentoring. One is structured, facilitated, and formal. The other is nonstructured, spontaneous, and informal. As we saw with the relationship, we might want to view these as two ends of a spectrum. However, we often find the two combined: Formal mentoring relationships often involve informal activities, and informal mentoring relationships sometimes make use of more formal strategies for development.

Formal Programs

Formal programs for mentoring are common today in the workplace, and increasingly in education. Churches and parachurch ministries are also beginning to develop mentoring programs, and I heartily encourage you to consider that for your congregation (see Establishing a Mentoring Program in Your Church, p. 231). Actually, some churches have been using principles of mentoring for years, even though they haven't used that term to describe their work. (A common designation is "discipleship." I'll draw some distinctions between mentoring and discipleship later). Here are five examples of formal mentoring programs:

- *In government.* The General Accounting Office (GAO) of the United States has a program called the Executive Candidate Development Program (ECDP), which pairs some of the GAO's 125 senior executives with between fifty and sixty ECDP candidates each year.

- *In a business.* At Rooney, Ida, Nolt and Ahern, an Oakland, California-based accounting firm, all one hundred employees are eligible to participate in a volunteer mentoring program overseen by the personnel manager. Twice a year, the company calls for volunteers to serve as mentors. Those who want to be mentored (called participants) give the personnel manager the name of five mentor candidates. Then a screening process attempts to match every participant with his first or second choice.

- *In education.* Several dozen Yale University students serve as volunteers in a science program called DEMOS (Daringly Educational Marvels of Science) for the New Haven, Connecticut, elementary schools. Working in teams of three, the volunteers visit a classroom twice a semester, putting on an hour-long demonstration related to science. They also help the teacher integrate the presentation into the curriculum, and meet with students after school for a weekly science club.

- *In parachurch ministries.* One of the oldest and most well-known programs for spiritual development is the 2:7 Series sponsored by The Navigators, a Christian organization based in Colorado Springs, Colorado, dedicated to fostering discipleship. The program takes its name from Colossians 2:7, which urges believers to be "rooted and built up in [Christ], strengthened in the faith as you were taught, and overflowing with thankfulness." The ten sessions in the series lay a foundation for one's faith by emphasizing fundamental beliefs, attitudes, and habits designed to bring growth in character as well as in biblical understanding.

Another program designed around the concept of mentoring is the Marketplace Mentors program, established in 1986 by Marketplace, a division of InterVarsity Christian Fellowship of Madison, Wisconsin. Marketplace pairs Christians who are just starting out in their careers with older believers in the same careers.

Formal (or facilitated) programs like these are encouraging to see. But they also can be difficult to execute. One of the hardest things is to get a workable match between a protégé and a mentor.

Informal Mentoring

By far, the most common form of mentoring is the informal approach. It is rarely called mentoring and tends to be overlooked (as well as undervalued). Nevertheless, you can find the principles of mentoring being practiced everywhere. For example:

- Two men serving on a church committee get together for coffee. The older man explains to the younger man how the committee operates, what its purpose is, and how the younger man might contribute. This is a form of informal mentoring.

- A mechanic invites a teenager to help him fix a car. They spend a day bent over the engine, the mechanic pointing out what is wrong with the car, and the boy handing him tools, pumping the accelerator, and occasionally even making needed adjustments under the mechanic's supervision. This is a form of informal mentoring.

- A student decides to pursue a particular major, largely because he is drawn to one of the professors. The student takes all of the professor's courses, regularly shows up at his office, and takes on special projects that the professor suggests. There is no official requirement that either the student or the professor ought to pursue this kind of relationship. It emerges naturally. It is a form of informal mentoring.

- A man in his late twenties becomes friends with a man who has just turned forty. They attend the same church. They see each other around town. They periodically get together for lunch. They go fishing together. During the next 15 years they build a close friendship, and the older man has a profound influence on the younger, who observes the older man's Christ-centered life up close as he lives it out in everyday activities. This is an unusually significant relationship, but it is still a form of informal mentoring.

A Difference in Expectations

Can you see some of the differences between formal and informal mentoring? Neither one is better. They just start out with different expectations. For instance, if you are an apprentice on a construction site, the company would pair you with an experienced man, and your agenda would be structured primarily along work lines. As time goes by, and depending on the chemistry between you and the experienced man, you might get into personal issues. But those would probably be secondary.

By contrast, if you and a friend get together, you have to develop your own agenda, since no one from the outside is imposing one on you. That's why I asked you to think carefully about your objectives in chapter 3. If you know what you want or need, you make it a lot easier for your mentor to help you. He has a base from which to work.

My guess is that most men reading this book are trying to establish a fairly informal mentoring relationship with someone. If that's the case with you, I suggest that you keep your expectations modest and flexible. Frankly, you are pioneering in territory that desperately needs to be conquered, but where there are few guides to lead you through the terrain.

As I cautioned at the conclusion of the last chapter, don't get hung up on whether the friendship that you and another man are building qualifies as "mentoring." Just pursue the relationship. Even those who run facilitated mentoring programs will tell you, a label means almost nothing. What matters is whether anything positive is rubbing off when one man deals with another.

Immediate Concerns vs. Long-Term Issues

A second distinction to be aware of as you set your agenda is the difference between immediate concerns and long-term, core issues. This is the distinction between the crisis and the chronic, felt needs and real needs, symptoms and diseases.

A guy comes to me and says, "Prof, I need help with my prayer life. I just can't seem to pray the way I should." So we agree to get together for prayer, three times a week for a month. However, over the next four weeks, he misses six of our scheduled appointments, shows up late for the other six, and leaves early from three of those.

Finally I ask him, "Hey, friend, if you want to develop a prayer life, don't you think you should make our prayer time a priority in your schedule?"

"What do you mean?" he asks. "It is a priority. Why, I've got it right here in my book. See? Three times a week: 'Hendricks for prayer.'"

"Yes," I reply, "I know it's in your book. But it's not in your life." He looks at me like I dropped a two-by-four on his head! So I point out, "Do you realize that you've missed half of our times together, and cut the other six short? If this were a course, do you think you'd be passing?"

You see, this guy has a problem with his prayer life because he's got a far greater problem, one that affects everything in his life: he's an undisciplined individual. Unless I address that, we could spend years trying to get his pray life in shape, but at the end of the time we'd still be stuck at square one. No, if I intend to really help him grow, I've got to do two things. First, I've got to help him recognize his fundamental need for self-discipline, then I've got to help him develop in that area.

Getting Down to Basics

Now I'm not disparaging the guy for seeking help with his prayer life. That's fantastic! Nor would I disparage you for approaching someone for help with a particular need that you have. But never forget that the agenda you bring is always the tip of the iceberg. There are always underlying issues—especially issues of character.

And that's the value of mentoring. It starts with the things you want to work on, and ideally leads to the things you need to work on. For example, you might start out wanting to understand the Bible, but you end up realizing that what you really need is to learn how to read. You might start out trying to get control of your finances, but you end up discovering that you've never learned the value of hard work. You might start out trying to stop sinning in a particular area, but you end up realizing that you've never learned to walk by the Spirit.

Fundamental issues like these tend to surface as you relate to a mentor. If he is a person of insight, he will help you address basic areas, so that you not only solve immediate problems, but in the process grow into an altogether different person—a wiser, more mature, more Christlike person.

Expecting Too Much—Or Too Little

This distinction between surface issues and core concerns has a lot of implications for how you and your mentor structure your time together. For one thing, it ought to temper your expectations. You may be a go-getter who really wants to go for broke in terms of your personal development. That's great! Just recognize that you always have to start with where you are. If your mentor is wise, that's where he'll start. Sure, you may feel like you are ready to take on any challenge, conquer any mountain. But before you start up Everest, be willing to climb a few foothills first to test your skills.

On the other hand, you may need to raise your expectations. You may be going into the relationship assuming that it will affect you in merely superficial ways. You think you're going to get a tune-up. But in reality, you're in for a major overhaul. That's the power of godly mentoring. It can change your life in ways you never imagined.

Setting an Agenda

Sooner or later, the man you perceive as your mentor is probably going to ask you, "How can I help?" Or else, you are going to say to him, "Here's how I need your help." Either way, when you get to that point, you are establishing an agenda. You are negotiating what it is that you want to work on, and what it is that your mentor will do to help.

How, then, do you establish that agenda? Keeping in mind the distinctions we have just made—between formal and informal mentoring and between immediate concerns and long-term issues—ask yourself questions such as: What do I want this person to do for me? What do I want to learn from him? How can he help me? What do I expect to be the outcome of spending time with him?

You should also refer back to your answers to the five questions posed in chapter 3, which can be personalized as:

(1) What do I want?
(2) What price am I willing to pay?
(3) How do I plan to accomplish my objectives?
(4) What is my personal dynamic?
(5) How do I learn?

Your answers to these questions, particularly the first, should get you started in identifying items you want to work on. Of course, it is altogether possible that you're struggling even to come up with answers to these questions. If so, that's a good place to start with your mentor. Tell him you need his help to think through these basic issues.

Do you and your mentor need to consciously and verbally agree on everything you're going to work on together? That's probably unrealistic and, in some cases, almost unnecessary. But as a general rule, the more concrete your agenda is, the more you need agreement on how you are going to accomplish that agenda. Moreover, the more you need to pay attention to the last two questions above: What is your personal dynamic, and how do you learn?

The Learning Contract

The need to arrive at a mutually agreeable agenda can be seen in the *learning contracts* that formalized mentoring programs often employ. A learning contract is a written statement that lays out the expectations of both protégé and mentor. Empire State College of the State University of New York has been using learning contracts since 1971 to create highly individualized degree programs for its students, who are mostly people in the workplace. The faculty for these students are referred to as "mentors." They negotiate a course of study with each student, draw up a learning contract with them, and then submit that contract to a dean for approval. This signed agreement helps to focus everyone's activity, clarify expectations, and measure progress.

You may not need to write up a learning contract with your mentor. The relationship may not call for that. But I will tell you this: The clearer you are about where you are going and how you are going to get there, the faster you will tend to arrive at your goals and the fewer problems you will tend to encounter on the way. (Frankly, I wish every educational institution required its teachers and students to define in writing what and how they intend to learn. It could transform the results overnight. The same holds true for churches.)

Some Suggested Activities

I want to encourage you to be as imaginative as you can be in thinking up an agenda for your development. Whoever said personal growth has to be boring? If it is, you have to wonder—how much growth is taking place?

But let me provide some sparks for your imagination and creativity with a handful of ideas. The projects and exercises below are not assignments—just a few suggestions to seed the clouds in hopes of provoking a brainstorm:

1. *Get on his turf.* Visit your mentor's workplace, his home, the places where he hangs out. If he travels, see if you can go on a trip with him. See him in action. Play the part of an observer. See what you can learn just by watching him "do his thing," especially when he's in his own element.

2. *Invite him onto your turf.* Let him come into your home, your workplace, maybe even show up at your son's soccer game where you happen to coach. Let him observe you. If he's a perceptive man, he'll pick up on things you never even dreamed of.

(These first two activities give both you and your mentor an appreciation for each other's background, preferences, and style. They can also help to lay a foundation for the relationship on which you can build as you spend more time together.)

3. *Take on a responsibility.* Run a program. Oversee a major purchase. Solve a problem. Deliver a package. Your mentor may or may not supervise you in this activity. But let him observe you in action. Then debrief with him, so that he can critique your performance—and character.

4. *Go through a process over time.* If you're involved in a course of study, a counseling situation, a family or personal illness, a relocation—anything that plays out over a period of time—that's a great opportunity to make use of your mentor. Let him be a sounding board. Ask him to critique you in the midst of the process. For example, what does he observe about your discipline, your tenacity, your problem-solving ability, your response to crises, your ability to size up people and situations, your learning style?

5. *Give a speech or other presentation in front of a group.* Then debrief with him.

Now this suggestion will appeal to some, but intimidate the socks off others. Research by people like the Dale Carnegie organization and other groups devoted to communication has consistently shown that the number one fear of American workers is the fear of public speaking. People worry about that even more than they worry about losing their jobs!

So why include it as an idea for mentoring? Because one of the most valuable things you can do for your personal and spiritual growth is develop your communication skills. You may or may not have gifts in teaching, persuasion, or other communication arts. It doesn't matter. Sooner or later, you're going to face a situation where you need to express yourself in front of a group of people—even if it's just a small group of two or three. To give the gospel, for example, or influence an important decision. Your mentor will be doing you an invaluable service if he instills in you the confidence to speak your mind and helps you learn to say what you have to say clearly and effectively.

I'll never forget a student I had in a preaching class at the seminary. He was assigned to come up with an illustration and then present it in front of the group. At the next class period, he was among the guys sort of shrinking down in their chairs, hoping I wouldn't call on them. But he was the first one I tapped. "OK, man, you're on!"

"Me, Prof?"

"Yeah, you."

He reluctantly made his way forward and started in. Then half-way through, he stopped cold. "Good night, Prof, I forgot the ending! Let me sit down."

"Naw," I said, "you can't sit down. Anybody here want him to sit down?" There was a chorus of no's. "Sorry, nobody wants you to sit down."

So he backed up to get another running start. Finally he remembered the rest of the illustration. When he went to sit down, the class burst into applause, which brought a huge smile to his sweating face.

I asked, "Is this the first time you've ever done that, pal?"

"Very first time, Prof."

"Fantastic!" I said. I was so proud of him. Then I asked, "Did you enjoy it?"

"No," he laughed, "it was horrible!"

But he got through it. And the next time he had to stand up before the group, he was a lot more confident. Today, he's one of the better communicators around.

Now obviously, this man was in training to become a preacher. He had little choice but to work on his public speaking skills. That may not be the case for you, and learning to speak in front of an audience is certainly not a requirement to be mentored. Still, I heartily encourage you to at least give it a try once or twice, under your mentor's tutelage. The best way to conquer a fear is often to just do the very thing you fear. But beyond that, the experience may open for you a whole new door to the world. If you doubt that, re-read the story of Jim in chapter 4.

6. *Do a leisure activity together.* Go to a ball game. Go water-skiing. Ride horses together. Play a game of chess. Visit a bookstore.

Attend a concert. Have a backyard barbecue with your wives or families. It's in moments like these, when your guard tends to be down, that some of the best teachable moments come along.

7. *Involve him in a significant decision you are making.* Are you buying a house or a car? Planning your life insurance? Trying to figure out where to send your kids to school? Changing jobs? Taking on a new role or assignment at church? Major choices like these call for wisdom. Your mentor should be able to supply some of that.

Remember that decisions are always values-driven. They reveal what matters to you. So allowing your mentor to help you think things through will surface your fundamental beliefs and commitments—whether positive or negative—and create opportunities for insight and growth. *You* need to make the decision, but your mentor can help to make it an *informed* decision.

8. *Pray and worship together.* I'd like to think that this would be a given, but that's not always the case. Men will work together and play together, but not always pray together. So let me challenge you to *ask* your mentor to join you in prayer. It's not the words that matter, but the worship that counts.

One of the beauties of prayer is that it reveals a man's heart. I tell you, I sometimes learn more about a man from his prayers than by any other means. Furthermore, when men pray and worship together, they bond. If you've been to one of the Promise Keepers gatherings, you know what I'm talking about. Men all over the country have hugged, laughed, and cried together as they joined in worship in outdoor arenas, vowing to live for God and their families.

Any Man Can

Now be honest with me—are there any of these suggestions that you *can't* do? Probably not. Most men should have no trouble doing all of them. My point is that the process of personal development does not need to be highly complicated or excruciatingly painful. It ought to be an adventure—literally, the adventure of your life! So why not get started right now?

Chapter Nine

CAUTION: MEN AT WORK!

Michael wore the expression of a basset hound as he sat in the car with Will, his high school buddy.

"C'mon, man, let's go in and get a burger," Will said, nodding toward the restaurant nearby.

"I'm not very hungry," mumbled Michael. He made no move to open the door.

"Look, he's gone, and that's that," Will replied, starting to sound a bit exasperated.

"Yeah, I know." Michael shook his head. "I know. But that's the problem. He's gone. He's not coming back. And the worst of it is, he didn't even say good-bye!" There was genuine bitterness in his voice, and he was staring out the window as if the world had suddenly taken on an entirely different look.

"You spend all that time with a guy," he continued, "and then one day—*Poof!*—he vaporizes."

Michael then assumed a different voice. " 'We're brothers, Michael—you and me. We're brothers in Christ, man!' 'I'm with you all the way, man!' 'You can count on me, man!' Yeah, right!"

Michael kept shaking his head. "What a lousy thing to do!" Finally he sighed and opened the car door. As he shifted his legs to get out, he muttered, "Well, that's the last time I trust one of these bozo youth leaders that the church keeps sending!"

Warning: Road Hazards Ahead!

This true story is tragic—but all too familiar. A bright, enthusiastic, energetic young man takes on a leadership role for the youth group in a church. He pours his time and talent into working with those kids, firing them up, challenging them in the faith, encouraging them in their relationships, helping them with their problems—until they think he's just the greatest. They invest all of their young, inexperienced loyalty in him. If he says it, they figure it's got to be right. If he does it, it's got to be cool. If he condemns it, it's got to be bad. In their eyes, he's the leader. He's the pacesetter. He's the man to follow.

Then one day, he's suddenly gone. Maybe he gets transferred, maybe he graduates from college or seminary, maybe he gets married and moves away. But he makes a catastrophic mistake: he forgets to put closure on his relationships. He walks out and leaves a giant hole in the hearts of his teenage troops. And for some of them, like Michael, it's a bad news item. They will never forget that their role model took off and never even bothered to say good-bye. I've seen it happen dozens of times.

It is experiences like this one that often give mentoring a bad name. "Don't bother me with this relational jazz," a guy will say in reaction to my call for men to form vital relationships. "Sorry—been there, done that! I tried it once, and it didn't work out. It sounds good, but it doesn't happen that way. People let you down. I can't take that again. So count me out!"

When I hear that kind of disillusionment, it makes me want to plant a sign at the front end of every relationship getting underway. The sign reads: "Caution: Men at Work!" You know what a construction project looks like, don't you? It's real messy. Lots of dirt and debris everywhere. That's what relationships can be like too. Why? Because all of us are still under construction—you and your mentor included. None of us will be fully complete until the Lord takes us home. So when we interact with each other, our unreconstructed flaws can cause problems for other people. As a result, it's best if we proceed with some caution.

So, having earlier described the benefits of mentoring relationships, let me now warn you about a few potential breakdowns—some barriers to surmount and some potholes to avoid. By anticipating these trouble spots, you stand a far greater chance of having a positive, productive journey with your mentor. Even if you already have a mentor, watch out for the following hazards, and consider the suggestions given in order to improve your current relationship.

Unrealistic Expectations

Unrealistic expectations can go both ways. You can expect more of your mentor than he is capable of delivering. He may demand more of you than you are capable of performing.

Just as unrealistic expectations cause a lot of men to shy away from serving as mentors, they also cripple the mentoring relationship. A guy comes to me and says, "Howie, I've been pouring my life into this kid for the last year, and I'm just worn out. I don't like it anymore."

I say, "Well, tell me about your relationship."

So he describes a scenario in which he's been getting together at least once a week with this young man, and talking on the phone with him about every other day. "It's gotten to the point where I'm not even getting my own work done!" he tells me.

Now that much interaction is an incredible investment of time and energy—far more than is probably necessary, unless these two men are in a highly structured environment such as a school or training program. So I ask why he thinks he needs to put in that amount of effort. He says, "Because when we started out, I wanted this fellow to know I was committed to him, so I told him I'd always be there for him. I had no idea that he would interpret 'always' as *always*!"

Both this man and his protégé are operating from an unrealistic perspective. If they have any hope of salvaging the relationship from burnout, they need to make some drastic changes. They need to cut way back on the amount of time, meeting less frequently, and with more clearly defined objectives. They also need to see that the purpose of mentoring is not for the mentor to carry the protégé, but for the mentor to help the protégé learn to walk on his own.

The crazy thing about expectations, though, is that they are usually insidious. You tend to be unaware of them—until they are unmet. Then you suddenly feel ripped off. Yet it's impossible for either you or your mentor to establish a relationship without bringing at least some expectations to it. Some you will be aware of and will be able to articulate to each other. In so doing, you allow each other to respond and determine together whether those expectations are realistic. But other expectations you will be unaware of, and eventually one or both of you will feel disappointment. If you are feeling that way toward your mentor, you need to stop and ask a few diagnostic questions:

- What did I expect to happen that hasn't happened?
- What grounds did I base my expectations on in the first place? Where did they come from?
- Did I ever communicate to my mentor what I wanted? Did he agree to provide that?
- In general, what am I hoping that this relationship will do for me? Is that hope realistic? Can any relationship satisfy it, or am I wishing on a star?

The best way to avoid disappointment is to clarify as much as you can up front. That's why we talked about setting an agenda in the previous chapter. If the two of you can reach agreement, especially in terms of goals and frequency of interaction, you won't be making assumptions that will come back to bite you later.

This point leads right into. . .

Unfulfilled Expectations

Even when your expectations are thoroughly realistic and mutually agreeable, sooner or later you are bound to be disappointed. No matter how perfect he may seem, your mentor will probably let you down at some point. He will miss an appointment, fail to make a phone call that he promised, ignore a report that you gave him to read, or give you a lot less input on a decision than you had hoped for.

Some years ago, our family was having dinner when the phone rang. My wife, Jeanne, answered, and I heard her tell the caller that we were eating. But a moment later, she returned to the table with a funny look on her face. "It's Wendell Johnston. I think you better take this one," she said.

I grabbed the phone and said, "Hello, Wendell."

"How're you tonight, Howie?" he asked.

"Fine. What's up?"

"Well, I don't mean to spoil your supper, but I've got a problem."

"Wendell, you know I'll do anything I can to help you," I told him.

"Well, I don't know if you can," he replied. "You see, I'm over here in Fort Worth (about thirty-five miles away), and I've got a room full of a few hundred people waiting for you to speak."

I had blown it! Pure and simple. I had agreed to speak months ago, had forgotten to check the calendar, and now I had left my good friend Wendell holding the bag. It was unintentional, and from my perspective inexcusable. But at that point, there was nothing I could do except apologize and feel pretty woolly. (Fortunately, Wendell and I can enjoy a good laugh about that blunder today.)

Your mentor is only human (just like you). In fact, the longer you hang around him, the more likely it is that the clay in his feet will become evident. He may make commitments to you that he doesn't keep. He may promise you more than he can produce. He may violate some of the very principles that he has held up to you. Don't be wiped out by it.

But don't excuse it either. When he fails to fulfill what the two of you have agreed upon, then you're going to have to do a brave thing: you're going to have to call him on it. Not in a pugnacious way, but in a straightforward way. "Hey, I thought we were supposed to get together? I really missed the time with you. It's important to me." Or, "You said you were going to write a letter to So-and-So on my behalf. He says he never got it. Did you forget to send it?"

The beauty of mentoring is that you have someone to look up to. But the risk and the inevitable reality is that this person who you think so highly of will also let you down. When he does, deal with it in a Christlike way and move on.

A Mentor Who Fails

Finally, like yourself, your mentor can stumble. What do you do if he stumbles badly and falls into sin?

There are no easy answers to this question. Every case is unique. But there are some general principles that apply across the board. One is, pray. Pray for your mentor, for God to work in his life to bring about repentance, forgiveness, and restoration. Also pray for yourself, for wisdom, sensitivity, and a sense of direction for what to do. Pray for patience too that God would keep you from just reacting, instead of responding. And pray for the grace to forgive him.

It's also a good idea to pull back from the agenda that you and your mentor have established. I'm not suggesting that you abandon the relationship. But if your man is struggling through deep waters of his own, how much of a resource can he be to you?

A third piece of advice is to learn from his failure. I've known guys whose heroes wiped out right in front of their eyes, and frankly, (this may surprise you) it was one of the best things that ever happened to the protégés. They had elevated these figures so high on the pedestal that only a catastrophic fall could correct their distorted perspective and redirect their focus on the Lord. It was a tough way to learn, but the lesson would stick with them forever: no man is invincible.

Learning from someone else's failure means paying attention to your own vulnerability in that same area (see Galatians 6:1). It also requires that you guard against becoming disillusioned with the faith or with the mentoring process. If your mentor has failed, that's a tragedy. But his lapse doesn't nullify the truth of God's Word or the value of life-on-life relationships. If anything, it underscores the need for men to keep short accounts with God, and to hold themselves accountable to other men.

Problems of Control

Mentoring is all about influence—one man influencing another. But influence, by its very nature, is rooted in the issue of power. If I influence you, it's because you are granting me the power to influence you. When you let someone mentor you, you are granting him the power to affect your life.

Can you see the inherent danger in this set-up? As long as your mentor respects your sovereignty as an individual and takes the Christlike posture of a servant-leader, you're OK. But what happens if he usurps control of your life and starts using you to accomplish his own agenda? What happens if you abdicate responsibility and become a puppet in his hands and a parrot of his words?

It is this very problem that has given mentoring, and the related process of discipleship, a bad press in some quarters. "I don't want anybody running my life!" people will say. "I don't want to end up being a pawn of somebody like Jim Jones or David Koresh."

To which I reply: Good! We don't need any more tragedies like that. There is one Lord, Jesus Christ. He is the only Person to whom we should ever cede total control of our lives. To hand over that authority to anyone else is spiritual adultery.

And yet we can't escape the fact that we need to let others influence and shape us. "Remember your leaders," urged the writer to the Hebrews, referring to leaders in the faith. "Consider the outcome of their way of life and imitate their faith. . . . Obey your leaders and submit to their authority. They keep watch over you as men who must give an account. Obey them so that their work will be a joy, not a burden, for that would be of no advantage to you" (Hebrews 13:7, 17). Scripture is unequivocal: The Lord wants us to place ourselves under the spiritual authority of godly leaders, for our own good.

So how can we do that without handing over too much control? Answering that question is itself a major part of the learning process. As boys grow into men, they have to establish their boundaries and learn to protect themselves. That comes by experience—often in the school of hard knocks. But let me suggest some principles that may help.

No Unlimited Commitments

First, whatever authority you relinquish to someone else should be *limited* and *temporary*. Many years ago, I went to my doctor friend with a tremendous pain in my side. He checked me out and said, "Hendricks, you've got a rock collection in your gall bladder! We're going to have to operate."

So I checked into the hospital. Before they put me under for the surgery, I signed a release form giving my surgeon permission to operate on me. But I wasn't signing my life away! I was merely allowing the medical personnel to sedate me for two or three hours in order to perform the surgery. It was a limited procedure.

In a similar way, as you place yourself under another man's influence, focus on a few limited objectives for a certain period of time. This is what I encourage my students at the seminary to do. From where I sit, I can see all kinds of things that they could work on. But I try to get them to target just a few key areas during their time in school. When we eventually graduate them—and we do graduate them—they still have a lot to work on, but hopefully they have made a few measurable gains.

An Outsider's Perspective

A second principle comes from Paul's relationship with Timothy. Remember the apostle's charge to his young protégé? "The things you have heard me say in the presence of many witnesses entrust to reliable men who will also be qualified to teach others" (2 Timothy 2:2). Have you ever noticed the context in which Paul gave instruction to Timothy? It was *in the presence of many witnesses*. In other words, Paul and Timothy's interaction did not occur in secret. There were other people around, observing what was being said and what was taking place.

Other people can be one of your best defenses against someone gaining too much control over your life. That's one reason I encourage mentoring to take place in groups, as well as one on one. It's a lot harder for an overly domineering mentor to force his will on a group than on an individual.

Never be afraid to check out anything your mentor says or does by consulting another trustworthy person. If you have doubts about what is going on, compare notes with someone whose judgment you respect. And pay special attention when someone tells you, "Hey, I think you're letting So-and-So rub off on you just a little too much."

I might add that you should always compare anything you hear—from your mentor or anyone else—with Scripture and the testimony of the Holy Spirit. If someone is telling you something that does not resonate with what the Bible and the Spirit say, it's off-base, no matter how good it may sound.

Whose Life Is It, Anyway?

One final way to test whether your mentor is exerting too much control over you is to *ask yourself whether you can regain control whenever you wish*. If you can, you're OK. If you can't, you need to reevaluate the relationship.

When Bill was in college, he had a friend who was participating in a group sponsored by a particular parachurch ministry. One spring break, this group decided to hold an event designed for evangelistic outreach. As the holiday approached, Bill asked his friend what his plans were.

"Well, I'd like to go home," the young man said. "In fact, I need to go home." He then described a serious situation that had come up in his family.

"Yeah, it sounds like you need to be there," Bill said.

"But I don't know if I can," the friend replied, much to Bill's surprise. He then explained that one of the leaders in the parachurch group, a man who had spent quite a bit of time working with him, was urging him to stick around and participate in the outreach event.

"He [the leader] says that staying around for this event is kind of a test of my commitment to Christ," Bill's friend told him. "If I go home, it's like I'm making my family more important than Christ."

That's an awful lot of control for one man to exert over another—probably too much, because the fellow had virtually lost his freedom. He was no longer being given the right to choose his priorities and make his plans. They were essentially being made for him. (Bill told him as much, and warned him to rethink his relationship with this man.)

Maybe the best way to avoid problems with control is to evaluate your prospective mentor before you ever initiate a relationship. Look to see whether he is encouraging people to go out from him, as well as inviting them to come in to him. Are they "graduating" from his program, or merely enrolling in it? Is he a useful transfer station along the way, or a warehouse for an ever-expanding collection of dysfunctional people?

In my experience, the people who run into the most problems with control are the ones who fail to take responsibility for their own development. When Paul said to the Corinthians, "Follow my example, as I follow the example of Christ" (1 Corinthians 11:1), he was shining a light on the footsteps of faith, so that the Corinthians would know where to walk. But some of us don't want to walk in Jesus' footsteps; we want someone to carry us in them. We don't want to follow as much as we want to be led. We'll never grow that way.

Take Charge of Your Life!

One of my favorite places to visit is Glen Eyrie, a retreat center in Colorado Springs operated by The Navigators. Situated next to the Garden of the Gods on the eastern slope of the Rockies, the Glen is hidden in a vale surrounded by spectacular cliffs of reddish sandstone. If you know where to look on one of these cliffs, you'll see an eagle's nest, perched several hundred feet above the canyon floor.

From time to time, the eagles hatch their young, and then the male spends all day circling over the territory, searching for food while the mother guards her nestlings. This goes on for weeks and months, until the young eagles have developed their bone structure and grown feathers. Then one day, in what seems like an act of utter cruelty, the mother gets her beak under one of her comfortable offspring and flips him right out of the nest.

He begins to fall. All the while the male is circling about screaming at the descending creature, perhaps hoping to scare it into action—as if it weren't terrified enough! Finally, he spreads his tiny wings and catches some air, hardly knowing what has happened. In that moment, the little bird averts death by acquiring a skill he will use the rest of his life.

Some who are reading this chapter are in free-fall. They have been pushed out of the nest in what feels like a terribly cruel and unfair way. But there is no other way. Eventually they must live their lives. And unless they take responsibility to spread their wings and fly, they will end up on the rocks, a casualty of their own inaction.

This matter of taking charge of your life is so important, and so crucial to effective mentoring, that I want to devote one final chapter to it as we conclude Part 1.

Chapter Ten

TAKING RESPONSIBILITY

When our family was quite young, we had a little ritual that our kids begged us to repeat as often as possible. We would line them up in the hallway, and one by one have them stand with their backs to the back of a closet door. Using a ruler on top of their heads, we would mark a line on the door and write the date and their heights. In this way we developed a simple growth chart. The kids begged us to measure their growth.

One time when I was leaving town on a trip, Bev, my second daughter, told me that while I was gone, she was determined to grow. (We had just recently charted her height.)

Sure enough, when I arrived back in Dallas and stepped off the plane, Bev ran to greet me with the exciting news, "Daddy! Daddy! Come home quick! You gotta see how much I growed!"

As soon as I arrived home, we got out a ruler and went to the growth chart to measure her progress. The distance between the new line and the most recent one couldn't have been more than a millimeter or two, but she jumped up and down, shouting, "See, Daddy! See, I told you! I *did* grow!"

Later that day, she and I got to talking in the living room. She asked me one of those questions that you wish kids wouldn't ask: "Daddy, why do big people stop growing?"

I don't know what I told her, but I'm sure it was very superficial. Probably something like, "Well, Bev, they don't exactly stop. They stop growing up, but then they start growing out!" You know, a nice dresser, but their middle drawer is sticking out!

Anyway, long after she was gone, God was working me over with that question. Why *do* big people stop growing? And is there any way to get them started again?

Could the answers to those questions have anything to do with mentoring? After all, I've suggested that a mentor is someone committed to helping you grow and realize your life goals. Is it possible, then, that the widespread frustration felt by many men today concerning their personal and spiritual development could be in any way connected to a lack of mentoring relationships? I'm convinced that it is.

Mentors—Keys to Your Growth

In the foreword to Ted Engstrom's excellent book *The Fine Art of Mentoring*, Gordon MacDonald points out that "in the past, mentoring happened everywhere. On the farm, a boy or a girl was mentored alongside of mothers and fathers and extended family members. From the earliest years, these mentors gave children a sense of 'maleness' and 'femaleness' and taught them what work was all about and how it was done, what character meant, and what were the duties and obligations of each member of the community."

But today, MacDonald observes, "What passes for people development happens in a classroom, and the certification of a person is by diploma from an institution rather than the stamp of approval from an overseer, a mentor. The criteria for judgment of people usually rests upon knowledge rather than wisdom, achievement rather than character, profit rather than creativity.

"And as long as that is true," he adds, "mentoring will likely be a second class matter in our value system."[1]

Are you feeling stunted in terms of your growth and development? If we were to stand you up against a growth chart, would there be any distance between where you are today and where you were, say, six months ago? One year ago? Five years? Ten years or more?

If the gains are negligible, perhaps you need to start looking for a mentor. A mentor can be a vital partner for your growth—spiritually, personally, and professionally. Such a relationship will not automatically transform your life. But it is one of the best means to that end. In fact, mentoring is one of God's primary means for bringing His children to maturity. Let me show you how that works.

The Process of Growth

The Bible tells us that the goal of life in Christ is that we become *like Christ*. Jesus told His disciples that "everyone who is fully trained will be like his teacher" (Luke 6:40). In other words, by following Christ, we will eventually become like Christ.

Likewise, Paul said that we have been predestined to be conformed to the likeness of Jesus (Romans 8:29). In fact, the purpose of the church is to help us in "attaining to the whole measure of the fullness of Christ" (Ephesians 4:13). So Christlikeness is our ultimate objective.

But please note: Christlikeness involves more than just "spiritual" categories; it includes everything in our lives. Jesus is Lord of *all* (Colossians 1:15, 17). Therefore, He wants us to become like Him in *all* areas of our lives—the intellectual, the physical, the social, and the emotional, as well as the spiritual. Is that your goal—Christlikeness in *every* area?

If so, then you need to know that the Bible tells us that becoming like Christ involves a *growth process*. We don't arrive at that goal overnight. Again, Paul said that the church exists to build us up until we reach maturity: "Then we will no longer be infants," but instead "we will in all things grow up into Him who is the Head, that is, Christ" (Ephesians 4:12–15).

Even Jesus "grew," we are told, in four areas: in "wisdom," the intellectual component; in "stature," the physical component; in "favor with God," the spiritual component; and in "favor with men," the social and emotional component (Luke 2:52). By growing in these various ways, He demonstrated that life is developmental. We are meant to mature, to increase our God-given capacities—*all* of them, not just the spiritual ones.

This principle was brilliantly illustrated in the life of one of my dear friends, who passed away not long ago at the age of eighty-six. The last time I saw her was when she came up to me at a Christmas party and said, "Well, Hendricks, I haven't seen you for a long time. What are the five best books you've read recently?"

Needless to say, she had a way of keeping you on your toes! Her attitude was, "Let's not sit here and bore each other. Let's get into a discussion. And if we can't find anything to discuss, let's get into an argument!"

She died in her sleep at her daughter's home in Dallas. When I went over to meet with the family, her daughter told me that the night before, this woman had sat down at her desk and written out her goals for the next ten years.

I love it! This woman realized that life is all about growing. In fact, the minute you stop growing, you start dying. She *never* stopped growing. The only thing that stopped her was when her body finally gave out.

Peter's final charge to his readers was, "Grow in the grace and knowledge of our Lord and Savior Jesus Christ" (2 Peter 3:18). So the question becomes: Are you committed to change and growth?

Stages of Growth

If so, you need to know that the Bible tells us that there are *stages* in the process of becoming like Christ. First John 2:12–14 indicates three categories of believers: children, young men, and fathers. These are interesting descriptions, because they are analogous to the three stages of biological growth: childhood, adolescence, and adulthood.

Each of these periods is marked by particular kinds of development. For example, a child is preoccupied with learning basic skills, such as talking and walking. An adolescent is developing independence and the ability to deal with the world and make decisions. An adult is concerned with making sense out of life and producing offspring. In a similar way, the apostle John seems to be saying that believers in Christ go through developmental stages in which they concentrate on certain things.

I invite you to read John's summary, and then ask yourself: "Which stage am I at?"

My guess is that most Christian men today are either at the childhood stage or the young man stage. But few ever attain to adulthood, spiritually speaking. Why is that? One reason is a fundamental misunderstanding of how growth takes place. You see, as Gordon MacDonald astutely pointed out, we've changed our model for Christian education.

Mentoring—A Forgotten Art

In the days when the church was just getting started and the New Testament was being written, boys were groomed into men through the relationships they had with older men. Call it mentoring, apprenticing, tutoring, whatever—the lessons of life were learned through life-on-life relationships. In fact, this seems to be the pattern for personal development throughout Scripture (see Mentoring Relationships in the Bible, pp. 180–181).

These mentoring relationships were carried on not only by people of faith, but by society in general. The method continued until about a hundred years ago, when the Industrial Revolution and other factors brought about a radical change in the way knowledge and skills are taught.

Nowadays, teaching means telling, and testing boils down to the student cramming as much information as possible into his head, and then regurgitating it onto a piece of paper during an exam.

I'll never forget the student I ran into at the seminary who was on his way to take a test. I started to engage him in conversation, but he said, "Don't touch me, Prof! I'll leak everything I know!"

That's not education. Yet how often we equate Bible knowledge with spirituality!

Back when I was in Wheaton College, I worked as a youth director in a church. We had a boy in the junior department who had memorized 600 verses, word-perfectly! Todd (not his real name) was amazing. You could give him any reference, and he had the verse down cold.

One day I was told that someone had been stealing money out of the junior department offering. So I appointed myself as a committee of one to investigate, and—you guessed it—our 600-verse prodigy turned out to be the culprit. I caught him red-handed.

So I took Todd into my office and confronted him with his wrongdoing. I even gave him a verse of Scripture to drive home my point—to which he proceeded to tell me that I had misquoted the verse.

Finally I said, "Do you see any connection between that verse of Scripture and your stealing from the offering?"

"No," Todd replied. "Well, maybe."

"What do you think is the connection?"

"I got caught."

This kid typified our flawed system of spiritual education. We tend to think that if someone has mastered the Bible, he's practically a spiritual giant. But from God's perspective, the name of the game is not knowledge—it's active obedience. It's not how much truth is in your head that counts, but how much is in your life. Hebrews 5:13–14 distinguishes between infants, who are not acquainted with the teaching about righteousness, and the mature, "who *by constant use* [or practice] have trained themselves to distinguish between good and evil" (emphasis added).

God is not impressed with how much I know (intellectually) of His Word; He wants to know how much like Christ I am becoming. In the spiritual realm, the opposite of ignorance is not knowledge, it's obedience. In fact, according to the New Testament's understanding of the term, to "know" and not to do is not to "know" at all.

And this is is where mentoring could save the day. It becomes ever clearer to me that we really don't need more books, tapes, broadcasts, sermons and the like to "teach" us how to live the Christian life. What we need are *relationships* with people who know Christ (experientially) and can help us know Him at our point of need. It's not enough to harangue someone with the exhortation to "follow Christ." We need mentors who can say, as Paul said, "Follow me, as I follow Christ," models who flesh out what life in Christ is all about.

Your Responsibility

So does that place all of the burden on mentors, to take us from one stage of growth to the next? By no means. It places a burden on you and me to go out and find people who can help us get to the next level.

Earlier I pointed out that there's a real similarity between finding a mentor and finding a job. In light of that overlap, Richard Bolles's words are instructive:

Many unemployed people have sat at home, waiting for God to prove that He loves them, by causing a job to walk in the door. It doesn't happen. . . . You *have* to take over the management of your own job-hunt or career-change, if it is to be successful. No one else here on earth is going to have such concern for how it turns out, as you do. No one else is going to be willing to lavish so much time on it, as you will. No one else will be so persistent, as you will. No one else has so exact a picture of what kind of job you are looking for, as you do.[2]

Change a word here and there, and Bolles could be talking about looking for a mentor. For that matter, he could be describing the kind of responsibility with which every person needs to pursue spiritual growth in general. No one else will do it for you. No one else can. No one else should.

So the ball is in your court. Let me close with four things you can do to meet the challenge:

1. Find a Mentor

Again, every man needs a Paul and a Barnabas, an older man and a peer. Don't get hung up with the age factor. Just look for men who you feel can help you grow and realize your life goals.

As I have emphasized repeatedly, finding mentors will take time and energy on your part, and you may have to wait a while for the right person to come along. But the effort to find that person will be worth it in terms of the growth you will experience.

2. Make Mentoring a Way of Life

By now, I hope you can see that we're not talking about finding one, single mentor for the rest of your life. That would be highly unusual. Even if you found such a long-term relationship, you still need several mentors throughout the course of your life. You need a variety of perspectives, and different men will contribute different things at different stages of your development. Therefore, you always need to be on the lookout for godly mentors. It should become a way of life.

Of course, you should keep in mind that mentors are by no means the only resource by which God intends to bring you to maturity. As I've noted, God always uses a constellation of factors to work in your life.

3. Find Mentors for Your Kids

If you are a father, you can do an invaluable service to your children by keeping an eye out for potential mentors for them. Obviously, as a parent you play the primary role in the development of your kids. But you can't provide everything. God never intended that you should.

So you're wise to look for teachers, coaches, youth leaders, other parents, and people in the workplace who are willing to take your son or daughter under their wing. That way, your children won't have to grow up and say what perhaps you've been saying: "No one ever built into my life."

4. Mentor Someone Else

In addition to a Paul and Barnabas, every man needs a Timothy, a younger man into whose life he is building. Whatever God has given you, you have an obligation to share that with someone who needs it. We've seen illustrations of this principle throughout the book:

- Paul tutored young Timothy in the faith; Timothy became a pastor and passed the truth along to faithful men under him.

- A man named Walt befriended me when I was a boy; I've given my life to reproducing Christ in the lives of my students.

- A man paid for Eugene Lang's college education; Eugene Lang offered to pay the tuition for the students at P.S. 121.

- Bill will tell you that many men have made a major impact on him; now he meets frequently with others to let them in on what he has learned (and continues to learn).

You Can Make a Difference!

If you stop and think about it, it really takes very little to make a substantial difference in someone's life. Just consider the people who have been significant in your life. Did it require them to have remarkable skill or knowledge? Sometimes, maybe. But more often than not, what mattered was that they were there, that they cared, and that they communicated that they cared.

Can you do that? Can you give someone an hour of your time? Can you tell him stories from your own life about situations you've faced? Can you encourage him to hang in there when things are tough, and stand by him as he fights his battles? Can you pray with him and for him?

The process is not that complicated. If only we could find a few good men who would be willing to give it a try! I want to ask you to be one of those men. If you will, come with me into Part 2, where we'll explore mentoring from the mentor's side of the relationship.

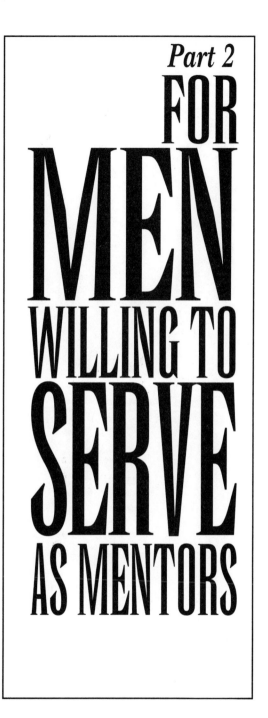

Part 2

FOR MEN WILLING TO SERVE AS MENTORS

Chapter Eleven

A CALL FOR MENTORS

History often turns on the smallest of factors. For example, in 1856, a New York lawyer named George Bissell was seeking shade under the awning of a drugstore when he happened to notice an advertisement for a patent medicine made from "rock oil," a byproduct of drilling for salt. That chance encounter gave him the idea for the modern oil derrick which opened the way to the international oil industry.

In 1986, a rare night of freezing temperatures settled over Florida's Atlantic coast, where the space shuttle Challenger awaited liftoff from Cape Kennedy. At sunrise, the launch proceeded. But 71 seconds into the mission, the billion-dollar spacecraft exploded, bringing the United States' space program to an abrupt halt. Investigators eventually blamed the tragedy on a tiny rubber O-ring, which malfunctioned after the unexpected cold turned it brittle and inflexible.

When we turn our attention to the first century A.D., we tend to think of the great events that transpired in Jerusalem as the defining moment of history. And, of course, they were: the appearance of the prophesied Emmanuel ("God with us") in the person of Jesus Christ, His three-year ministry of healing and His call to righteousness, His crucifixion and subsequent resurrection, and the launch of the worldwide body of Christ through the bold outreach of the early church.

The Man Behind Paul

These matters rightly dominate the spotlight of history. Yet an often overlooked but crucial hinge on which history turns is to be found about two hundred miles northwest of Jerusalem on the tiny Mediterranean island of Cyprus. Cyprus was the home of an unassuming Jew named Joses, or Joseph, and it is this man who merits our attention. We don't know how Joses came to faith in Jesus; perhaps he was among the 3,000 visitors to Jerusalem at Passover who responded to Peter's proclamation of the gospel (Acts 2). Whatever the circumstances, the message of the Messiah took root in his life, and he began to identify with the early church.

As an indication of his commitment to Christ, Joses sold some or all of his property on Cyprus and brought the proceeds to Jerusalem, where he donated them to the church's benevolence fund. Following custom, the church leaders responded by giving Joses a new (or Christian) name, Son of Encouragement, or Barnabas (Acts 4:36–37).

Now how is it that Barnabas—a relatively minor character in Scripture—could be said to have changed history? The answer is, because Barnabas came to the aid of Saul (later known as Paul) after his dramatic Damascus Road experience and mentored him in the faith. Were it not for Barnabas, who knows what would have happened to Saul—or to the early church? Certainly none of the leaders at Jerusalem wanted anything to do with him. As far as they were concerned, he was Public Enemy Number One, no matter what happened on the way to Damascus. "But Barnabas," the account reads, "took him and brought him to the apostles" (Acts 9:26–27), defending Saul's claim of conversion, and negotiating access for him to the fellowship of believers.

Nor did Barnabas' influence end there. Later, he and Paul traveled together to spread the gospel, and Barnabas apparently promoted Paul to the forefront of leadership: "Barnabas and Saul" (13:7) became "Paul and his companions" (13:13). Later still, Barnabas challenged Paul over the apostle's treatment of young John Mark (15:36–38). Just because he was known as the Son of Encouragement did not mean that Barnabas avoided conflict.

So while we rightly think of Paul as the strategic spokesman for Christ in the New Testament, we must never forget that behind Paul there was a Barnabas. In fact, Paul seemed to be echoing Barnabas when he wrote to Timothy, "The things you have heard me say in the presence of many witnesses entrust to reliable men who will also be qualified to teach others" (2 Timothy 2:2).

By mentoring Paul, Barnabas was engaging in a ministry of multiplication (see the diagram, Barnabas: A Ministry of Multiplication, p. 141). The world has never been the same, which demonstrates that every time you build into the life of another person, you launch a process that ideally will never end.

Where Are the Leaders?

Do we need a ministry of multiplication today? Absolutely, because the world is screaming for leadership:

- We need leaders in our homes. Not long ago James Dobson, psychologist and head of Focus On the Family, produced a timely videotape that asked a perceptive but haunting question: "Where's Dad?" I can think of few questions that America needs to be asking itself more than that one. You look into home after home today, and you see mom and the kids, but no father. Where is he? At work? On the road? On the golf course? Out of the picture? Wherever he is, too many kids are growing up without any significant presence of a father in their lives. It's as if Dad has abdicated his role as a parent.

  In fact, *New York Post* film critic Michael Medved points out that by the age of six, the average American child will have spent more time watching television, videotapes, and motion pictures than that child will spend *in an entire lifetime* talking to his father.[1] In other words, *Hollywood is raising the next generation!*

  No wonder the American family today is unraveling like a cheap sweater. No wonder only half of all children now live in a stable home with both their biological mother and father, according to the United States Census Bureau.

  What happens to children whose families don't make it? Psychologist Judith Wallerstein, reporting on a long-term study of the emotional effects of divorce, finds that "almost half the children of divorces enter adulthood as worried, angry, under-achieving, self-deprecating, and sometimes angry young men and women."[2]

  Do these reports alarm you the way they do me? It's a fact of history that no nation has ever survived the disintegration of its home life. Once the home goes, it's just a question of time before it all goes.

- We need leaders in our churches. Do you realize that only 6 percent of senior pastors today believe they have the gift of leadership?[3] Meanwhile, the average church in America is sustained and operated by only 15 to 20 percent of its membership.

  No wonder researchers find that more than two-thirds of the 350,000 Protestant congregations in the United States have either plateaued or are in serious decline.[4] No wonder that since 1980 there has been *no growth* in the proportion of the adult population that can be classified as "born again." As Charles Colson, president of Prison Fellowship, told one journalist, "If this were a business, you'd be contemplating Chapter 11 [bankruptcy]."

- We need leaders in our society. In politics, in business, in education, in medicine, in science, in law, in the military—the landscape is littered with the bodies of "leaders" who have forfeited their right to lead because they have not been people of integrity. They have not been people we can trust.

  As a result, says Warren Bennis, Distinguished Professor of Business at the University of Southern California, "At the heart of America is a vacuum into which self-appointed saviors have rushed. They pretend to be leaders, and we—half out of envy, half out of longing—pretend to think of them as leaders."

Bennis is right. The pedestals are largely empty today. The heroes and models have vanished. I'll never forget the little kid I encountered in a barbershop. "Hey, son, when you grow up, whom do you want to be like?" I asked him.

He looked me straight in the eye and said, "Mister, I ain't found *nobody* I want to be like!"

Can you hear the death cry of a potential Timothy? No one to look up to. No one to follow. No one to pass along, as Paul passed along to Timothy, the truth that leads to life in Christ. I can think of no greater tragedy! But if we want to produce a Timothy, then we need to produce a Paul. And if we want to produce a Paul, then we need to find a Barnabas. My friend, could God be calling you to that role, the role of a mentor?

A Man of Influence

I often hear older men complaining about the younger generation. But my question is, "What are *you* doing to impact a young person in a positive, Christlike way?" You cannot change everyone, but you *can* affect someone. You *can* be a man of influence.

It's like the story that business titan Jack Eckerd tells of the man walking along a beach, who came upon a pitiful sight: thousands of beautiful starfish washed up by the tide, now drying and dying in the hot sun. So the man reached down, picked up one of the limp creatures, and flipped it back into the sea. He continued his walk in this manner, pausing every few feet to grab another starfish.

Presently another man came by and remarked on this curious activity. "Why are you doing that?" he asked.

"I'm trying to save the starfish," the man replied.

At this, the other man laughed and swept his arm to indicate the thousands of starfish that littered the beach. "Why bother?" he said cynically. "It won't make any difference."

But even as he spoke, the beachcomber was tossing another starfish into the surf. He watched it disappear beneath the waves, then turned and said, "It made a difference for that one."

There is probably little you or I can do to change the many looming factors that hinder us in our efforts to produce men of excellence today. But God is not asking us to save the whole world. That's God's responsibility. Our responsibility is to do the best we can to bring our own lives under Christ's lordship and then influence the handful of people God brings our way to do the same. That will make a difference—maybe not for everyone, but at least for someone.

Why Aren't You a Mentor?

So why is that not happening? Why is the need for life-on-life relationships between older and younger men going largely unmet today? If I asked you, "What keeps you from serving as a mentor to another man?" what would be your response? I'll tell you what are the four most common answers men give to that question:

"I don't care."

First, many would-be mentors simply aren't interested in the process. They don't see any compelling need or feel any great urgency. Add to them the many men who respond to almost all appeals for action with apathy.

I can almost understand why. In a world with so many needs, so many problems, so many desperate cries for help, a person can easily reach "compassion overload." You know, one more crisis comes along and he just yawns. "So what else is new?" is the attitude. Thus he succumbs to the inertia of indifference.

And you see it everywhere. An older guy sits in his office, surrounded by younger men just watching his every move. He doesn't realize it, but for them, he sets the pace. Yet if you asked him, "Hey, Jim, have you ever thought of inviting some of these guys out to lunch to find out what's really going on inside, what they're really looking for in life?" he just gets that look on his face that says, "Why bother?" Essentially, his attitude is, "Who cares? You can't save the world. Besides, I won't be around anyway."

Then there's the man who is skeptical of the process. "I can't see that just getting together with a kid is going to make much difference," he says (and it is interesting to note that this man tends to deal with most people on an "as needed" basis). "Besides," he says, "I'm a pretty busy individual. I've got my own needs to attend to. Is this really the best use of my time?" If he's been burned once or twice by someone who didn't pan out, he may add, "Why waste time on a kid whose life is going nowhere?"

If you fall into this category, let me be honest: I'm not interested in talking you into doing something that you fundamentally don't want to do. At the same time, I make no apology for trying to light a fire under whatever spark of motivation might be there. When it comes to mentoring, the stakes are so great, and the benefits—for you, for other men, and for society in general—are so enormous, that I fairly froth at the mouth just talking about it!

That's not because I've read some books on mentoring or because someone came along and said, "Hendricks, here's something else you need to get involved in." No, it's because mentoring is the story of my life. I am the product of a core of individuals who built into my life ever since I came to Jesus Christ some sixty years ago. I thank God that they never looked at me and said, "I don't care." If they had, I could have been just like that boy in the barbershop.

In the end, caring derives from only once source—the heart of God. That's why I say, if you claim the name of Christ, then you need to display the concern of Christ for people.

"I feel inadequate."

The second reason why men beg out of the mentoring role is also the most common: they have real doubts as to whether they can pull it off.

This is what Pete Hammond has discovered in the Marketplace Mentors program. He and Bill were once invited to speak at a brown bag luncheon with some guys in their twenties. During his remarks, Pete challenged the group to seek out older men as guides and mentors.

But then one man at the table challenged Pete with a perplexing problem. "I've been trying to find an older man for a long time," he said with some exasperation, "but it just doesn't seem to happen! It's like every time I try to get something going, they find an excuse to shut it down. You're saying 'Find a mentor,' but I'm wondering, 'Where are they?' "

"Let me let you in on a little secret," Pete replied, glancing around the room. "You guys scare the pants off some of us older men sometimes," he said with a chuckle.

The group looked somewhat disbelieving.

"I'm serious!" Pete went on. "Look at you! You're young. You're strong. You're healthy. You're virile. You're handsome. You dress well. You've got all this energy, and all these opportunities. An older guy looks at all that and he thinks, 'There's no way I can keep up with these guys! What do I have to offer?' Somehow, you've got to convince him that you value his input."

Does that scenario describe you? Perhaps you feel inadequate to serve as a guide or a role model. Perhaps the real reason you are reading this chapter is because some young man placed this book in your hands following a request that you "mentor" him (whatever that means!). He may have even said something like, "Here, just read this book—especially Part 2. It'll explain what I'm talking about."

Of course, you were too polite to refuse him. So here you are. And though you would never admit it out loud (least of all to him), the fact of the matter is, you are scared speechless! You realize that this kid has got expectations for you, and you're convinced that there is no way you could ever live up to those expectations.

If that's the case, may I assure you that you are not alone. Most men in our culture do not see themselves as mentor material. They are persuaded that they don't have what it takes: "I don't know anything"; "I don't have any training"; "I can't teach"; "I'm not very good at relationships."

I've heard all the excuses. But I'm convinced that most are based on misguided perceptions and unrealistic expectations about the mentoring process. For example, take the notion that younger generations automatically discount whatever older people say. This is a holdover from the infamous "generation gap" of the 1960s.

But the reality is, an older man almost always has the advantage in dealing with someone younger. Just go into the workplace and observe how younger men tend to view their elders. They look up to them; they pay them deference. Sure, you can find cases of disrespect, and occasionally you'll hear some whippersnapper dismiss an older colleague as "that old coot." But a remark like that reveals far more about the younger man's insecurity than anything about the older man.

Some of us have got ourselves older than we really are! You know, our bodily functions may be to the point where, as someone has said, if something is working, it hurts; and if it doesn't hurt, it probably isn't working! So we just assume that the young lions no longer fear our roar, and we retreat to our den.

But may God grant us the staying power of Caleb, who, at age eighty-five, was still leading the charge in the conquest of Canaan! "I am still as strong today as the day Moses sent me out," Caleb boldly announced to the Israelites. "I'm just as vigorous to go out to battle now as I was then. Now give me this hill country that the Lord promised me that day." Yes, there were fierce warriors and fortified cities to be faced, "but, the Lord helping me, I will drive them out just as he said" (Joshua 14:11–12).

All around you are young men facing giants. They need a champion of the faith to help them conquer their God-given territory.

But you say, "I have nothing to offer!" May I challenge that assertion? The older you are, the more likely you have:

- *Experience.* You know how the world works. Hopefully, you have acquired what Proverbs calls *wisdom,* meaning "the skill of living."

- *Knowledge.* Certainly in your area of expertise. But how about knowledge of Scripture? Or other literature? It tends to be older men who can ask, "Have you read such-and-such a book? It's got the answer you're looking for."

- *Access.* To people, including other maturing Christians. To networks. To information. To authority.

- *Money.* Jesus challenged us to use our wealth to populate heaven (Luke 16:9), which forces us to ask, how much are we investing in people? Even buying lunch for a young man in order to have conversation with him can be a powerful thing. Did it ever occur to you that unless you pay, it might never happen? He may feel that he can't afford it.

- *Resources.* Over time, you probably have acquired more resources than you realize—in most cases, certainly, more than your prospective protégé. By "resources" I mean useful assets such as homes, cars, offices, tools, personal libraries, and even cash. Using these possessions to help another man grow is one of the best ways I know to be a faithful steward of what God has given you.

- *Friendship.* If nothing else, you can offer companionship. The journey from boyhood to manhood can be ever so lonely, which is why we often hear disillusioned young men say, "All I wanted was for someone to be there."

- *Time.* The older you get, the busier you get—but the more control you tend to have over your time. This is especially the case if you are near or in retirement. (By the way, never forget that retirement is a cultural, not a biblical concept. You may retire from your company; indeed, you may not have an option. But you will never retire from the Christian life, which means that until the day you die, someone somewhere ought to have the benefit of gleaning from your life.)

- *Yourself.* God created you as a unique, valuable individual. In fact, your very person is your most valuable asset, so don't overlook it. God has made you with your special slant on life, your unique bent and style. No one else is exactly like you. No one else can match your unique contribution. Are you willing to just "be yourself" in the company of a younger individual?

I could add other items to this list. The point is to stop believing the lie of the devil that says you have nothing to offer. It's not true! If you are in Christ, you always have something to give to other people. How do you find out what that something is? You'll never know until you get involved with other people.

One final point related to feelings of inadequacy concerns your own family. You may have had failures—perceived or actual—with one of your own children, so that you now feel unqualified to step in and help any other young person. If so, consider that the painful lessons you've learned may actually be the greatest thing you have to offer.

Imagine if we could talk to some of the "fathers of failures" in Scripture, such as Manoah, the father of Samson (Judges 13:2); Eli, the father of Hophni and Phinehas (1 Samuel 2:12–17, 22–25, 34); Samuel, the father of the corrupt judges Joel and Abijah (8:1–3); or David, the father of immoral Amnon and rebellious Absalom (2 Samuel 13:1–14; 15:1–16). Do you think any of them might have something to teach us? The same could hold true for you.

I don't want to minimize genuine feelings of fear or inadequacy. But one of the main reasons we are starving for mentors today is that many men who could serve as excellent mentors are afraid to see themselves in that role. Would it help not to use the terms "mentor" or "mentoring"? Fine, describe things in a different way. Labels matter very little; but lives matter a lot. So call it what you will, the objective is to build a relationship that impacts another man's life.

"No one ever asked me. "

A third reason some men are standing on the sidelines with respect to mentoring is because they've never been recruited into the contest. Some may be new to the game and unaware of their responsibility. Others may be waiting for someone else to take the initiative and approach them about serving as a mentor.

If that is your situation—if you are holding back because no one has ever asked you—then let this book serve as a personal invitation. I challenge you to get involved in mentoring.

More importantly, young men all around you are asking for your involvement. Do you recognize that? Believe me, younger men *want* to be mentored. Everywhere I go, they ask me, "Where can I find a guide, a coach, a father-figure, a mentor?" Meanwhile, older men are asking, "Where can I find a ministry? What can I do to really make a difference for Jesus Christ?" Hmmm . . . do you suppose there might be some possibilities here?

Of course, the most compelling reason to get involved in mentoring relationships is because God is asking you to do it. Proverbs 13:20 says that "he who walks with the wise grows wise." That presupposes that the wise are willing to let someone benefit from their wisdom.

Or consider Jesus' final command: "Go and build buildings." No, He said to go and *build men,* to make disciples—learners—who would follow His ways (Matthew 28:19). The Lord was describing a ministry of multiplication. And if I understand my New Testament correctly, there are only two things God is going to take off this planet. One is His Word, the other is His people. Therefore, if you are building His Word into people, you can be confident that you are building a legacy that will last into eternity.

"I don't know how. "

Of all the reasons given for not serving as a mentor, the plea that "I don't know how" is the easiest to surmount. Technique can be taught.

Of course, first you may need to unlearn some myths that you may have acquired along the way. One of the most common is that the mentor does all the giving. That's not true. In the next chapter I'm going to show you that mentors stand to gain as much if not more from the relationship as their protégés.

Another is that everything depends on the mentor. That's not true either. A mentor is like a man flying a kite. The kite does the flying, and the wind creates the lift. All the man has to do is hold the string with just the right balance of pull and give. If he draws the string too tightly, he puts stress on the kite that can rip it apart. But if he lets out too much line and the wind dies, the kite will begin to fall.

Thus mentoring is a bit of an art. But it's not that difficult. Almost any man can learn to do it. In fact, mentoring goes on around us all the time. It's just that we usually don't recognize it for what it is. But if we realized what was happening and were more aware of the process, we could make a far greater impact on others, as well as get a lot more out of it ourselves.

Would you be willing to give it a try?

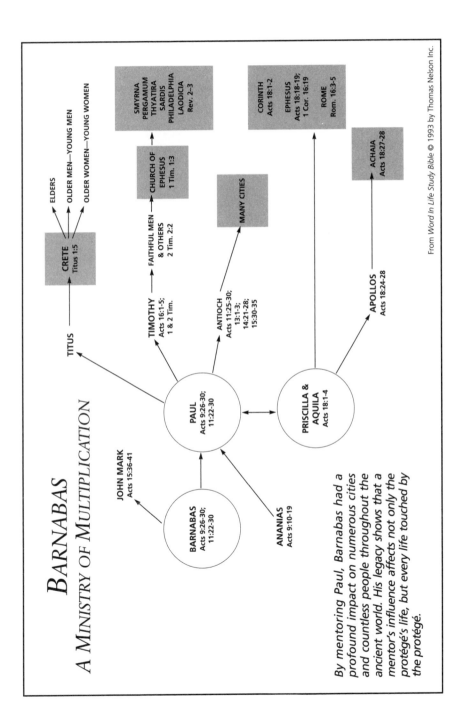

BARNABAS
A MINISTRY OF MULTIPLICATION

BARNABAS
Acts 9:26-30;
11:22-30

JOHN MARK
Acts 15:36-41

ANANIAS
Acts 9:10-19

PAUL
Acts 9:26-30;
11:22-30

TITUS

CRETE
Titus 1:5

ELDERS
OLDER MEN—YOUNG MEN
OLDER WOMEN—YOUNG WOMEN

TIMOTHY
Acts 16:1-5;
1 & 2 Tim.

FAITHFUL MEN
& OTHERS
2 Tim. 2:2

CHURCH OF
EPHESUS
1 Tim. 1:3

SMYRNA
PERGAMUM
THYATIRA
SARDIS
PHILADELPHIA
LAODICIA
Rev. 2–3

ANTIOCH
Acts 11:25-30;
13:1-3;
14:21-28;
15:30-35

MANY CITIES

PRISCILLA &
AQUILA
Acts 18:1-4

APOLLOS
Acts 18:24-28

ACHAIA
Acts 18:27-28

CORINTH
Acts 18:1-2

EPHESUS
Acts 18:18-19;
1 Cor. 16:19

ROME
Rom. 16:3-5

By mentoring Paul, Barnabas had a
profound impact on numerous cities
and countless people throughout the
ancient world. His legacy shows that a
mentor's influence affects not only the
protégé's life, but every life touched by
the protégé.

From *Word In Life Study Bible* © 1993 by Thomas Nelson Inc.

WHY BE A MENTOR?

People who have run for public office tell me that the only thing worse than losing an election is winning one, because then you have to govern. The Old Testament leader Moses discovered something of this principle after the Israelites' dramatic departure from Egypt.

Two months after crossing the Red Sea, the people arrived at Mount Horeb (believed to be in the southern Sinai Peninsula). Horeb was a familiar spot to Moses. Here the Lord had revealed Himself in the burning bush, calling Moses to deliver His people from bondage and bring them to the mountain so that they could worship Him (Exodus 3:1–12).

While the people made camp, awaiting the Lord's appearance, Moses set up a court to hear the backlog of cases that had already built up during the Exodus journey. There must have been many, for as soon as the sun rose, people began lining up for Moses to settle their disputes. All day long he listened and passed judgment. In fact, he was still at it long after sundown.

Jethro to the Rescue

Who knows how long this wearisome pattern might have continued? But fortunately for Moses, his father-in-law Jethro happened to be visiting. Apparently he sat all day watching his son-in-law hold court. Then, as they ate a late dinner, Jethro asked the weary leader a question.

"What is this you are doing for the people? Why do you alone sit as judge, while all these people stand around you from morning till evening?"

"Because the people come to me to seek God's will," Moses explained. "Whenever they have a dispute, it is brought to me, and I decide between the parties and inform them of God's decrees and laws."

Do you get the picture? Out of a group that some estimate to have been as many as 2 million people, Moses was the only man in the lot certified to pass judgment. I live in a city of 1 million people. Imagine me being the only judge for the whole town! Moses may have had twice that load.

No wonder his father-in-law replied, "What you are doing is not good!" (Somehow I think the same thought may have been running through Moses' mind at that point!) "You and these people who come to you will only wear yourselves out. The work is too heavy for you; you cannot handle it alone."

Do you have an in-law like that—always glad to critique your performance? You know, it never occurs to him that even though you weren't good enough to marry his daughter, you still managed to father the brightest grandchild on earth! I guess that's why some men define a close relative as one you only see at funerals.

At any rate, Jethro did more than highlight Moses' problem; he gave him some practical ideas for solving it: "Listen now to me and I will give you some advice, and may God be with you." Jethro then described the principle of delegation, encouraging Moses to appoint leaders under him who could judge the minor cases, while Moses would handle only the most difficult matters. "If you do this and God so commands, you will be able to stand the strain, and all these people will go home satisfied" (Exodus 18:14–18, 23).

Delegation may seem like the obvious solution to you and me, but it ran somewhat contrary to the thinking of that day. Nevertheless, Moses listened to his father-in-law's wise counsel, and the record shows that Jethro's approach became the cornerstone of Israel's judicial system.

Now this exchange between Jethro and Moses is a classic study in mentoring. But I wonder, what was it that caused Jethro to step in and help his son-in-law? Was it purely an altruistic response to an obvious need?

Perhaps. But if we read between the lines and look at Jethro in light of his culture, I think we can guess at some additional motives. For one, Jethro probably wanted Moses to succeed even more than Moses did. To understand why, consider the fact that Jethro was a priest of the Midianites (Exodus 18:1). This tribe, like the Israelites, was descended from Abraham. But they also were idol-worshipers. Nevertheless, Jethro apparently feared the Lord (18:11–12), and he recognized that the success of Moses' venture would go a long way toward vindicating his faith.

Furthermore, Jethro had a vested interest in seeing the people survive the desert journey to the Promised Land. As a lifelong resident of the Sinai, he knew better than anyone the perils that awaited them. He also knew that the best man to lead them through this terrain was Moses, who had had forty years of experience tending Jethro's flocks in the area. It was critical that this leader remain in good health, and not "wear out" himself and the people, as Jethro put it. Otherwise, the migration could end in disaster.

Both Men Gain

Why would Jethro care what happened to the Israelites? Again, I believe his motives went beyond human compassion. Certainly that was involved. But in Jethro's world, the measure of a man's life was determined by how many descendants he left behind, especially males. To our knowledge, Jethro had only one son (Numbers 11:29). So Moses was an additional link to a legacy.

Do you see how this incident between Jethro and Moses highlights the motives of a mentor? At first glance, it would seem that Moses was the chief beneficiary of Jethro's counsel. But if you stop and think about it, Jethro had a lot to gain as well.

The same principle holds true for you. In the last chapter, I encouraged you to open the door to the possibility of influencing the life of some young man. But if you are like many men, you may have been thinking, "Great, Hendricks, just what I need! One more obligation to add to my list of 386 other things I don't have time for! Why should I extend myself for someone else when I can't even keep up with my own needs? Is this just another appeal to sign up as a Do-Gooder, or is there something in it for me?"

The answer is unequivocally yes, there is a great deal in it for you— possibly even more than what's in it for a young person. And there need be no shame in acknowledging that. Frankly, it's a rare individual who participates as a mentor solely out of altruistic motives. Obviously, concern needs to be there; unless you genuinely care about someone, you have a hard time serving him.

But mentoring is like parenting, in that there are some built-in rewards to the process. To an outsider, child-rearing may appear to be nothing but sacrifice. All the giving would seem to be one-way, from parent to child. But those of us who have raised children know otherwise. For example, there is no greater joy than to feel a little child's arms grasping your neck as he or she says those magic words, "I love you, Daddy." That is a moment beyond compare!

In a similar way, you may be assuming that mentoring is a one-way street, in which all the goodies flow to the protégé. I assure you, the truth is just the opposite. God has built into the process some definite rewards that can make it extremely satisfying. And there is nothing wrong with pursuing that satisfaction.

The Benefits of Being a Mentor

Let me suggest what some of those benefits are. Most of them are intangible; but that makes them no less invaluable. Here are five positive gains to consider: (1) a close relationship with another man, (2) personal renewal, (3) a sense of self-fulfillment, (4) enhanced self-esteem, and (5) an impact through your life.

A Close, Personal Relationship with Another Man

Consultant Bobb Biehl is a master at the art of asking good questions. One of his most profound is: "Who will attend your funeral without looking at his watch?"

A question like that kind of redefines the meaning of friendship, doesn't it? I hate to think of how many men are going to die having had numerous acquaintances, but few, if any, real friends. Will that be the case for you? It doesn't have to be. One of the outstanding contributions of the Promise Keepers movement is its call for men to pursue vital relationships with a few other men. Mentoring is one way to accomplish that objective—particularly peer mentoring (see Peer Mentoring, pp. 32–34).

Perhaps the premier example of peer mentoring in Scripture is the friendship between David and Jonathan. Humanly speaking, that relationship didn't stand a chance. By all rights, Jonathan should have succeeded his father, Saul, to the throne of Israel. But God rejected Saul in favor of David. So Jonathan and David should have been rivals. Instead, they became inseparable friends, forming such a close association that the Bible describes the soul of Jonathan being "knit" to the soul of David (1 Samuel 18:1).

What a refreshing alternative that is, given all the "friendless American males" who populate our society today. And what a healthy model for men to pursue in light of the profoundly confused and disturbing picture of male relationships gaining credence in our culture.

One encouraging sign that men are rediscovering the value of life-on-life relationships are the many small "covenant groups" that have started to meet together during the past few years. For example, I have some friends in Dallas who have been meeting every Tuesday morning for coffee and prayer for about twenty years, without fail. Imagine the bonds they have forged! Likewise, Bill knows some men who have been meeting quarterly in Chicago for about a dozen years. They've seen each other through every imaginable extreme of life, both positive and negative.

All of these are examples of peer mentoring—men about the same age and at a similar level of maturity who have bonded together to support each other and grow together. Relationships like these—committed, honest, lasting over time—bring the greatest joy and provide the greatest benefits. They are not always easy to sustain, but those of us who participate in them will tell you that they are worth all the effort.

However, it is not just peer relationships that offer the benefits of friendship. Mentoring a younger man has its own level of affection and intimacy—especially if the relationship is about development rather than control.

For one thing, meeting regularly with a younger man will keep you connected to the younger generation. That's one thing I love about being around my students (who somehow keep getting younger!). They keep me plugged into what's happening. It's very easy at seventy-plus years of age to think that you've seen it all, done it all, or know it all. But five minutes around a kid in his twenties will convince you otherwise.

And just as you can help interpret what the world *has been* to your protégé, he can help interpret what the world *is becoming* to you. He can be a tremendous source of information, keeping you up-to-date on current issues, questions, problems, opportunities, developments, and trends. In an information society, who among us can afford not to have another set of eyes and ears scouring the terrain for useful and meaningful data?

In addition, a younger man can often serve as a useful sounding board to bounce ideas off of. When Bill was in his teens, he worked for six summers at Pine Cove, a Christian retreat and conference center near Tyler, Texas. At that time, the executive director of Pine Cove was Don Anderson. Don had a tremendous heart for kids. He also had a dream—to create a senior high camp on a lakefront property, built around water activities such as skiing, boating, and sailing. In an environment like that, kids would have a ball while the staff helped them consider the claims of Christ.

Bill, who was passionate about water-skiing, immediately fell in love with Don's concept. But what caused Don to soar in Bill's estimation was when he brought Bill into his office one day, unrolled a set of blueprints, and asked Bill what he thought. Bill was overwhelmed that Don would consult him about what he thought of the property, the program, and the overall plan. Meanwhile, Don was tapping a valuable resource. After all, who better to comment on a camp for teens than a teenager?

There is one other benefit often overlooked in committing oneself to a younger person—accountability. We tend to think of accountability primarily in terms of peer relationships. But have you ever considered the built-in accountability of answering to a younger man, and serving as his role model?

This is more powerful than you may realize. I've heard men admit to great struggles in the area of lust and infidelity, but they chose the way of purity because of the men following after them. "I just couldn't do it when I thought about them," they have said. "I kept thinking, 'What would So-and-So think of me if I committed this sin?'"

This was exactly Paul's line of thinking when he said that he consciously exercised self-control, like an athlete disciplining his body, "so that after I have preached to others, I myself will not be disqualified" (1 Corinthians 9:27). That's amazing. He was not only accountable to Christ, he was accountable to Christ's people. Is the same thing true for you?

Personal Renewal and Revitalization

In the same 1 Corinthians passage, Paul likened the Christian life to a race. Not a hundred-yard dash, but a marathon. I can testify from personal experience that that's exactly what it is—a life-long race.

Unfortunately for many of us, the longer we run, the less energy we have to finish well. Some of us are fading in the stretch. This is especially a temptation for men who reach what is called "retirement." Retirement is where they give a man a gold watch and lots of free time to look at it. They put him out to pasture to play with the toys he's accumulated.

As a result, many men over age fifty-five are reaching for the bench, sliding for home. They are caving in at the very time when they ought to be tearing the place apart for Jesus Christ. That's one reason I believe so strongly in mentoring. It helps younger men mature and older men rejuvenate. Why? Because we grow most in the process of helping others grow.

No one knows this better than elderly people who volunteer to work with children and young people. One seventy-eight-year-old widower who puts in several hours a week with kids at an elementary school through a program run by the American Association of Retired Persons says, "I could never have survived the long agony of my wife's death if I didn't have 'my kids' at school. My hours with them gave me the strength to go on— because they needed me."

By the way, this is why we need more interaction between the generations in our churches. Somewhere along the way we decided to segregate everybody by age groups. That has certain merits, but one of the downsides is that it isolates the generations from each other. In a culture where the extended family has been reduced to the nuclear family and even the single-parent home, churches could have a profound impact if they counteracted that trend.

A Sense of Self-fulfillment

Earlier we looked at Jethro and surmised that he may have helped Moses because he wanted to leave a legacy. How interesting then to read Moses' words in Psalm 90, which were written sometime during the Exodus journey. "The length of our days is seventy years," he wrote, "or eighty, if we have the strength; yet their span is but trouble and sorrow, for they quickly pass, and we fly away" (Psalm 90:10).

Moses was telling us that life is fleeting. How then ought we to respond? "Teach us to number our days aright, that we may gain a heart of wisdom," Moses prayed. But also: "May your deeds be shown to your servants, your splendor to their children. May the favor of the Lord our God rest upon us; establish the work of our hands for us—yes, establish the work of our hands" (90:12, 16–17).

Do we hear an echo of Jethro in Moses' prayer? We certainly have testimony to the fact that almost every human being has a built-in longing to leave a heritage for the next generation. That longing grows deeper as one grows older. Mentoring is a means for fulfilling that desire.

As a teacher, I can tell you that nothing satisfies quite like the sense of accomplishment that comes from developing another individual. To take a person who has raw talent and limited experience, and work with him to shape his expertise, hone his skills, and launch him into productive work—that's a privilege I wouldn't trade for the world!

In fact, my greatest joy as a professor is to see my students excelling in the arenas to which God calls them. When they succeed, I succeed. When they break new ground, I feel like a part of the team. When they win praise and acclaim, I feel a swell of pride, knowing that I've had a strategic part in helping them along the way.

But sometimes I wonder whether as a society we have any appreciation left for the development of people. I often hear business executives mouth the old bromide that "our people are our most important asset." But if that's true, then it's fair to ask, what are you doing to cultivate that asset? What specific, practical plans and budgets do you have in place to identify and build the strengths of your people, and place them where they can be most effective?

And if those questions apply to business, how much more to the local church? If you are a pastor, I challenge you to consider: Is your church a net consumer of human resources, or a net producer of them? Are you building a great church, or great people? Are you building people only to the extent that they serve the purposes and programs of your institution, or in light of the gifts and opportunities that God has given to your people? Ephesians 4 speaks to this very issue.

The development of people is not a burden, it's a blessing. It is one of the most fulfilling activities of which I'm aware. And mentoring is all about people development. David recognized this truth when he wrote, "Since my youth, O God, you have taught me, and to this day I declare your marvelous deeds. Even when I am old and gray, do not forsake me, O God, till I declare your power to the next generation, your might to all who are to come" (Psalm 71:17–18). That's a prayer that every mentor could stand to pray.

Enhanced Self-esteem

In former times, the older a man got, the more deference he was paid. That's not always the case anymore. I'm meeting an increasing number of men in their senior years who look completely defeated, as if life has run over them like a Mack truck. Their self-esteem is just shot. Yet the irony is, they have as much to offer as ever—though they can hardly believe it.

Psychologist Erik Erikson called this the tension between generativity and self-absorption, or stagnation. A man either generates new relationships, new ideas, new products, and new growth, or he dies. He descends into a wallow of self-absorbed isolation as the world passes him by. The antidote, says Erikson—and this is similar to David's prayer in Psalm 71— is to *care,* to reach out with commitment toward the relationships, ideas, products, and so on that mean so much to the man—particularly by cultivating the next generation. It is this caring that keeps the man alive and active, rather than stagnant.

You see illustrations of this all the time. Some old guy will look like he's at death's door, when one day he's presented an opportunity to speak to a group of young people. Suddenly his strength returns, he summons his inner resources, and he performs at a level far beyond what anyone would have expected. He literally receives energy from the bright young faces in front of him.

The same can hold true for you, whatever your age. Nothing bolsters one's self-esteem like knowing that someone cares about and is paying attention to what you do and say. In a mentoring relationship, your young protégé may hang on your every word, and watch your every move. Sometimes that can be intimidating, but it is also exhilarating.

The Confidence of Having Made a Difference with Your Life

Two lines run through every man's life: a lifeline, and a purpose line. The lifeline marks biological progress; the purpose line marks the spiritual progress. Once the purpose line begins to taper off, it is just a question of time before the lifeline will do the same. What a tragedy, then, that for many men, we can already write their epitaph: "Here lies John. Died, age 39. Buried, age 69."

I can think of at least two reasons why a man might lose his purpose in life at such a relatively young age. One is great failure. A guy is breezing along in his thirties, working through his career, raising his family, enjoying life. Then suddenly—*Wham!*—he hits forty and his world comes unglued. So what does he do? If he's like many men who lack spiritual sensitivity, emotional maturity, and the support of mentors and friends, he's liable to take a long dive off the cliff. It may be an adulterous affair, an ill-advised career move, a poor business decision, or some other foolhardy escapade. The bottom line is, his life may end up on the rocks, shattering his relationships, his dreams, and his self-esteem.

For some men, life is essentially over at that point. They feel like their failures have been so great that they are out of the contest. The best they can do is quietly limp toward the finish line.

If this describes your life, may I suggest that becoming a mentor offers a ray of hope for you. Obviously you need to get your life back together before you make a commitment to coach another man. But don't assume that your failures automatically disqualify you from having a significant impact on another individual. There is a redeeming satisfaction in knowing that someone else will have the opportunity to learn from your mistakes. Indeed, sometimes the best teachers are those who have walked the paths of pain and can warn others about staying away from danger.

The other thing that can steal a man's purpose in living is great success. I see men all around me making headlines, making fortunes, making history—but not making a difference. Not as God measures significance. As a result, they are gaining the whole world, but losing the vitality of their own souls.

Remember David's prayer? "Even when I am old and gray, do not forsake me, O God, till I declare your power to the next generation, your might to all who are to come" (Psalm 71:18). Somehow David was not impressed by his crown, his kingdom, his wealth, his wives, or even his incredible talents as a ruler, a warrior, a builder, a musician, a poet. The only thing that really mattered to David was, "What does God think of me?" That determined his purpose.

Clearly, David was not a perfect man. But he was a purposive man. He knew why he was put on this earth. No wonder he was described as a man after God's own heart (1 Samuel 13:14; Acts 13:22).

I like the way my friend Bob Buford has put it: at some point, a man has got to move from success to significance. Otherwise, he's a dead person walking around in a body. Mentoring is one means of making that move, because it forces a man to think, not about the acquisition of material resources, but about the unleashing of spiritual resources in another individual's life. That can make a difference—for now, for eternity.

A Compelling Question

In fact, the most compelling question that every Christian man must ask is this: What am I doing today that will be an influence for Jesus Christ in the next generation? The stakes involved have never been higher. Both the church and society are facing an unprecedented crisis of leadership. Yet all the evidence suggests that leaders cannot be produced apart from some form of mentoring.

So it boils down to this: We cannot hold onto the world, we can only hand it to others. It's as if you are a father with your arms wrapped around your young son's shoulders, helping him get the feel of the bat as older brother lobs a ball across the plate. Swing and miss. Swing and miss. Swing and connect. Swing and miss.

There is no glory in that moment—only hints of glory as a pattern is established. It may be years before little Casey can swing on his own and connect with the ball. It may be years more before he ever hits his first run. But the pattern is established.

Someday, he will stand at the plate where the balls are hard and fast. It's a game where they call real strikes, and some men strike out. One team will win, and the other will lose.

When your son hits that home run in the game that counts, you may not be around to see it. But there will be a piece of you in that swing. That's your reward for leaving the world in good hands.

Chapter Thirteen

WHAT A MENTOR DOES

Years ago, I traveled deep into the Brazilian rain forest to visit missionaries in the Amazon jungles. It was an outstanding trip, but physically rugged. This was long before roads had been bulldozed through the rain forest, and it took us several days by dugout canoe to reach our destination, deep in the bush.

On my return from that remote locale, the Indians indigenous to that area presented me with several gifts. One was a chief's headdress made of vividly colored feathers. Another was a dried specimen of a piranha (my boys especially liked this), the infamous Amazon fish whose schools, when set to a feeding frenzy, were supposedly capable of stripping the meat from a cow in less than a minute.

A third gift was a long, slightly tapered pole. It was fashioned from paper-thin strips of what appeared to be bark, and wound with twine into a tight spiral that was held together by some sort of glue or pitch, hardened over a fire. At the larger end of this dark brown pole was carved a knot of dark wood, about the size of a man's fist. A small hole had been bored in the middle of this end piece.

Several days and some flights later, I arrived back home at Love Field in Dallas. This was in the days before jet travel, when you disembarked outside onto a stairway rolled up to the aircraft. I made my way down the steps and strode across the tarmac to the terminal, briefly glancing back at the plane. The propellers had stopped, and baggage handlers had the cargo doors open and were pulling out the luggage. All of a sudden they stopped and gathered around.

The guy in the plane was handing down my pole. I could see the men looking at each other, laughing and shaking their heads, obviously curious as to what this crazy thing was. One of them held it up and looked through the end. Another seemed to act as if it were an oversized pool cue. I was beginning to worry that they might damage it. But finally they put it on the baggage cart and went on with their work.

At home, my kids were no less mystified than the baggage handler as to what this contraption might be. "It's a blowgun," I told them.

"A blowgun? What's that?"

How to Use a Blowgun

"It's how the Indians hunt monkeys," I said. "Come on, I'll show you," and we headed for the garage. I brought out a quiver of very thin sticks, each about ten inches long, with a fine point on one end. These were the darts. Attached to the quiver was a cotton-like ball of silky fibers. I took a few strands of this material and wadded them around the end of one of the darts.

"The Indians dip these darts into poison that they get from a frog," I explained. "Then they use the blowgun to shoot at the monkey. The poison paralyzes the monkey, and it falls out of the tree. Watch!"

I pushed the dart down into the hole in the large end of the blowgun, which was the mouthpiece, and lifted the weapon to my mouth. Aiming at a dart board set against the wall, I blew as hard as I could. The dart shot out the other end and drilled into the target. After a moment of stunned silence, my kids shouted, "Wow! Do it again!"

At this point in the book, you may be in a somewhat similar position as the baggage handlers and my children. I have been talking about "mentoring" and encouraging you to get involved in "mentoring relationships." But you may be thinking, " 'Mentoring'? What's that?" And even though I have told you in a general way what the purpose of mentoring is, you may still be mystified as to how the process works.

Those baggage handlers at Love Field were holding exactly the right equipment to hunt monkeys. They just didn't know it. They had never seen a blowgun in their lives. And even if I had told them what it was, they wouldn't have had a clue as to how to use it.

How to Be a Mentor

In the same way, you probably have the right equipment, the right skills, to mentor someone. But that doesn't mean you are aware of what you possess. And even if you were, you might not know how to use it to impact another man's life.

So having exhorted you to pursue the mentoring process, let me explain *how* to pursue it. In this chapter I'll clarify what I mean by a mentor. Then in the remaining chapters, I'll give you a template and some tools for establishing and cultivating mentoring relationships.

Let's begin with a definition. It was Charles Kettering who said that a problem well-defined is a problem half solved. So I want to define what a mentor is and distinguish his influence in a person's life. This is easier said than done, because fundamentally the term *mentor* is not a "pure" term at all, but a metaphor, a figure of speech that describes someone in a certain type of relationship.

The First Mentor

The original person named Mentor is a figure in the *Odyssey,* an epic poem by the Greek poet Homer. Mentor is the male guardian and tutor of Telemachus, the son of the poem's central character, Odysseus. While Odysseus is away fighting at Troy and then finding his way home, Mentor raises Telemachus into manhood.

It is also worth noting that from time to time in the poem, Athena, goddess of wisdom and the arts, assumes the form of Mentor—which adds some interesting possibilities to our understanding. For example, the tale ends with Odysseus and Telemachus engaged in a pitched battle with the townsmen, most of whom have been acting as suitors to Odysseus' wife during his prolonged absence. The combined strength of father, son, and their allies is so effective that they not only regain control but threaten to wipe out the entire village. But just as the heroes are poised to blot out their enemies, Athena appears and demands that Odysseus end the battle:

"Son of Laertes and the gods of old,
Odysseus, master of land ways and sea ways,
command yourself. Call off this battle now,
or Zeus who views the wide world may be angry."

He yielded to her, and his heart was glad.
Both parties later swore to terms of peace
set by their arbiter, Athena, daughter
of Zeus who bears the stormcloud as a shield—
though still she kept the form and voice of Mentor.[1]

Thus, Mentor seems to have a connection with peacekeeping, arbitration, and the preservation of community. The combatants listen to him. He stands above the fray, and his wisdom (or is it Athena's?) rules the day.

I leave it to you to read Homer's *Odyssey*. Then you can make of Mentor what you will. The point is that he is the origin of our metaphorical term *mentor*. And like all descriptive terms, *mentor* means different things to different people: master, guide, exemplar, father-figure, teacher, trainer, tutor, instructor, leader, counselor, coach. There are many possibilities. (For more discussion of the term *mentor*, see What Is a Mentor?, pp. 165–166.)

Mentoring Is Defined by the Relationship

That being the case, we have to define a mentor not in terms of any formal roles that he carries out, but in terms of the *character of his relationship* with the other person, and the *functions* that that relationship serves. For example, earlier I defined a mentor somewhat loosely as a person committed to helping you grow, keeping you growing, and helping you realize your life goals. Notice that the relationship is characterized by the mentor's commitment, and its function is developmental—the growth of an individual.

Is this too abstract? Let me get very practical. A mentor serves his protégé (or follower) in any of several key ways:

- *He is a source of information.* He knows things—particularly things about life—that the protégé does not.

- *He provides wisdom.* In the Bible, wisdom means "the skill of living." Or, as someone has put it, wisdom means knowing what to do *next*. The mentor applies truth to life in a way that makes sense and works.

- *He promotes specific skills and effective behaviors.* There is often a practical edge to the mentoring relationship. The protégé comes away knowing how to do certain things that he couldn't do before.

- *He provides feedback.* The mentor is more than a mirror; he is a commentator. He has an informed point of view. He not only sees, he sees what matters.

- *He coaches.* In our culture, *coach* may be as close to a synonym for *mentor* as we have. The job of a coach is to prepare an athlete to win a contest. The job of a mentor is to prepare a protégé to win at life.

- *He is a sounding board.* It costs nothing to ask the question, "What if . . . ?" But it may cost everything if a person goes ahead without asking that question. The mentor provides a protégé the opportunity to test ideas and intuitions before they become agendas and attitudes.

- *He is someone to turn to.* In times of personal problems and crises, we need people whom we trust and respect. A mentor engenders that kind of confidence.

- *He helps devise plans.* Whether one is charting a program for spiritual growth, plotting a career path, deciding on an education, or contemplating marriage, a mentor lends perspective and practical advice.

- *He nurtures curiosity.* Mentors tend to open doors rather than close them. They show us the possibilities, the opportunities, the unexplored. They seem to have a fondness for asking, "Have you noticed . . . ?"

We could easily add to this list. It is meant to be suggestive, not exhaustive. Nor does every mentor fulfill all of these functions—though some fulfill all of them and more. But every mentor offers at least some of them.

So what is a mentor? Perhaps a better question is, when does a man become a mentor? You see, *what matters is not so much whether you see yourself in that role, but whether someone else sees you in that role.* The perception of the protégé goes a long way toward defining the relationship.

Tom and Richie

Let me illustrate. Tom, twenty-eight years old and a carpenter, lives with his wife, Julie, and two small children in a starter home that they bought before they had kids (while Julie was still employed). Down the street lives Richie, a teenager who lives alone with his mother. His parents are divorced.

One Saturday Tom is shooting baskets in his front driveway, using a backboard set up over his garage. As he turns from a rebound, he notices Richie walking by. Richie has paused ever so slightly to watch Tom, but as soon as Tom notices him, Richie starts walking again.

On an impulse, Tom stops and says, "Hey, you wanna shoot some hoops?"

It takes Richie only a second or two to respond, "Sure, I guess so."

So they start trading the ball and taking shots. Pretty soon they are into a game of horse, and before they realize it, half the afternoon has gone by.

Finally they stop and Tom gets a couple of sodas. They sit on the porch and talk about the Pistons and the Bulls. Richie mentions his trading card collection. Then Tom recalls the day he shook hands with Nolan Ryan. They both talk about whether right-handed pitchers or southpaws have the greater advantage. On and on they go, sports being the hot topic. Eventually Richie says it's time to go, and they say good-bye.

But a few days later they are back in the driveway, shooting hoops. The routine continues week after week, almost always followed by a post-game discussion. For a while, the conversations are pretty much limited to sports and the weather and other superficial topics. But gradually the talk shifts to more substantive issues. Tom asks Richie about school and his friends. Richie talks from time to time about his home life. Tom tells Richie about some of the jobs he is working on. Richie meets Julie. One day, he starts asking Tom about girls.

In this manner, the relationship deepens little by little. In the course of time, Tom tells Richie that he and Julie are Christians, and explains what that means. Not long after that, Richie prays to receive Christ. Tom introduces him to some kids at his church, and Richie begins to get active in the youth group.

Several years go by, and Richie is ready to graduate from high school. Now he's talking with Tom about what he should do with his life. His grades won't qualify him for college, and he's thinking about applying for a job in construction. But Tom points out that to earn a decent wage, Richie needs to get some training. Tom describes his own experience at a vocational school and how helpful that was for him. He even takes Richie to visit one of his former teachers there, and the man gives Richie a tour of the school.

As a result, Richie enrolls and learns how to work on consumer electronics. This leads to an entry-level job with a growing company. Before long, Richie is promoted and transferred to another city. At about the same time, Tom and Julie sell their house and move to another neighborhood. Tom and Richie exchange a couple of postcards, but neither one is a letter writer. So eventually they lose touch with each other. For all practical purposes, the relationship has run its course.

Now the interesting thing is that twenty years later, when Tom is in his fifties, I could run into him at a seminar on mentoring and ask him, "Are there any guys you feel you've really influenced in a significant way?"

He might scratch his head and say, "Well, Dr. Hendricks, there was Larry, a guy on our construction crew. I led him to the Lord, and I guess I really helped him save his marriage. And there was a guy named Hal in my church. We used to get together for prayer a lot. And I coached my kid's little league team, and there was a boy—I forget his name—who just thought I hung the moon. He wanted to be exactly like me when he grew up. So I guess I must have made an impression on him.

"But other than that, I can't think of anyone. I mean, I've tried to be friendly with kids and younger guys. You know, shoot hoops and stuff, talk with 'em, that sort of thing. There was a guy down the street who used to come over sometimes. But really, Dr. Hendricks, with the exception of those two or three guys I mentioned, I really couldn't say I've been what you've been calling a 'mentor' to anyone. I'd like to. That's why I'm here, to learn how."

The Impact of a Mentor

Meanwhile, I could run into Richie, who is pushing forty, and I could ask him the question with which I began this book: "Who are the people who have helped to make you who you are today?"

And without a moment's hesitation, Richie would shoot back, "It was a guy named Tom. I'll never forget him. He lived down the street from me, and we talked about *everything*. I mean, there was nothing I couldn't ask him. He wasn't preachy or a know-it-all. He just listened and always seemed to have a slant on things that made me think.

"I would have followed that man anywhere! He was the most godly person I've ever met. He's the guy who led me to Christ. I mean, when nobody else cared, he gave me the gospel. He's the guy who got me started in a church. He's the guy who told me I ought to begin reading the Bible and praying. He's the guy who showed me what a real father and husband is supposed to be.

"He's also the guy who kept me from making the mistake of blowing off my education just to get a job. I mean, my whole career happened because he took me over to a vocational school and insisted that I at least apply. I didn't even think I could get in!

"I don't know whatever happened to him, but there's hardly a day that goes by that I don't say a little prayer, 'Thank you, Lord, for Tom!' I don't know whether I'm all that clear on what you mean by a 'mentor,' Dr. Hendricks, but if you're talking about somebody who has really made a difference in your life, then I guess Tom was that person for me. Is that what you mean by a 'mentor'?"

Same relationship, two completely different perspectives. But it is Richie's perception that proves determinative.

By the way, I can assure you that this scenario is played out time and time again. Young men look up to older men in ways that older men can hardly even imagine. In fact, if older men had the slightest idea of the influence they actually have, to say nothing of the influence they could have, relationships between men in this country would be transformed. Indeed, books like this one would hardly be needed, because men would already be engaged in vital relationships.

It's important to try to define what a mentor is, but I caution you not to get hung up in words and concepts. Tom and Richie wouldn't have had a clue that they were involved in a mentoring relationship. But they still experienced the benefits. The main reason I define mentoring in this chapter is to help you become intentional about serving other men in a significant way.

How About You?

There is a Richie out there who needs what you have to offer. In the next chapter, I'll help you go about finding him. But first, you may be wondering whether you are cut out to serve as another man's mentor. Let me close with a brief inventory of questions that you can use to evaluate your suitability:

(1) Are you a man of patience? That is, do you take the long-range view?

(2) What is your area of competence? In what skills are you qualified, and what is your specific area of expertise?

(3) How strong are your interpersonal skills? Are your relationships generally healthy?

(4) Are you process-oriented? That is, are you capable of sticking with a person over time, while he develops?

(5) Are you willing to take risks?

(6) Are you willing to accept responsibility to help someone else grow?

(7) Is your character worth emulating? Would God approve of someone adopting your behaviors, attitudes, values, language, and mannerisms?

(8) Are you willing to make time for someone else?

(9) Is there any sin or unhealthy situation that you have not addressed, that could possibly damage your relationship with another person?

(10) Have you settled the question of Christ's lordship over your life? Are you fundamentally committed to honoring Him in every area?

Your answers to these questions alone do not certify that you would make the perfect mentor. But they will provide you with direction. They can help you gain a reasonable estimate of what you have to offer and where you should be careful.

One word of caution: In answering these questions, don't psych yourself out with ideals. You can get so enamored with high standards that you automatically disqualify yourself. For example, take question #3: "How strong are your interpersonal skills?" You might be thinking to yourself, "Good night! I'm no Dale Carnegie! I have a hard enough time just saying good morning to my wife! And I have no training as a psychologist! I can't read what's in another person's mind. I could never serve as a mentor." But the reality is, if you can carry on a conversation, you might do just fine.

Obviously you need to pursue high ideals. God calls us to that very thing. But He also knows that none of us is perfect, and that we all have limitations as well as strengths. Those weak spots need not necessarily eliminate us from serving as mentors. The fact is, most men are actually capable of far more positive influence than they realize.

WHAT IS A MENTOR?

Mentoring is a relational process [in which a] mentor, who knows or has experienced something . . . transfers that something (resources of wisdom, information, experience, confidence, insight, relationships, status, etc.) to a mentoree, at an appropriate time and manner, so that it facilitates development or empowerment.

Paul Stanley and Robert Clinton (*Connecting*)

In modern-day terms, mentors are influential, experienced people who personally help you reach your major life goals. They have the power—through who or what they know—to promote your welfare.

Linda Phillips-Jones (*The New Mentors and Protégés*)

Defining mentoring is sort of tough, but describing it is pretty easy. It's like having an uncle that cares for you for a lifetime, and wants to see you do well. He's not your competitor; he's there to support you, not to compete with you or discourage you. He's not your critic as much as he is your cheerleader.

Bobb Biehl (1993 Promise Keepers workshop)

The mentor relationship is one of the most complex, and developmentally important, a man can have in early adulthood. The mentor is ordinarily several years older, a person of greater experience and seniority in the world the young man is entering. No word currently in use is adequate to convey the nature of the relationship we have in mind here. Words such as "counselor" or "guru" suggest the more subtle meanings, but they have other connotations that would be misleading. The term 'mentor' is generally used in a much narrower sense, to mean teacher, advisor or sponsor. As we use the term, it means all these things and more. . . .

Mentoring is not defined in terms of formal roles but in terms of the character of the relationship and the functions it serves. . . . We have to examine a relationship closely to discover the amount and kind of mentoring it provides.

Daniel Levinson (*Seasons of a Man's Life*)

For the Christian, "mentoring" has objectives in the real world that are beyond the stuff of legends. "Discipling" is a close synonym, with these differences: A discipler is one who helps an understudy (1) give up his won will for the will of God the Father, (2) live daily a life of spiritual sacrifice for the glory of Christ, and (3) strive to be consistently obedient to the commands of his Master. A mentor, on the other hand, provides modeling, close supervision on special projects, individualized help in many areas—discipline, encouragement, correction, confrontation, and a calling to accountability.

Ted Engstrom (*The Fine Art of Mentoring*)

Chapter Fourteen

How to Spot a Protégé

There's an old cliché in business that if you build a better mousetrap, the world will beat a path to your door. That may be good inspiration, but I wouldn't recommend it for implementation, at least in today's marketplace. Nowadays, if you build a better mousetrap, *you'd* better be the one beating a path—to the door of your customer (unless you plan to warehouse a lot of mousetraps). People today don't care what you've got to sell—no matter how good it may be—nearly as much as they care about their own needs. The only question they have about your product is: "Do I need it?" Period. If not: "Leave me alone!"

I'm afraid something of that mind-set carries over into the realm of personal development, including mentoring. You can't just "hang out your shingle" as a mentor and expect a prospective protégé to ring your doorbell. Instead, you have to go ring his doorbell, figuratively speaking. Otherwise, you may be like the guy with a better mousetrap: great product, but no takers. Why? Because he's sitting back waiting for customers to find him, instead of him going out to find potential customers.

An Active Search

For many men, however, finding a protégé is a bit like looking for the proverbial needle in a haystack. In fact, it's worse than that: it's like looking for a needle in a haystack full of needles. After all, is there really *any* man who *doesn't* need a mentor? How, then, do you qualify your prospects?

Or are you supposed to just grab the first young man who comes your way, shake his hand, and say, "You lucky dog! Guess what! I'm going to mentor you!"? I wouldn't recommend that approach.

On the other hand, I wouldn't recommend that you wait for him to drop into your life, either. As I've indicated, you may wait forever. While it's true that countless young men are starving for the leadership of older men, it is also true that most of them are unlikely to ask for it.

Therefore, you've got to be proactive about seeking out a younger man to work with. By "younger man," I mean a man who is younger than you are. As a rule of thumb, protégés tend to seek out a mentor who is between six and fifteen years older than they are. So a teenager will tend to gravitate toward a man in his twenties or early thirties. A guy in his thirties will tend to look to a man in his forties or early fifties. A man at fifty-five will pay attention to a man in his sixties or seventies. Obviously there is nothing set in concrete about these age spans. Boys in their adolescence have been known to be profoundly influenced by men in their sixties or seventies. And peer mentors influence each other even though they are roughly the same age. But in this chapter, I'm primarily concerned with mentoring relationships where there is a noticeable age gap.

Finding a younger man to influence is not as difficult as it may sound. Indeed, it may not be difficult at all. But it probably won't "just happen." Remember that Barnabas intentionally went after Saul (or Paul) and brought him into the fellowship of believers (Acts 9:27). Likewise, Paul intentionally recruited Timothy to join him in his travels (16:1–3).

In the same way, as you consider the many young men around you—in your workplace, in your church, in your neighborhood and community—I encourage you to be intentional about identifying potential protégés. Ask yourself: which ones look like someone who could use what you have to offer?

What About "Potential"?

Now notice: I am not asking which ones have potential. That's a ludicrous question. *Everyone* has potential. That's part of what it means to be created in God's image. God has a blueprint, a design, an intention for every one of us. So we can never look at someone and say, "Well, forget him. He's hopeless. He doesn't have what it takes." My friend, humanly speaking, which of us does have what it takes?

Furthermore, if you go by the criterion of "potential," you tend to end up with a bias toward a certain kind of person—the one who happens to look promising *at the time you evaluate him*. As a result, you tend to "move with the movers," as they say. But that's a shotgun approach to people development that misses more often than not.

For example, suppose you run across someone who may be brilliant, but nevertheless seems erratic, lacking in judgment, unsteady, undependable, rude, and overly fond of drink. One of his friends even describes him as having "jaywalked through life." You might easily reject any idea of mentoring such a man, but in the process, you would be letting go of a young Winston Churchill.

Or suppose you meet a teenager who does not appear to be a particularly bright student, is not very verbal, is independent to the point of being antisocial, comes off as arrogant, acts defiantly in school, and occasionally even throws temper tantrums (such as hurling a chair at a tutor). How would you assess that young man's "potential"? Most of us would say that he probably won't make it. That's certainly what Albert Einstein's high school teachers thought.

Or suppose you had a student who turns in papers that really only merit a "C." His ideas sound a little kooky, and you think, "This kid will never amount to much. He likes to dream of starting something big, but after he graduates and gets into the real world, he'll change his tune real fast." If you took that attitude, you'd be letting go of a Fred Smith, whose idea for Federal Express, the dominant player in the overnight delivery industry, was hatched when he was a junior in college.

Am I suggesting that every young man you run into is a potential Churchill, Einstein, or Fred Smith? No, I'm asserting something of far greater significance: Every young man you run into has been called into existence by the Creator-God. Never take that lightly! It means that God sovereignly built into him exactly the "right stuff" to become the unique individual that God intends him to be. Your task as a mentor is to look for that "right stuff" and help bring it out so that the young man fulfills God's intention.

What does that say about the five qualities I mentioned in chapter 4, the ones that mentors tend to look for in a would-be protégé: a goal-orientation, a desire to increase his capacities, initiative, an eagerness to learn, and personal responsibility for his own development? Clearly, these are vital when it comes to personal and spiritual growth. Ideally, I'd like to see all five in a prospect. But I wouldn't rule out a man just because he lacks some of these traits or is weak in some of them. I have to realize that where he is now may bear little resemblance to where he might be ten, twenty, or thirty years from now. Moreover, I may enjoy speculating about his future, but I've got to pay attention to his present: What has he got to work with right now, and what I can build on?

Who Can Use What I've Got?

Therefore, in identifying a prospective protégé, the fundamental question to ask is: *Who looks like someone who could use what I have to offer?*

Remember the relationship I described between Tom and Richie in the last chapter? Richie was essentially looking for someone with time and a listening ear. Tom was able to offer that—and did. Of course, Tom wasn't even aware of his profound influence on Richie. But let's suppose that Tom had read this book and been looking for someone to work with. The relationship might well have started exactly as it did. But as it developed, Tom could have said to himself, "This guy needs time and a listening ear. I can offer that. Richie just might be a prospect."

Meanwhile, Tom might have bypassed some other teenager who needed other things—things that Tom couldn't offer. For instance, a kid at Tom's church might have been looking for answers to deep, intellectual and philosophical questions about Christianity. That wasn't Tom's forte. Another kid in the community might have needed a place to live, essentially a surrogate home. But that wouldn't have been an option for Tom, as he and his growing family were already packed into their tiny house. Another kid might have needed money—like the kids at P.S. 121 that Eugene Lang helped (see chapter 2). But trying to offer help like that would have been beyond Tom's means.

Can you see that the person you want to link up with is the person who can make the best use of what you have to offer? That's why it is so important for you to know what you can and can't give. To do that, you need to stop and take inventory. You need to know yourself, your gifts, your resources, and your limitations. To help you evaluate these, you might want to use the list that begins on page 137, or the questions on pp. 163–164, or some of the assessment tools and inventories listed at the end of this chapter.

You also need to stay in prayer about whom God would have you spend time with. Do you realize that Jesus Christ spent *all night* in prayer before He chose the Twelve? (Luke 6:12-13) And Paul told Timothy that he constantly remembered him in prayer night and day (2 Timothy 1:3). Somehow, I think that pattern was established even before the apostle asked Timothy to join him.

Let's say that you've gotten to the point where you are looking at a prospective protégé. How do you tell whether he can use what you have to offer? Let me give you two sets of questions to ask—six diagnostic questions to ask the prospect, and six reflective questions to ask yourself about the prospect.

Questions to Ask Your Prospect

These questions are probes to gather information. You are dealing with many unknowns, so the point is to find out some basic facts that will enable you to make informed decisions. You don't need to ask these questions in exactly the way they're stated. Use your own words and your own personality. You may even be able to get at some of these things in other ways. I certainly wouldn't recommend firing these questions at a younger man as if you were interrogating him in a police line-up. It may take weeks or even months to ferret out some of his answers, and some things you may never know. After all, he always has the right to remain silent.

1. "What would you like to do with your life?" This is often a fun place to start with someone, because the question is open-ended, relatively non-threatening, and offers clues as to the young man's general outlook. However you ask it, you are trying to get at his plans, goals, dreams, and passions. What does he want out of life? What are his expectations? What does he hope to become?

2. *"You seem to really be interested in such-and-such. Tell me about that. What else are you interested in?"* Obviously, you are trying to discover the young man's interests. Often these will surface on their own. He'll tell you about a book he's reading, a game he has played, an adventure he took part in, a project he is working on. Pay particular attention to the things he is *passionate* about—the subjects and situations that really engage his energy and emotion, that get him worked up, that make him vocal, that command his time and attention, and that show that he cares. That passion is a clue to his motivation and natural bent.

3. *"What are you good at?"* Every person has certain skills and abilities. Like interests, these may be self-evident. On the other hand, they may not always be developed. At any rate, dig around to see if he has unusual capacities that no one knows about. The classic example is the kid who does poorly in academic subjects at school, but happens to be a mechanical genius with his hands. Or the young man who is awkward in relationships, but is endowed with an extremely good memory and an eye for detail. You have to pay attention to discover subtle but significant abilities like these.

4. *"Tell me a little of your history."* You can probably ask this question in more subtle ways. The point is to find out what this guy's story is. Where did he come from? What are the highlights (and lowlights) in his life? What people and incidents have been significant to him? What tragedies has he had to go through? What factors seem to account for who he is? People don't just fall out of the sky. They emerge into the world. Every one of us has a unique story to tell. By discovering your prospective protégé's, you'll gain valuable information about what part you might play in his life.

5. *"Tell me about your family."* The man's parents, brothers, and sisters are all part of an important group in his history—his family of origin. From your perspective as a potential mentor, his relationship with his father may be the most telling. It holds a lot of clues about his attitudes toward topics like authority, work, God, women, and what it means to be a man. Also pay attention to how his siblings have turned out. Sometimes that can tell you a lot about the stock that he comes from.

Another key factor that is often overlooked is his heritage and roots.

Today we think of "family" in terms of the nuclear family. But in Scripture, "family" takes into account not only mom, dad, and the kids, but the extended family—grandparents, aunts, uncles, cousins, and other living relatives—and beyond them, one's ancestors. It appears from the record, particularly in the Old Testament, that a man's familial roots play a significant role in shaping who he is.

6. *"Do you have faith in God?"* At some point, you want to gain an understanding of the man's spiritual condition. He may volunteer information here; he may not. But you want to determine where he stands in regard to the faith. Does he even believe in a God? If so, has he placed his faith in Jesus Christ for salvation? If he has not, that alone is no reason to reject him as a protégé; in fact, your relationship with him may be a great opportunity to win him to the Lord (see pp. 76–77).

If he is already a believer in Christ, you'll want to assess how far he has progressed in the faith.

Questions to Ask About Your Prospect

The following questions are reactions to the information you have gathered, questions you should ask yourself. If you have taken the time to get to know your prospect, you'll have a lot of data to work with. But you still need to determine whether you can help him.

1. *"In what ways is this young man like me?"* The more you have in common with someone, the easier it is to relate to him, and the more you are likely to impact his life. It's not that you can't help someone who is quite different from you. But you'll find that the differences often make it harder to communicate and relate. So, do you see any aspects of yourself in this person? Do you have a lot in common? Or nothing at all? Do you find it easy to spend time with him, or is it a strain to be around him, and to find anything to say?

2. *"What are his needs, as I see them?"* You might generate a list of needs and then rank them according to how critical they are. For instance, what would you say are his top three needs, the three issues that will keep him from moving ahead? Another way to ask this question is to back off and look at the big picture. Here you want to ask, "What does this guy *really need*?"

For example, we saw earlier that Tom might have determined that what Richie *really needed* were time and attention. Obviously Richie had many other needs. He needed a dad, a stable home life, and probably some help in school, among other things. But by sizing up the overall picture, Tom would have been able to identify two simple but strategic concerns—ones that he could do something about.

3. *"Do I respond to this person's need or situation?"* At some point, you've got to look at your own reactions to this individual. You've got to be honest. Does he move your heart? Do you feel motivated to do something? Does something in you get activated so that you genuinely *want* to get with him?

Don't try to manufacture feelings and motives that aren't there. Just pay attention to what is there, because that is one way that God may be speaking to you, telling you either to get involved more deeply, or not.

4. *"Does he seem to want my help?"* Mentoring is not about selling ice cubes to Eskimos. Remember the question: Who looks like they could *use* what you have to offer? You need not press yourself on someone who really doesn't want you. So you need to ask yourself whether you have any indication that this young man is seeking you out, responding to your initiatives, or soliciting your assistance. If he is doing that, then it's a good sign. You may be able to help him. If not, that's OK. There is probably someone else out there who has needs you can meet.

5. *"Is this the right time for me to help this fellow?"* Timing is everything. Sometimes a qualified mentor shows up too early to be of much help to a young man. Sometimes he shows up too late. In evaluating your prospect, you need to consider whether the moment is ripe. This is another reason to be in regular prayer, asking God to open your eyes to men whom He has prepared for you to serve.

6. *"If I were to put everything I know about this guy into a story, how would that story read?"* Again, every person has a unique story to tell. Stories have a beginning, a middle, and an end. You are coming into this young man's life somewhere in the middle of the tale. What has happened so far? Based on what you know, what would be your hunch as to how it will all come out? Likewise, stories have characters and plot development. Who are the significant characters in your prospect's life? What is the plot

so far? Is there a central conflict? Is he trying to surmount certain obstacles or solve certain problems? Can you see any way in which you might fit into the story?

Decision Time

As you are answering all of these questions, you may be asking an overarching one: "What am I supposed to do with all of this? This seems like a lot of brain work! What's the payoff here? Where is all this leading?" The answer is that it is leading to a point of decision. Sooner or later, you will have to make some choices as to whether this relationship will go deeper and, if so, in what ways. In short, you have to decide how much of yourself you are able to give to this person.

There are essentially four options. The first one is, you may decide that the relationship is not for you. If not, don't be ashamed or afraid to acknowledge that. You actually serve the other person by saying, "No, I really can't help you." You don't serve him by stringing him along under false hopes and pretenses.

A second option is that you may decide to take a wait-and-see approach, or to proceed with caution. The issue of timing may affect this. As you look down the road, you may sense that your help will be more useful in six months, or a year, or three years. In that case, you might sort of "maintain" the relationship until conditions are ripe for something more involved.

A third possibility is to decide that yes, this relationship will work, but only if you enforce some cautions and limitations. I sometimes work this way with certain students at the seminary. For instance, a guy may have an unhealthy tendency to try and hold people's attention. If I let him, he would eat up hours of my time. I'm willing to work with him, but I don't have hours to give him. So I tell him, "I can meet with you for one-half hour, once a month. For that half-hour, buddy, I'm all yours. But I can only give you that half-hour." Then I instruct my secretary to help me keep on schedule, and when his half-hour is up, she tells me my next appointment is waiting, and I escort him to the door. It's a win-win arrangement for both of us.

The final option—and the one you always hope for—is the realization that the relationship is going to work well. You sense that you can probably have a real impact on this person's life. When that happens, praise God and then pray that He gives you the wisdom to be a guide and the grace to be a servant. In the next few chapters I'll give you some practical suggestions on how you and your protégé can make your interaction productive.

But as you conclude this chapter, I want you to stop and draw up a list of potential candidates for a mentoring relationship. Who might God be drawing into your sphere of influence? Any names or faces come to mind? Don't be too quick to say "yes" or to say "no."

The ideal mentoring relationship is perhaps the "natural" one—the situation where the mentor naturally, almost effortlessly offers what he has to offer, and the protégé naturally, almost instinctively takes what is offered and makes good use of it. We saw an illustration of that in Tom and Richie. Nothing was forced. No one was coerced. There wasn't a lot of pressure to follow a script or make something happen. The relationship simply developed over time and ended up marking Richie for life.

This suggests that as you look for a protégé, try to find situations where the relationship comes together as naturally as possible. Mentoring should be a dance, not a drill. Above all else, it should bring joy, not grief.

ASSESSMENT TOOLS & INVENTORIES

Church leaders today have access to a growing number of formal instruments and inventories designed to show people's strengths, gifts, interests, personalities, and other characteristics. These tools can be helpful in evaluating how a mentor can best serve a protégé. In fact, putting the protégé (as well as the mentor) through an assessment process can itself can be a valuable growth experience, as it provides insight into how the person tends to function.

Brad Smith of Leadership Network in Tyler, Texas, has compiled the following list (by no means exhaustive) of assessment vehicles. Note that in addition to the items listed, new tools are constantly being developed by churches and organizations. You might check with your local Christian bookstore, denominational headquarters, or leading churches to find out what is most current, effective, and appropriate for your needs.

Spiritual Gifts Assessments

These are usually inventories based on the lists of spiritual gifts in Romans 12, 1 Corinthians 12, and Ephesians 4. Examples include:

- *Basden-Johnson Spiritual Gift Analysis,* by Paul Basden and Lee Johnson, McCart Meadows Baptist Church (817-370-9900).
- *Discover Your Gifts Manual and Workbook,* by Charles R. Shumate and Sherrill D. Hayes, Christian Reformed Church (616-246-0764).
- *Houts Spiritual Gift Inventory* (charismatic and non-charismatic versions available); available through the Charles E. Fuller Institute (818-449-0425).

Some spiritual gift tests are part of a complete lay mobilization curriculum, such as:

- *Network: The Right People . . . In the Right Places . . . For the Right Reasons,* by Bruce Bugbee; available through Zondervan (800-876-7335), or Network Ministries International (800-588-8833).

- *Mobilizing Your Spiritual Gifts Series, Unleash Your Church,* by Paul R. Ford; available through the Charles E. Fuller Institute (818-449-0425).

Natural Gifts Assessments

These tools measure gifts and motivations present from birth, usually as indicated through an autobiographical interview and from observation of consistent behavior. Examples include:

- *The System for Identifying Motivated Abilities (SIMA)®,* by Art Miller, People Management Inc.; available through the Ministry by Design Division, David McKnight (612-337-9550).
- *Motif,* by Ralph Mattson, DOMA Inc. (612-895-1544).

Personality Style Assessments

These measure various aspects of the personality, such as temperament, role preference, leadership style, learning style. Examples include:

- *DiSC* (formerly *Performax*); available through the Carlson Learning Company (800-777-9897); or see the book, *Understanding How Others Misunderstand You,* by Ken Voges and Ron Braund.
- *Meyers-Briggs Type Indicator (MBTI);* requires certification through the Association for Psychological Type (816-444-3500); or see the book, *Please Understand Me,* by David Kirsey and Marilyn Bates.
- *Role Preference Inventory,* by Bobb Biehl, Masterplanning Group Intl. (800-443-1976).
- *Styles of Influence,* by Gene Getz, Center for Church Renewal (214-423-4262).

Interest Assessments

These compare a person's level of interest in various fields, and cover areas such as values, career interests, work space, and lifestyle desires. Examples include:

- *Holland's Self-Directed Search* (assessment booklet) and *The Occupations Finder;* available through Psychological Assessment Resources, Inc. (800-331-TEST).
- *Canμbell Interest and Skill Survey (CISS);* available through NCS Assessments (800-627-7271).

Ministry Match and *Chemistry Match,* by Steve Johnson, uses a multi-construct instrument that incorporates elements from #1–4; contact The Profile Group (303-745-2097).

Chapter Fifteen

YOU CAN DO IT!

Occasionally I come across people who object to the whole concept of mentoring because they can't find the word "mentor" in the Bible. "You're just importing the latest fad from the business world," they argue. "You're just putting a secular label on the biblical concept of discipleship."

Am I? I'll grant that the word "mentor" does not appear in Scripture. But I can't agree that mentoring is a fad of recent origin. As we've seen, the original Mentor dates from Homer's *Odyssey*, which takes us back more than eight hundred years before Christ. And the role that Mentor carried out—bringing up young Telemachus while his father was away at war—happens to be the pattern by which children have been brought to adulthood in nearly all societies throughout history—except for our own.

An Age-Old Pattern

In fact, mentoring was the primary means of instruction in Bible times, as Scripture attests. I've already mentioned several examples of mentoring relationships: Jethro and Moses, Jonathan and David, Barnabas and Saul, Paul and Timothy (and see Mentoring Relationships in the Bible on the next two pages).

We also know that in Jewish homes of that day, particularly in the Old Testament era, children learned most of their skills from their parents, members of the extended family, and neighbors in the community, using a hands-on methodology. As a result, most people followed in their parents' footsteps. Sons inherited the occupations of their fathers, and daughters took on the responsibilities of their mothers.

MENTORING RELATIONSHIPS IN THE BIBLE

Mentoring was a way of life in Bible times. It was the primary means of handing down skills and wisdom from one generation to the next. So it's not surprising that Scripture gives us numerous examples of mentoring relationships. The list below shows some of the more prominent. By studying the passages indicated, you can learn a lot about the principles and practice of mentoring. (Also see the diagram Barnabas: A Ministry of Multiplication, p. 141.)

In the Old Testament

Jethro and Moses (Exodus 18)	Jethro taught his son-in-law the invaluable lesson of delegation.
Moses and Joshua (Deuteronomy 31:1–8; 34:9)	Moses prepared Joshua to lead Israel into Canaan.
Moses and Caleb (Numbers 13; 14:6–9; 34:16–19; Joshua 14:6–15)	It appears that Moses groomed Caleb for leadership, and inspired in him an unswerving faith in the Lord's promises.
Samuel and Saul (1 Samuel 9–15)	Samuel not only tapped Saul to become Israel's king, but tried to shape his character as well. Even when Saul rebelled against the Lord, Samuel kept challenging him to repent and return to God.
Samuel and David (1 Samuel 16; 19:18–24)	Samuel anointed David as king and gave him refuge from Saul's murderous plots.
Jonathan and David (1 Samuel 18:1–4; 19:1–7; 20:1–42)	An outstanding example of peer mentoring, Jonathan and David remained loyal to each other during the troubled days of Saul's declining reign.

Elijah and Elisha (1 Kings 19:16–21; 2 Kings 2:1–16; 3:11)	The prophet Elijah recruited his successor Elisha and apparently tutored him in the ways of the Lord while Elisha ministered to Elijah's needs.
Jehoiada and Joash (2 Chronicles 24:1–25)	The priest Jehoiada helped Joash—who came to the throne of Judah when he was only seven years old—learn to rule according to godly principles. Unfortunately, Joash turned away from the Lord after his mentor died.

In the New Testament

Barnabas and Saul/Paul (Acts 4:36–37; 9:26–30; 11:22–30)	Barnabas opened the way for Saul to associate with the church after his dramatic Damascus Road conversion.
Barnabas and John Mark (Acts 15:36–39; 2 Timothy 4:11)	Barnabas was willing to part company with Paul in order to work with John Mark. Later, Paul came around to Barnabas's point of view, describing John Mark as "useful to me for ministry." John Mark is believed to have been the primary author of the gospel of Mark.
Priscilla and Aquila and Apollos (Acts 18:1–3, 24–28)	Tentmakers Priscilla and Aquila served as spiritual tutors to Apollos at Ephesus. As a result, Apollos became one of the early church's most powerful spokesmen for the gospel.
Paul and Timothy (Acts 16:1–3; Philippians 2:19–23; 1 and 2 Timothy)	Paul invited Timothy to join him during one of Paul's missionary journeys. Timothy eventually became pastor of the dynamic church at Ephesus.
Paul and Titus (2 Corinthians 7:6, 13–15; 8:17; Titus)	Paul, along with Barnabas, apparently won this Greek-speaking Gentile to the faith and recruited him as a traveling companion and coworker. Titus became a pastor and, according to tradition, the first bishop of the island of Crete.

The Greeks took a slightly different approach. They looked upon the raising of young children as a menial occupation. Therefore, they delegated it to slaves. When a boy became six, he was assigned a *pedagogue* or tutor, a slave who raised him until puberty.

Paul refers to this role in Galatians 3:24–25, where he likens the Law to a harsh disciplinarian, or tutor *(pedagogue)*, as opposed to Christ, who offers grace. Likewise, he told the Corinthians that "even though you have ten thousand guardians (or *pedagogues*) in Christ, you do not have many fathers, for in Christ Jesus I became your father through the gospel" (1 Corinthians 4:15). In both cases, he was referring to slaves who essentially had the same role as Mentor in Homer's *Odyssey*. (For other Bible passages related to the concept of mentoring, see pp. 191–192.)

Mentoring vs. Discipleship

What's the difference then between mentoring and discipleship? They are closely related, but not exactly the same. Both involve instruction based on a relationship. But discipleship involves a call, a direct invitation from the teacher that borders on a command. Jesus told the fishermen Peter and Andrew, "Come, follow me," and "at once they left their nets and followed him" (Matthew 4:19–20). Then he ran into their colleagues, James and John. Again, "Jesus called them, and immediately they left the boat and their father and followed him" (4:21–22). The same pattern was repeated with the rest of the Twelve.

The word *disciple* means "learner." In Jesus' day, teachers roamed the ancient world recruiting bands of "learners" who then followed these masters and adopted their teaching. Sometimes the disciples became masters themselves and developed their own followings. But Jesus' command to His followers to "go and make disciples of all nations" (Matthew 28:19) is distinctive in that Jesus remains *the* Master, *the* Discipler. He wants people who are recruited to the faith to remain *His* disciples, *His* learners.

Discipleship, as we know it today, tends to narrow its focus to the spiritual dimension. Ideally, it should touch on every area of life—our personal life and lifestyle, our work, our relationships. But discipleship always looks at these areas by asking the question, how do they relate to Christ? How does following Christ affect my personal life, my work, my relationships, and so on?

Mentoring, at least when practiced by Christians, certainly ought to center everything on Christ. But mentoring is less about instruction than it is about *initiation*—about bringing young men into maturity. Whereas the word for *disciple* means "learner," the word *protégé* comes from a Latin word meaning "to protect." The mentor aims to protect his young charge as he crosses the frontier into manhood.

For my own part, I do not make a hard and fast distinction between discipleship and mentoring. There is a great deal of overlap. But I like the concept of mentoring because it focuses on *relationships.* That is what we are missing in education today, whether we're talking about formal instruction in schools and universities, or informal instruction at home, in the church, and in the community. Men are not involved in vital relationships the way they once were.

As a result, boys are growing up with no concept of what it means to be a male. Many have poor role models, or even no role models, for what constitutes a godly husband and father. Most are going into the work world with a distorted picture of work. And because our culture has few means of inviting young males into the circle of men, countless men are living in fear of other men. They don't know what is expected, or what to expect. The worst of it all is that we are passing down to the next generation a giant void about what it means to be a man in Christ.

So it really doesn't matter what you call it. The point is, we need older men and younger men *relating* in such a way that younger men grow as older men guide. That is the historical pattern. It also happens to be the biblical pattern.

Attracting a Protégé

Now we can't go back to the days of old and re-create all the factors that accounted for mentoring and its benefits. The world has changed too much for that. But human nature and need have not changed. The desire and need for mentoring relationships remain as great as ever. How, then, can you recapture something of this ancient art and practice it in ways that benefit men around you? Let me suggest five simple strategies for attracting younger men into your sphere of influence.

Pray for God to Point Them Out

Prayer always ought to be our starting point for any form of personal or spiritual development. Prayer gets us properly aligned with God before we align ourselves toward another individual. That vertical relationship with Christ comes first; then the horizontal relationships with other people.

But as we pray, we need to ask God to open our eyes to potential candidates. In light of the question we looked at earlier, we might ask, "Lord, who looks like someone who could use what I have to offer? Open my eyes to see that person." Likewise, you might go back to the list of potential candidates I asked you to draw up at the end of the last chapter, and pray through that list. "Lord, is there a guy on this list whom you want me to pursue? Is there a name here that I need to pay attention to?"

I'm convinced that if you pray for a Timothy, sooner or later God will probably send one into your life. In fact, God may have done that already. The reason for praying is so that you will *recognize* him. Prayer acts as a sort of filter or lens that helps you see people in a different way. God can use your prayer to screen out all but the most likely candidates, so that you have direction as to who to pursue.

Start with Your Area of Expertise

One of the most natural ways to initiate a relationship that could lead to mentoring is to start with what is familiar to you. By doing so, you will feel the most comfortable and competent. You can also avoid the tension that often exists when relationships are just getting formed.

When you see a younger man in need in an area in which you have ability or training, offer to give him a hand. For example, maybe you hear a guy at your church tell your prayer group that he is struggling with his taxes, and you happen to be an accountant. Can you offer to stop by his house and give him some suggestions? You don't have to do his taxes for him. Just be a support as he works through the situation.

Or maybe you're a plumber, and you overhear a friend at the barber shop talking about his aged mother's run-down house and its faulty heating system. He says that someone wants to charge her $80 just to come and tell her what's wrong with it. You may not be qualified to repair the unit, but perhaps you can at least determine the problem. Why not suggest to your friend that he take you with him over to his mother's, *so that the two of you* can look at her furnace.

Another way to initiate relationships through your expertise is to teach what you know. Are you a lawyer? Maybe the young married couples in your church could use a workshop on setting up a will. Are you a paramedic? A group of college kids could probably stand to learn something like CPR or the Heimlich maneuver. Are you a special education teacher? Maybe you could teach a high school kid how to sign.

The point is, not only is there intrinsic value in offering people your expertise: you meet needs and impart knowledge. But you also open the door to the possibility of an ongoing relationship with a younger individual. If you go into it on the lookout for a potential protégé, you just might find one. At the very least, you enrich other people's lives.

Place Yourself in Proximity to Younger People

If you want to attract younger men, you've either got to bring them onto your own turf, or you've got to go out and meet them on their turf. You'll meet a lot more of them if you go where they are.

One of the best ways to accomplish that is to volunteer to work with young people. Serving as a leader with Cub Scouts or Boy Scouts is an obvious choice. Another one is coaching for a Little League or soccer team. But there are countless other possibilities as well. Teaching a Sunday school class or assisting with the church youth group. Instructing at a summer camp. Serving as a docent at a children's museum or reading children's stories at the library. Volunteering at a local school (many elementary and secondary schools around the country have recently introduced formal mentoring programs, so this is a live option).

Whatever you can do to get next to younger people, do it. I'll meet a guy who says, "Hendricks, you're always telling us that young men are dying for a mentor, but I've never met one." Then I look at where this man spends his time, and it's all with men his own age. At the office, on the golf course, at church. He hasn't been around anybody younger than he is since college, with the result that he's out of touch. He's isolated in a comfortable cocoon with his colleagues and peers. Don't let that happen to you!

Set Up "Low Risk" Opportunities for Interaction

It's good to meet a younger man on his own turf, but sometimes the way to get to know him is to get him *off* his turf and *out* of his element. When he has a "home field advantage," he may be so highly influenced by his environment that you never find out what he's really like.

This is the strategy behind Outward Bound and similar programs. They'll take a team of executives into the wilderness, and suddenly the dynamics of the group will change. Some guys who seemed like big shots back in the office are suddenly less confident, while other men who ordinarily look passive assume new leadership. I'm not suggesting that you have to go rock climbing or white-water rafting to get to know a man. I only mean to encourage you to set up "low risk" opportunities where relationships can be established. By "low risk" I mean situations where no one has to perform, no one is going to be judged. The purpose is to have a good time and enjoy each other's company.

For example, you might invite a group of younger men over to your house for a cookout. Tell them you'll provide the fire, they can bring the meat. Or take three or four guys hunting or fishing. Or organize a men's night out to the ballpark. Or schedule a workday at your church to tackle some special projects. You might end the day with something relaxing, like an ice cream feast or a dip in someone's pool.

Use your own imagination to decide what works for you. The purpose of these encounters is twofold: to have fun, and to spend some time with younger guys to see if you strike a chemistry with any of them.

Invite a Likely Prospect to Join You Informally

Once you've got a specific guy in view, you'll need to give him some one-on-one attention. Again, keep this activity "low risk." You might offer to buy him lunch. Or take him golfing with you. Or invite him to tag along to some special event or convention that you are attending. Or call him up and ask him to lend you a hand with some project you've got going, such as moving boxes, or trimming tree limbs, or picking up a load of firewood.

By initiating these kinds of offers, you are *inviting* this young man into your circle, onto your turf, with no strings attached, and with no (or at least low) expectations. That's extremely valuable for him, and it gives both of you a chance to interact more closely than in a group setting. The relationship may go no deeper. You may just remain friends, or even drift apart. But at least you've observed your man up close and given him the opportunity to do the same with you.

Auditioning Men for Manhood

Perhaps as you consider these various suggestions, you are wondering, "What's the point in all of this? These ideas seem like just a lot of socializing and being a good guy to some younger men. What will doing these things accomplish?" The answer is that you are gradually auditioning younger men for initiation into manhood.

If that sounds overly dramatic, consider this. Most societies down through history have had rites of passage to mark major transitions in life. I'll never forget a recent trip that Jeanne and I took to Israel. While visiting the Wailing Wall in Jerusalem, we witnessed five bar mitzvahs taking place. What an incredible experience to watch these young Jewish boys being hoisted onto the shoulders of a father, an uncle, a family friend, who then danced around that sacred square while bystanders clapped and the women threw candy. I turned to my wife and said, "Sweetheart, those boys will never forget this day!"

Do we have anything in American culture that comes close to replicating that? I'm afraid not. Our secular society has virtually eliminated the rituals of life, with the result that many men no longer know where they stand. They're left to wonder: "Am I a boy, or a man? Do I know enough, or not? Am I competent, or not? Do I have respect, or not? Do I matter, or not?"

You can help answer those self-doubts by inviting a young man into your world. In many ways, you control the "blessing," as authors Gary Smalley and John Trent have so appropriately put it, that bestows on him a place in society.

"But what you are suggesting sounds so simple," you may be saying. "Invite a kid to lunch. Take him to a ball game. Bring him along on a bass boat. Those sound awfully easy."

You're right! They *are* easy. I'm not talking about brain surgery, here! I'm talking about things that almost any man can do. That's why it's so tragic that so many men *aren't* doing them—and aren't making the most of it if they are.

Can You Buy a Man a Cup of Coffee?

You see, I keep challenging men to become mentors, and a guy will say to me, "Brother Hendricks, I don't think I can do that. I just don't have what it takes."

Oh, really? Can you buy a young man a cup of coffee?

"Yeah."

Can you invite him to sit next to you at the company picnic?

"Yeah, I can do that."

Can you ask him to ride with you in the car while you take your mother-in-law to the airport?

"Yeah, I suppose I could probably do that."

Good! You're well on your way to establishing a mentoring relationship.

"But what good will it do?" I hear someone asking, still not convinced. Let me respond with another question: What good does it do to spend time with your children when you come home from work? I mean, "all" you are doing is throwing a softball around. "All" you are doing is making doll voices. "All" you are doing is rolling on the floor with a baby making goo-goo eyes at you. What good will that do?

A Handsome Gain

The answer is: plenty! God has been gracious to us in that He has made the most significant pieces of life to be the most simple. They are things that almost anyone can do. Their significance may seem paltry in the moment. But it's in the aggregate, over time, that the gains mount up and become visible. It's like putting a dollar in the bank every day. A dollar? So what? But give it a year, five years, ten years, a lifetime—and compound the interest—and you've got a handsome gain!

Furthermore, in the end, what matters is not your estimate of whether the time you spend with a younger man has been profitable; it is *his* estimate that counts. I can assure you that if he happens to be someone whose heart and life have been prepared by God to receive the unique contribution that you have to make, your interaction will have been not simply worthwhile, but invaluable.

Bill's good friend, Dolphus Weary, head of Mendenhall Ministries in Mendenhall, Mississippi, grew up in grinding poverty in rural Mississippi in the 1950s and 1960s. As a black, Dolphus experienced firsthand the terrible effects of the racism of that era. By the time he reached adolescence, he had come to believe that "no matter what I do, no matter how hard I work, I'll always be second-class here. The system is rigged against me, and I'll always make just enough to get by, but never enough to get ahead. That's the way it is here, and it's never going to change."

No wonder Dolphus determined, like many black youths, that if he ever got the chance, he would leave Mississippi and never come back. But that chance never came, and by the time he was ready to finish high school, Dolphus assumed that he was destined for a life of menial labor.

But God had a purpose for Dolphus Weary's life. He would take him out of Mississippi—but eventually bring him back for service. One of the crucial turning points occurred during a frenzied basketball game between Dolphus' school, Harper High, and the other black school in the county, New Hymn:

> At half time we were beating them on their own court 45 to 12. It was a joke! So they asked if their coach could play with them. He had been a star player at Mississippi's largest black college. We said okay.
>
> Ten minutes later, we were in a whole new ball game! Our guys were still shooting okay from the floor, but defensively we were in trouble. Their coach scored again and again. And their players, instead of looking grim, were getting excited. Their home court crowd was also screaming as the player-coach cut our lead to two points.
>
> With thirty seconds left, they called time out. The goal was for him to hold the ball and take the last shot. So we went into a man-to-man defense. Since I'd always thought I was a good defensive player, I

wanted him. I knew that the one thing in the world he wanted was to make that shot, tie the score, and send the game into overtime. He dodged left—I was there! He looked around for a chance to pass—no way! He dribbled down the court—I took after him! The clock ticked down to five seconds. When he finally went for the shot, I went up with him. I was a great jumper. He changed his shot in midair, the ball hit the rim—and bounced away!

The crowd went wild! They wanted to stone us! But then something incredible happened. We were all heading for the locker room when this coach from New Hymn came up and put his hand on my shoulder and said, "Have you ever thought about playing college ball?"

I was stunned! What with the noise and the emotion of the moment and all, I thought maybe he was joking. But when I looked into his eyes, I could tell he was serious. And the significant thing was the touch—just a real sense of confidence and respect he communicated to me. My own coach had never said or done anything like that.

But I immediately started thinking up all kinds of excuses why it couldn't happen. "Me? No way! I'm too short. And I don't have a very good outside jump shot. And I'd have to switch to guard. And . . ." I was going down a list of objections.

But the guy kept talking to me there in the hall. And for the first time in my life, I started feeling that maybe I did have what it took to play college ball. If I did, I might be able to use that as a way to pay my tuition.[1]

The coach asked one simple question: "Have you ever thought about playing college ball?" It was a question anyone could have asked. But no one did, until God brought this man from New Hymn High School into Dolphus' path. That single question prompted a chain of events that ultimately took Dolphus through college, into the ministry, and back to Mississippi to bring the hope of the gospel to his hometown community. Today, Mendenhall Ministries is a premier model for countless other groups around the country on how to deal with deep-seated poverty from a Christian perspective.

There is a Dolphus Weary somewhere in your life, some young man who is trying to surmount what seem like overwhelming obstacles. They may be obstacles of racism, such as Dolphus encountered. They may be obstacles of low self-esteem, limited resources, crippling personal problems, or the consequences of foolish mistakes. Or they may be what many of us regard as "minor" obstacles, just part of the "hard knocks" to be endured in growing up.

Whatever that young man's obstacle is, you could be a bridge over it. But he can't cross that bridge without your invitation. That's why he's waiting for you to say, "Can I buy you a cup of coffee?"

THE BIBLICAL BASIS FOR MENTORING

New Testament Passages Referring to Modeling

He appointed twelve—designating them apostles—that they might be with him and that he might send them out to preach. (Mark 3:14)

. . . but everyone who is fully trained will be like his teacher. (Luke 6:40b)

Therefore I urge you to imitate me. (1 Corinthians 4:16)

Follow my example, as I follow the example of Christ. (1 Corinthians 11:1)

Join with others in following my example, brothers, and take note of those who live according to the pattern we gave you. (Philippians 3:17)

Whatever you have learned or received or heard from me, or seen in me—put it into practice. And the God of peace will be with you. (Philippians 4:9)

Let the word of Christ dwell in you richly as you teach and admonish one another with all wisdom, and as you sing psalms, hymns and spiritual songs with gratitude in your hearts to God. (Colossians 3:16)

You became imitators of us and of the Lord; in spite of severe suffering, you welcomed the message with the joy given by the Holy Spirit. And so you became a model to all the believers in Macedonia and Achaia. The Lord's message rang out from you not only in Macedonia and Achaia—your faith in God has become known everywhere. Therefore we do not need to say anything about it. (1 Thessalonians 1:6-8)

We did this, not because we do not have the right to such help, but in order to make ourselves a model for you to follow. (2 Thessalonians 3:9)

Don't let anyone look down on you because you are young, but set an example for the believers in speech, in life, in love, in faith and in purity. (1 Timothy 4:12)

You, however, know all about my teaching, my way of life, my purpose, faith, patience, love, endurance. . . . (2 Timothy 3:10)

In everything set them an example by doing what is good. In your teaching show integrity, seriousness and soundness of speech that cannot be condemned, so that those who oppose you may be ashamed because they have nothing bad to say about us. (Titus 2:7-8)

Remember your leaders, who spoke the word of God to you. Consider the outcome of their way of life and imitate their faith. (Hebrews 13:7)

Not lording it over those entrusted to you, but being examples to the flock. (1 Peter 5:3)

Dear friend, do not imitate what is evil but what is good. Anyone who does what is good is from God. Anyone who does what is evil has not seen God. (3 John 11)

Chapter Sixteen

LEARNING & GROWING TOGETHER

The process of mentoring is like a man flying a kite. The kite does the flying, but it needs the man's help to take advantage of the wind. Kites don't fly on their own— unless they are out of control, in which case they are completely at the mercy of shifts in the wind and the downward pull of gravity.

In a similar way, you as a mentor can help a younger man take advantage of prevailing conditions so that he soars to new heights of personal growth and achievement. This requires intentionality on your part. That is, you are not in the relationship as a leisure activity. You are not like a little boy flying a kite to pass the time of day. You are more like Benjamin Franklin, who purposely launched a kite in hopes that lightning would strike it. You want your man to be energized by his involvement with you. That requires some leadership on your part.

In this chapter, I want to suggest some ways that you can structure your interaction so that it goes beyond having a good time, to having a "growth time." Now when I say "structure," I'm not talking about a contrived relationship—you know, where you and your protégé just follow a script, just connect the dots, without really engaging your personality and passion. Who's got time for that?

No, I'm talking about *active and willful participation* on the part of both of you. *Both* of you want to be there. *Both* of you are engaged in the process.

A Learning Contract

The place to start is with some sort of *learning contract*. A learning contract is a statement of the agenda and expectations of both protégé and mentor. It may be a formal, written document, or it may be informal and verbal. The nature of the relationship and the type of growth involved will determine which it should be.

For example, if I were helping a student learn to teach a course, I would probably require some sort of written agreement that stipulates the what, when, where, and how of our work together. Otherwise, we would have nothing to check our expectations, and no mutually agreeable way to measure his progress. Learning to teach a course is such a complex assignment that we could easily get our wires crossed. Without a written agreement, he might come to me, saying, "I thought you were going to do such and so," and I would start backpedaling, "I never said that! I never agreed to that!" Better to put it in writing.

However, a written learning contract is not really necessary when the relationship is informal and the agenda is fairly low-key. I'm not going to ask a guy for a formal learning contract just because he calls me up every other month to talk about issues in his job or marriage. On the other hand, if the relationship is going to be intentional, somewhere early on there has got to be a clear statement of what the demands are, and what the purpose is for spending time together.

This need not be burdensome or intimidating. It can be something as simple as the protégé asking, "Hey, can I have lunch with you next week," and you reply, "Sure. What's up?" Maybe he says, "I've got a job opportunity that my boss wants me to look at. I need some input." And you say, "Great! I'll be glad to give you my two cents' worth. Let's meet at 11:45, and I need to be out of there by 1:15. Will that work?"

The nice thing about that interchange is that it gives you some idea of what to expect, and what to prepare for. It also lets the protégé know what your limitations are in terms of time.

Another example of an informal learning contract would be where you agree to help a guy develop a new skill. Say it's writing. Your man has some ability as a writer, and you've challenged him to cultivate his talents. Finally he says, "OK, I'll work on my writing if you'll help me." So you say, "Fine, how much do you want to do?" He might say, "Well, it would take me about a month to put an essay together." So you say, "OK, let's try something for the next four months. You write up an essay and send it to me. I'll read it, and then we'll get together and discuss it. We'll do four essays like that and see where we stand. Does that sound reasonable?"

That's a useful agreement. It's verbal, it's informal, but it's clear. It's intentional. It's a lot more effective than just saying, "You know, you really ought to work on your writing," and then leaving the guy without a clue as to how you're going to help him.

By the way, in establishing a learning contract, I would caution you against making any open-ended commitments. Don't promise to meet with a guy weekly without putting an end-date on the agreement. Set a date for reevaluation and readjustment. That way, both you and your protégé have a "no-fault" means of buying out of the situation if things don't work out. And even if they do, circumstances inevitably change: schedules change, other commitments change, new demands come along, goals are achieved. By setting an end point to the learning process, you allow for flexibility. You also establish a deadline to shoot for.

An Agenda

One of the most important parts of setting up a learning contract is establishing an agenda. I'm afraid "agenda" has become a dirty word in some circles, largely because of its association with "hidden agendas." In addition, some people argue that agendas make a relationship contrived and rigid. Their attitude is, "Don't cramp my style, man! Don't force me into anything. Let's just let it happen. Let's just 'relate.'"

Well, if "just relating" enabled people to grow and develop, then I would say, "Fine, go to it!" We could take the pews out of our churches and the desks out of our schools, and replace them with futons and pillows on the floor, and man, we'd be in business!

But the process doesn't work that way. If you are trying to get somewhere, you've got to know where you are going and how you are going to get there. If you are trying to grow, or to help someone else grow, you have got to know what the learning objective is, and how you are going to accomplish it. That's what an agenda is. A statement of purpose, and a plan for achieving it.

And I say, put it all on the table. Don't hold back. If you are the protégé, tell me what you want. Tell me what your hopes are, your fears, your uncertainties, your doubts. Tell me what you'd like me to do. I can say yes or no to that, but I can't read your mind. On the other hand, if I'm in the role of a mentor, I've got to lay my cards on the table too. Here's why I'm in this. Here's what I think you need to do. Here's what I recommend. I don't need to (and can't) tell you everything that's in my mind and on my heart. But to the extent that it affects your learning and growth, and my participation in that, I need to be as up front as I can be. Nothing hidden. No surprises.

The Protégé's Part

So having said that, how do you establish an agenda with your protégé? I've addressed this from the protégé's point of view in chapter 8. Here I would add two things. First, whatever you do, make sure that your protégé drives the agenda, not you. He may need your help in setting it; in fact, your first great contribution may be helping him—I hate to say "forcing" him—to think through what he wants and needs. But you must let *him* determine that. You cannot determine that for him.

This may be a shocking concept for you. But I offer it as one who has spent the last forty-five years or more trying to help students learn. You see, in the academic world, we bring students in and set the agenda for them. We tell them, "Here, learn this body of material. Show up to these classes. Read these books. Write these papers. Follow this schedule. Take these exams. Rate your progress with these grades. When you're done, we'll give you a degree. And by the way, here's your tuition statement."

Then we wonder why students are bored out of their gourd in class! We violate one of the fundamental laws of education: people only learn what they can use. If information has no use, people won't learn it. They may write it down, they may file it, they may be able to regurgitate it on an exam; but that doesn't mean they've learned it.

Learning involves change. The learner is a different person as a result of the learning process. If he's not, then what's the point? But *he* is entirely in control of the change that takes place. That's why the more the learner establishes the agenda, the more learning will take place. And the more you can get your protégé to define what his objectives are—*his* objectives—the more productive your mentoring will be.

The Mentor's Part

This brings us to a second point. I'm not suggesting that your protégé understands everything about his needs or how to meet them. That's where you come in. Let him determine what he wants to work on, and even how he wants to tackle it; but then you suggest ways to improve on his agenda.

For example, say your man tells you he really wants to become a student of God's Word. He's decided that his lack of familiarity with Scripture is crippling his spiritual development. So he needs to learn what's in the Bible, and he really wants to go for broke. He tells you that his plan is to study through the entire Bible in a year.

You know what I'd say to a person like that? First of all, I'd affirm him like crazy. "Hey, pal, that's tremendous! You're absolutely right. You'll never grow apart from the Word. Good insight!"

But then I'd suggest a slight change in his approach. "You know, there's a lot in the Bible. Sixty-six books, in fact. Unless you are conducting an overview, studying the entire Bible in one year would require you to plow through five and a half books a month. You think that's realistic? How about if you started with one book a month? I'll work with you. In fact, let's start with something manageable, like the gospel of Mark. Sixteen chapters. It's about the life of Christ. Why don't you read the entire book this week, and let's get together next week to talk about it. We'll devote the next five weeks to Mark. How about it?"

Do you see what I'm doing? I'm trying to build success into his plans. I know from experience that he can't do any kind of in-depth study of all sixty-six books of the Bible in a year's time. If he tries, he'll just get frustrated and probably bail out. He's never been down this road, so he doesn't realize what he's taking on. I don't want his good intentions to end in a bad experience. So I offer a more realistic alternative that has greater promise of success. Of course, he may decide to reject my advice. That's OK. He'll figure it out sooner or later. But at least I've let him know that I stand with him in his efforts.

Strategies to Promote Growth

Discussion of an agenda leads to a question that I am often asked when I challenge men to serve as mentors: "Howie, I can see the value of influencing a younger man. But to be honest, I wouldn't know what to do. It's not that I can't hold a conversation or offer advice. But what do I do over the long haul? Where do we go after the relationship is established and we're past the superficial stuff?"

I can appreciate that concern, but to be honest, it is largely without foundation. If you are careful in setting your agenda, you are unlikely to run out of things to say and do. However, it helps to have some practical strategies up your sleeve. So let me suggest a few possibilities.

Get Your Protégé Involved

Your overarching principle should be *active participation*. Get your protégé involved in as much hands-on learning as you can. He doesn't need to sit and listen to you by the hour. He needs to do something that engages his mind and skills.

One of the best ways to accomplish that is to give him a manageable responsibility that relates to his abilities and learning objectives. For example:

- If he's trying to learn to communicate, have him make a brief presentation to a group of people.

- If he wants to learn to teach, sign him up to teach a class or to train someone in a particular skill.

- If he wants to develop leadership skills, let him run a meeting.

- If he wants to develop critical thinking, have him analyze and evaluate a need or problem.

- If he wants to learn to write, have him write an essay or a report.

- If he wants to work on his management skills, have him mediate a conflict that two subordinates are having.

- If he wants to learn more about being a servant, have him drive the church bus for several weeks.

Hand Off Responsibility the Right Way

Now in handing your protégé a responsibility like one of these, don't just dump it in his lap and walk away. That's not mentoring. That's irresponsibility. In fact, mentoring has gotten a bad press in some quarters because so-called mentors essentially use their protégés to do their grunt work. That's criminal! That doesn't build people; it demeans them.

The way to help your protégé learn the most from a delegated task is to follow this four-step approach:

1. *Brief him on the assignment.* Go over what is involved, what he is expected to do, and what he must do to prepare.

2. *Practice the assignment.* This can be part of the briefing process if the assignment is relatively simple. He can rehearse out loud what he plans to do. But if the task is substantial or complex, it pays to go through a dry run once or twice before he actually has to perform.

3. *Let him execute the task.* Step back and let him do his thing.

4. *Debrief with him on what happened.* From the standpoint of learning, this is the most crucial step—and also the most neglected. When a man completes an assignment, that's one of the most teachable moments there is. People always say that experience is the best teacher. That's not exactly true. *Evaluated* experience is the best teacher. Unfortunately, we often let this golden moment slip by, because as soon as we finish an assignment, we want to check it off and move to the next one.

The exception, of course, is if a guy blows it. Then he is certain to hear about it from others. As mentors, though, we should be doing just the opposite: *When he succeeds* we should get together for a review right away. That helps him find out what he can *learn* from his success. (I'll say more about how to deal with your protégé's successes and failures in a moment.)

Provoke His Thinking

The point of debriefing is to reflect on experience. That's one of the chief values of the mentoring relationship. It provides an ideal forum for a young man to stop and take a look at his life in terms where he is and where he wants to go. So in addition to giving your protégé responsibilities, let me suggest five other "tools" that you can use to provoke his thinking. You can make these tools formal or informal, as you wish. Their purpose is to promote reflection and insight, and to surface needs, issues, and possibilities.

The Case Study

A case study is a report that documents what someone has done in a particular situation. For years, many of the top business schools in the country have been using case studies to train future managers for the situations they will face in the marketplace. You can do something similar with your protégé by locating an article, book, or video that documents a situation related to his concerns.

For example, say your man is wrestling with how to deal with people of another race. Dolphus Weary, whom I mentioned earlier, struggled with that same issue, and has written his story in a book entitled *"I Ain't Comin' Back."* You and your protégé could read that biography as a case study in racial reconciliation.

The key to making use of a case study is to ask the right questions, such as: How is this situation like the protégé's? How does it differ? What are some of the key factors that determined the outcome? Who are the key people involved, and what did they do? What are the major lessons to be learned from this case study?

The Critical Incident Report

A "critical incident" is a momentary snapshot of a person's life, and the critical incident report is the "candid camera" that records that moment. You and the protégé can discuss it to evaluate its meaning for his growth and benefit.

For example, a young man is teaching a Sunday school class, when all of a sudden a child on the front row falls out of his chair into an epileptic seizure. Kids start screaming, and someone yells to call a doctor. Meanwhile, the teacher kneels down, places his finger into the ailing boy's mouth, and keeps him from biting his tongue. After a minute or so, the seizure calms, and the boy starts breathing normally again.

Now suppose that Sunday school teacher were your protégé. What an incredibly teachable moment this would be! You could ask him to write up a one-page report of this incident, which you would discuss with him. The report would document what happened (*who, what, when, where, how*), and then give the fellow's reaction to what happened—what he felt, what he discovered about himself, what he would have done differently—and anything else he cares to say.

Critical incidents need not be dramatic, but they need to be a slice from the man's own experience. They may report on a success, a partial success, or a major setback. By reconstructing and reflecting on these moments *with your help*, your protégé can learn a lot about himself: how he relates to people, how he handles stress, how he responds to the unexpected, what his tendencies are. The critical incident report is like extracting a sample from his life for laboratory analysis. It doesn't tell you everything, but it shows you a lot about what was going on at a particular moment.

The Reading List

Earlier I said that people only learn information that they can use. If that's true, then it becomes critical to steer people toward the information they need. As a mentor, you can do that for your protégé.

Now we often hear that people don't read much anymore, particularly men. That may be so. But men always find time to read what matters to them, and what holds their interest. If a guy has dedicated himself to growing in a particular area, he has no problem reading something that pertains to that area—as long as he can use it.

So instead of just telling your protégé that he should read more, recommend specific books that relate to his agenda. For example, remember the guy who wanted to get into the Bible? There are some very helpful titles in this area (Bill and I have a whole bibliography of these in our own book *Living by the Book*). Or maybe your man is grappling with career issues. Christian writers such as Art Miller, Ralph Mattson, and Lee Ellis have done a lot of superb writing on that topic. Or perhaps he is struggling to become a better father. A Christian bookstore will have a whole shelf of titles on this area.

Name almost any subject, and someone somewhere has probably written on it. As a mentor, you can do your protégé an invaluable service by recommending books that have been helpful to you or by conducting a little background check on your own to come up with a handful of possibilities.

In making recommendations, I wouldn't just hand the guy a list of titles and send him on his way. I would read my own copy of the book, and then discuss it with him when we got together. That way, I could see whether he is picking up on what the author has said, and making use of the information. And don't limit yourself to books when you think of a reading list. Keep in mind periodicals, audio and videotapes, even on-line databases—the possibilities are endless, because we live in a multimedia world and are surrounded by a sea of information. Help your protégé navigate toward a harbor, so that he locates what he really needs. Even the simple act of clipping a pertinent item from the paper and mailing or faxing it to him can be valuable. It tells him that his growth is on your mind. That's incredibly motivating!

The Interview

Do you have access to people who are experts in an area of interest to your protégé? Can you think of someone whose take on life is exactly what your man needs to hear? If so, I suggest that you arrange for your protégé to meet this individual face-to-face. It will be an unforgettable experience for him.

One of Bill's older friends was telling him about an elderly veteran of World War II, who survived the infamous Battan death march largely because one of the soldiers on the perilous journey read out loud from a pocket Scripture he was carrying. Bill asked to meet with this man and hear his account first-hand. Imagine the impression such an individual can make! By telling his incredible story of faith and courage, he can pass along a godly legacy to future generations.

In arranging for the interview, don't just tell your protégé to "go see So-and-So." Help to set the stage. You may need to make a call or write a letter of introduction, or even act as a host in putting the two of them together. Prepare your man beforehand by briefing him on who the interviewee is, and why he is a worthwhile resource. You might even ask what topics your protégé plans to discuss or what questions he intends to ask. (You may also have to inform the person being interviewed why you are sending someone to meet with him, and how he can help.)

After the interview, talk with your protégé about what he heard and what he learned. And remind him to write the interviewee a follow-up letter, or make some other gesture to thank him.

The Field Trip

Most of us associate field trips with something we did in grammar school. They were a heaven-sent answer to classroom boredom. But field trips are not just for kids. They are one of the best ways to engage adults in the learning process.

I well remember the student I had in a counseling class who came to me and said, "Prof, have you got anything a little more challenging?" I guess he was finding my lectures to be a bit tedious.

So I said, "Yeah, I think I can find something." Then I called up my friend at the Dallas juvenile delinquency center and said, "Hey, Joe, I've got a student who needs an education."

"I've got the picture," he replied. "Send him on over."

So I sent the student to the center. My friend arranged to have him put in a cell with a fourteen-year-old kid who was billed on twenty-six major counts. The state was waiting for him to turn sixteen so they could try him as an adult and put him away for good.

This little criminal was sitting with his feet propped up on the window sill when my student was brought in. As soon as the door clanked shut behind him, the kid turned and said, "Every day they send somebody in here with a different line. So what's yours?"

"Prof," the student told me later, "I just about lost it right there!" Remarkably, he was never bored in class again.

There is something about a *place* that can transform a person's receptivity toward learning. Just think about some of the possibilities that an astute mentor could find by taking his protégé to visit a prison . . . the New York Stock Exchange . . . a construction site . . . the emergency room of a hospital . . . the newsroom of a major metropolitan daily. Or consider what one could learn by visiting the stables of a horse ranch . . . the Holocaust Museum in Washington, D. C. . . . the flight deck of an aircraft carrier. Wherever people are engaged in the drama of life, there are lessons to be learned.

The same holds true for national landmarks and symbolic sites, such as Gettysburg, Ellis Island, the Vietnam War Memorial, or Pearl Harbor.

The lessons become especially memorable if you or your protégé have a personal connection with the place you visit. I could take you to Arlington National Cemetery, across the Potomac from Washington, D.C. You would no doubt be curious to visit the graves of President John F. Kennedy and his brother Robert. But if I then took you to an out-of-the-way section of the park and pointed out my father's grave, your impression of our tour might take on an entirely different significance. Suddenly we would not be talking about death in the abstract, but as a reality that hits close to home.

In addition to these five tools, there are countless others that you can use to stimulate your protégé's thinking: journals, time audits, schedules, budgets, role play, family histories, weekend retreats, and wilderness expeditions, to name just a few. The purpose of any activity should be to get the person *actively participating* in the learning process. Maximum learning is always the result of maximum involvement in a meaningful activity.

What If He's In over His Head?

But a lingering question remains. Experience can be an excellent teacher, particularly when it is immediately followed by evaluation. But what happens if, in carrying out an assignment, the protégé starts heading for failure? At what point should you as a mentor step in and rescue him? Or should you just let him crash and burn, and then help him pick up the pieces?

Coaches face this dilemma all the time. Should they pull their quarterback from the game because he's thrown two or three interceptions, and the team is now down by 21 points? Should they bench their star basketball center because he's missing shots that he normally makes with ease? Or should they leave these athletes in the contest, even if it means losing, in order to teach important lessons about competition and failure?

Obviously, there are so many variables to consider in any given situation that there are no hard and fast rules in this regard. But let me suggest three rules of thumb to take into consideration. First, if your protégé is a complete novice and he is headed for disaster, think twice about letting him wipe out. He stands a real chance of being shattered by the experience.

Help the Novice

Have you ever heard of the father who wanted to teach his little boy to swim? He threw him into a pool and let him flap and flounder until, gasping for air, the tiny swimmer managed to regain the side of the pool, where the father passively stood by. The man's attitude was, "My boy needed to learn how to swim. So I gave him two choices—either learn to swim, or drown."

Bill knows a man whose father did just that. What a cruel means of instruction! That boy may have learned to swim, all right. But he also learned to mistrust his father, and to fear learning in general. That's not the way to help a person develop.

Protect Others

A second principle is that if other people stand to be severely affected by your protégé's failure, you have a responsibility to step in and protect their interests. Imagine a student pilot flunking his flight courses and then being certified to fly. Would you want him at the controls when you hop on a plane? Of course not. You'd want him shipped back to basic training. But the person you would really want to put in the hot seat would be the flight instructor who passed him in the first place.

In a similar way, you must careful that your protégé is not placed in a situation where he is in over his head, thereby endangering other people. Bill recalls a situation when he was on the work crew at Pine Cove Conference Center that illustrates what I'm talking about. The crew had been assigned to clear a path through a heavily wooded area. At the work site, the work crew leader spent some time explaining the workings of a chain saw purchased specifically for the job. He showed how to use it, and then each teenager on the crew was allowed to try his hand at sawing through a log on the ground.

With that bit of training accomplished, the project began in earnest. Two guys worked with the chain saw, while the rest hacked down smaller trees and cleared away underbrush. The crew worked all morning, trading off on the chain saw every once in a while.

Shortly before the lunch break, two workers were sawing on a massive pine tree. They had cut three-quarters of the way through one side and were now making the final cut from the opposite side. Suddenly the crew leader bounded over to the boy working the saw and firmly pulled him away from the tree, killing the saw at the same moment.

"Run for it!" he shouted at the top of his lungs, and the crew scattered in all directions.

Ever so slowly, the pine tree began to wobble. Then a mighty crack was heard and the tree crashed to the ground—right where a group of the workers had been standing a moment earlier.

The two boys whose saw cuts had brought down the tree stared in disbelief. "Wow!" exclaimed one of them, "I thought that tree was going to fall the other way. What happened?"

"Look at your cuts," the crew leader said, pointing to the stump. The larger cut had been made on the side of the tree facing the crew—the exact opposite of what it should have been.

"You were lucky," said the crew leader, "and I should have been paying more attention. I'm just glad nobody got hurt." He mopped his brow with his shirt and finally said, "Let's go eat lunch."

When you delegate responsibility to a younger man, you are not excused from liability. Ultimately, you are responsible for what happens. So you need to have confidence that your man can and will come through for you. You also need to make sure that no one will be seriously harmed if he doesn't.

Consider the Consequences

That brings us to a third rule of thumb: You must step in if you are unwilling to face the consequences of failure with him. Learning often requires that a person take risks, and genuine risk always means there is a possibility of failure. That's OK. Failure is sometimes a part of the process. But if your protégé fails, he's got to know that you will stand by him. That's where a lot of his confidence comes from. If the risks involved won't allow you to do that, then you'd better cut the assignment short before he gets into trouble—and tell him why.

For example, suppose you are working with a younger man in your company, trying to help him develop as a public speaker. He seems to be making progress, and one day he comes to you with a proposal: "I know that our department is making a presentation next month on the status of the Omega project. Do you think I could make the main pitch?"

"Boy, I don't know," you say with some hesitation. "That's a pretty important meeting. All the senior executives are going to be there, you know. And something like that is traditionally my job as division director."

"I know," he replies. "But look at it this way. If I make the presentation, it will show that you are grooming people in your department. Besides, I've worked up these really nice visuals to illustrate what we're doing." He shows you some graphs and charts, and you agree that they look impressive.

"Well, OK," you finally say. Then as an afterthought, you add, "But why don't you make a practice run next week to the department."

"Sure!" he says enthusiastically, and runs off to start preparing.

But at the department meeting the following week, he falls flat on his face. He's poorly organized, his attempts at humor bomb, and his audio-visuals don't look nearly so good projected on a big screen as they did on crisp color laser prints.

So you call him in for a debriefing. "Look, I think I better handle the meeting next month," you tell him. "You've come a long way. But I'm uneasy after your presentation this morning. Neither one of us can afford to drop the ball in front of the executive committee. I'm certainly not willing to take that chance."

Your junior colleague may be terribly disappointed and feel like a failure, but you are doing him a service. He can always try again later, after he's developed some more. But you do not serve him well by setting him up to fail, and then disavowing any responsibility when he does.

Helping Your Protégé After a Setback

Speaking of failure, how do you help your protégé handle it? First of all, it's important to help him acknowledge honest feelings of disappointment, regret, and lowered self-esteem. Let him vent some emotion after he blows it.

Are there any lessons to be learned from his failure? Probably. Chief among them is the one attributed to Thomas Edison, who spent two years building dozens and dozens of prototypes in an attempt to invent the light bulb. At the end of each failed experiment, he allegedly said, "Well, we now know what *doesn't* work." That's really what failure tells you: what doesn't work.

Finally, no matter how badly your man stumbles, at some point you need to remind him that somehow the sun will still come up tomorrow. His failure has not brought the world to an end. Life goes on—and so must he.

Bless His Success!

The ideal time to work heavily with your protégé is not after he fails, but after he succeeds. Mentors often miss this, because they assume that success is its own reward. Nothing could be further from the truth. It may be true that failure is the back door to success, as one person has put it— but why sneak in the back when the front door is wide open? Success is the key that unlocks that front door.

You see, often we learn far more from our successes than we do from our failures. Failure only shows us what doesn't work; success shows us what does. Therefore, we need to analyze what happened to discover the "success factors," the elements that account for a positive outcome. Pay special attention to the clues that reveal: your protégé's motivations and passions; the conditions under which he operates best; the subjects and interests that stimulate his best efforts; the skills and abilities that he uses to achieve his objectives; and the ways that he ideally relates to people.

Factors like these are the keys to his destiny. They indicate what he uses to do his best work, and therefore what he needs to perform well in the future.

Bury your protégé's failures, but build on his successes.

And whatever you do, celebrate them. Create little rituals and ceremonies to honor his achievements. Take him out to dinner. Have him stand for a round of applause in front of his colleagues—or yours. Give him a token of his accomplishments—a book, a plaque, a small gift. Praise him in front of his wife and his children. This is "the blessing" that he so desperately needs to mark his progress.

Chapter Seventeen

PROBLEMS & PITFALLS TO AVOID

I want to dispel a myth. The myth is that if men form vital relationships with one another, those relationships will essentially be free of problems and conflict.

Now most of us know instinctively that that has to be a myth. Experience tells us that whenever two or more people get to know each other on anything deeper than a superficial level, they are bound to run into differences of opinion. Furthermore, they will invariably find things that they don't particularly like about each other.

Yet even though we know that in our heads, many us want to believe, deep down in our hearts, that somewhere, somehow, problem-free relationships are possible. We may even encase that hope within a bit of sidewalk spirituality. *After all,* we may reason, *didn't Jesus say that "wherever two or more are gathered, there am I in the midst"? And didn't He pray that we would all be one? And didn't Paul pray that believers would all agree?* And then we conclude, *So if we're all believers and all walking with the Lord, how can there be problems and conflict?*

Union vs. Unity

The answer is, because union and unity are not the same. You can tie two cats together with a rope and throw them over a clothesline. You'll have union, but you won't have unity!

Or take marriage. As someone has said, marriage is great; it's living together afterward that's the problem. A couple is united in marriage. Their union is legal, emotional, financial, and physical. But that union doesn't mean they won't have problems—only that they get to work through their problems together.

The same is true in the church. Just read the book of Acts. You'll find problems and conflicts all the way through. Believers were committed to the same faith, but sometimes they were in sharp disagreement over the practice of that faith. In Acts 6, it's a problem of certain elderly widows being left out of the church's meals-on-wheels program. In Acts 11, Peter is called on the carpet for giving the gospel to Gentiles. In Acts 15, the whole church gets into a rhubarb over the growing numbers of Samaritans and Gentiles infiltrating the body of believers.

And at the end of that chapter, we find Barnabas and Paul in a spat of their own, over a young disciple named John Mark. This is highly instructive for our discussion of mentoring, because it shows a mentor and a protégé with strong differences—so strong that the text says each went his own way (15:39). Was that the end of their faith? Of course not. Was it the end of their relationship? Hardly. In fact, Paul eventually came around to Barnabas' way of thinking concerning John Mark (2 Timothy 4:11).

All I'm saying is that problems and conflicts between believers are inevitable, even between men who are highly committed to each other—even between you and your protégé. So just expect them—indeed, accept them as a part of the learning process. Problems need not divide you. If anything, they should unite you in an honest search for a way to work things out.

In chapter 9, I discussed four categories of problems often encountered in mentoring relationships: unrealistic expectations, unfulfilled expectations, failure on the mentor's part, and issues of control. I discussed these primarily from the protégé's point of view, but I think you can read between the lines to draw application for yourself as a mentor. In this chapter, I want to discuss three more areas that often create problems for mentors and their protégés.

Problems of Time

One of the most common areas of frustration has to do with time. For example, the relationship may seem to require too much time for you as a mentor. In fact, it's interesting that this complaint is frequently given as a reason not to engage in mentoring at all: "There's no way I can be a mentor. I haven't got the time!"

Only you know your schedule and your priorities, so only you can determine whether you actually have time to give to a younger man. But I would say two things to this issue. First, the older you get, the more control you tend to have over your time. So if you *choose* to serve as a mentor, you are likely to find some discretionary time somewhere to give to the relationship.

Second, mentoring can actually take far less time than most men realize. Obviously, you could pour as much time into your protégé as you cared to. That would be true for any relationship. But mentoring is a situation where great gains can be realized for a relatively small investment. Why? Because there's an agenda, a purpose for getting together. This is not just a party time; it's a growth time. Furthermore, it's the protégé whose growth is on the line. That puts the monkey on his back to pour himself into the process. If anyone should be complaining about a lack of time, it ought to be him, not you.

When You Seem to Have Little Time

If it is you, there are several possibilities for what may be wrong. One is that you are doing all the work. If that's the case, you need to stop and revise your learning contract. You are mentoring your protégé; he's not mentoring you. Therefore, *he* needs to be doing the lion's share of the labor.

This brings up a fundamental law of mentoring: Do nothing for your protégé that he can do for himself. Otherwise, you cripple him by making him dependent on you.

Another possibility is that you and/or your protégé are operating from unrealistic expectations about what is involved. Again, the solution is to go back to your learning contract and check to see whether the agenda is reasonable, or too ambitious. If either one of you is asking too much, you need to reevaluate and scale back the expectations.

I'm not opposed to an ambitious set of learning objectives. If you've got a hard charger who wants to go for the gold, that's great! More power to him—if he can pull it off. Some can. But if he's got a highly ambitious plan mapped out, you may need to consider whether you alone can service all of his expectations. It may be that you need to contract to fulfill just a part of his agenda, and then help him solicit other people to fulfill the rest. Nobody says you have to do everything.

There's an additional possibility. The feeling that mentoring is taking too much time may actually be the result of not having enough time. In other words, the relationship feels rushed. You and your protégé are always scrambling to get things done. If that's the case, it may be that you have not budgeted enough time required for the agenda.

However, it's also possible that instead of a problem, you've got a blessing on your hands. One sign that the relationship is extremely satisfying and productive is the feeling that there's never enough time for it. You just can't get enough. That's a good problem to have. In fact, I'm not sure I'd change much.

I tell budding preachers at the seminary to leave their audience "longing, not loathing." That is, stop speaking just at the point where your people are satisfied. You want them to say, "No, no! Keep going!" You want them longing to come back for more. The same principle applies to your time with your protégé. Leave him longing, not loathing. Bring your sessions to a halt just at the peak of his motivation, just at the point of saturation. You never want to get to where you or your protégé are saying, "Boy, I'm glad that's over with. I thought we'd never finish!"

When Your Protégé Has Little Time

There is one final time-related problem. What do you do if your protégé can't seem to find time for the relationship? He doesn't show up for your sessions. When he does show up, he's late. He doesn't put much time into his work. On the whole, you get the sense that his mind is elsewhere.

That's a strong possibility. He may, in fact, be distracted by a problem he is struggling with. If you sense that, you might explore it with him: "Hey, Jim, it seems to me that sometimes your heart is just not in our times together. Sometimes I can tell that we're not on the same page. Is there something going on that I should be aware of? If so, I'd really like to help you with it, if I can." You never know what you might find under that rock when you turn it over. Whatever it is, there's a good chance it will lead to a teachable moment.

If your man genuinely can't find time for the relationship—for whatever reason (and there can be many)—he may need to reevaluate whether right now is the best time to be involved in a mentoring relationship. There's no shame if he says, "I need to pull back. I've got some other business I need to take care of in my life right now." In fact, you may need to give him permission to withdraw so that he can take care of his priorities.

Jealousy

Jesus told His followers that eventually they would do bigger and better things than He had done (John 14:12). Are you willing to have your protégé outdo you? Is it OK if he becomes more successful than you are?

The literature is filled with examples of mentors who simply could not deal with their protégés' mounting success. For example, the film *Amadeus* alleged that Antonio Salieri, an eighteenth-century court musician, was driven by jealousy to plot the death of his outstanding pupil, Wolfgang Amadeus Mozart. Likewise, the pioneer of psychoanalysis, Sigmund Freud, became so embittered at the growing acclaim of two of his followers, Carl Jung and Alfred Adler, that he reworded some of the footnotes in his writings to avoid crediting them.

These may seem like extreme cases, but I've known men in my own life to cynically disparage the accomplishments of their former protégés. Some have even resorted to dirty politics to block their success. Yet when challenged, these embittered men deny it, though they can hardly disguise their envy. "Look at him eat up all that praise," they'll say with contempt. "It's sickening! He's way overrated. Why, he wouldn't have gotten this far if it hadn't have been for me."

Do you think you're immune to that attitude? If so, I recommend a close reading of 1 Samuel 18. When King Saul returned from defeating the Philistines, women greeted him with tambourines and dancing. That was the usual way of celebrating victory, and this should have been a joyful occasion. "Saul has slain his thousands," they chanted, cheering him wildly. But then they added, "and David his ten thousands" (verse 7).

Scripture tells us that "Saul was very angry; this refrain galled him.

'They have credited David with tens of thousands,' he thought, 'but me with only thousands. What more can he get but the kingdom?' And from that time on Saul kept a jealous eye on David" (vv. 8–9).

Do you fear that a protégé may someday capture your kingdom? Let me tell you something: he very well may! In fact, if you've done your job right as a mentor, he shouldn't have to capture it. Maybe he should inherit it, and build on your legacy far beyond anything that you could imagine. That's the ideal you should be shooting for. Are you prepared for that?

Envy is like poison to a mentoring relationship. And in all candor, I have to tell you that this poison is polluting many in the body of Christ today, nipping in the bud the cultivation of new leaders. We've got too many men building their kingdoms, when they ought to be building Christ's kingdom. As a result, they have no interest in a ministry of multiplication. They can't be bothered with reproducing themselves in the lives of younger people. "Why train my competition?" is the attitude.

You know what the Bible says about that? It's an attitude directly from the pit. "Such 'wisdom' does not come down from heaven but is earthly, unspiritual, of the devil" (James 3:15). James is warning us about harboring bitter envy and selfish ambition in our hearts. If that describes you, then you need to repent of that before it ruins your life. You need to pray that God replaces the hellish poison of envy with the pure water of His wisdom (5:17).

It's hard to see someone surpass us. No question about it. It resurrects every fear we've ever had about our self-worth, our competency, and our significance. As the crowds start chanting someone else's name, it dawns on us that they have forgotten ours. That hurts.

So what do we do with that hurt? The devil holds out the salve of envy. The Lord holds out the salvation of grace. Which one we choose determines whether we end our days in jealousy or joy.

A Lack of Motivation

Have you ever swallowed a soft drink after all the fizz has gone out of it? Blah! It's pretty disgusting! It becomes sweet and syrupy, and altogether unsatisfying. Sometimes mentoring relationships end up like that. Either the mentor or the protégé (or sometimes both) loses interest, and the thing goes flat. The motivation seems to evaporate. For example:

- One or the other can't find time for the relationship.
- The sessions are boring and unproductive.
- Assignments are not carried out.
- More time is spent analyzing the relationship than doing productive work.
- The discussions drift away from the agenda onto rabbit trails and superficial matters.

There are many possible reasons to explain why the energy might be draining away. To look at them all would require a comprehensive examination of human motivation. For our purposes, it is enough to consider the advice of the tall Texan I ran into shortly after I moved to Texas many years ago. He listened to me quote the old saying that "you can lead a horse to water, but you can't make him drink."

"You're wrong about that, son," he replied. "You can always feed him salt."

What an insight into human nature! You can never force a man to change. You can only provide a climate in which change becomes increasingly desirable. If your man has lost motivation, the question you need to be asking is not, "What's wrong with this guy?" or even, "What's wrong with me?" Rather, "What can I do to rekindle his passion, so that he *wants* to make strides in his life?"

You see, you can temporarily motivate him through rewards, guilt, or even deception. But that's not compulsion, that's coercion. You are merely imposing outside factors that make your agenda temporarily attractive to him. But there's no internal commitment to it.

The better way is to seek out his *intrinsic* motivation, the internal factors that trigger his interest and effort, and then put him in situations that stimulate those factors. I alluded to these internal triggers in the previous chapter, only there I called them "success factors." Your protégé's success factors are a function of his God-given bent. They are actually the keys to his motivation. Help him discover those, and he'll have little difficulty staying motivated, because a man always prefers to function according to the way God has wired him. It's as natural as breathing.

The Mentoring Life Cycle

There is one other factor to consider as you troubleshoot a lack of motivation. It may be that the relationship has run its course. This brings us to the issue of the life cycle of the mentoring relationship.

Unlike parenting or marriage, mentoring relationships are rarely permanent. They go through a fairly predictable series of stages. Experts differ on how many stages there are. I'm going to suggest that there are three. By recognizing this life cycle, you can anticipate certain dynamics in your relationship with a protégé.

I call the first stage *definition*. This is the initial period, during which the relationship is being defined, and everything is tentative. The protégé is checking out the mentor, the mentor is sizing up the protégé. Each is deciding whether to commit himself to the other, and under what terms. If they decide to proceed, this stage comes to an end with some sort of agreement to work together, such as a learning contract.

The second stage is *development*. This is usually the longest and most intense period of the relationship. Mentor and protégé interact in ways that help the protégé grow and develop. They tend to meet regularly, or at least at key points along the way. This period is like a house or building under construction, with dirt flying, hammers banging, and power saws whining. The protégé is hard at work, accomplishing his agenda under the mentor's guiding hand.

But at some point, the structure is essentially complete—the protégé has effectively accomplished his agenda. It is not that he has reached full maturity, but he has fulfilled the objectives for which he needed the mentor's help in the first place. That brings the relationship to its third and final stage, the point of *departure*.

Departure may be sudden or it may take a while. But sooner or later the mentoring comes to an end. There are several common ways that this happens. The most difficult is through a painful break. One day there is a conflict. Mentor and protégé go back and forth, perhaps as in previous disagreements. Only this time, the conflict escalates until one of the parties decides, "I'm out of here!" Perhaps this was the case with Barnabas and Paul in Acts 15.

I've seen the impetus for this break to go both ways. A mentor will say, "Well, if that's the way you feel, why don't you just go do your thing." And the protégé says, "I will!" And he does, and they never really get back together. On the other hand, the protégé might say, "Look, it's time I did it my way." And the mentor says, "Go ahead," and so the protégé goes off on his own. There may be a reconciliation later on, or there may not. But the break is clear, even if it is not clean.

A second possibility is that the protégé sort of drifts away. His need for the mentor is no longer critical, so he contacts him less and less. We saw an example of this earlier in the relationship between Tom and Richie. After Richie's employer transferred him, the two men exchanged a few letters, but before long their contact died out. Richie had moved on in his life, and frankly, so had Tom. All that remained was a set of positive memories, particularly on Richie's part.

A third possibility—and this can occur whether the break is sudden or gradual, heated or "cool"—is that the relationship can go through a period of redefinition, in which the two men become associates or colleagues, rather than mentor and protégé. The ground between them becomes much more level, and they interact more as equals. In a way, this is the ideal outcome. It indicates that the mentor has done his job. He has helped his *former* protégé step up to his own level. He has helped him become his own man. In fact, it's possible that the two men will develop a peer-mentoring relationship, similar to the one Fred and Jerry have (pp. 32–34).

Such is the mentoring life cycle. There is no standard timetable for how long this cycle or its stages take to complete. Some experts estimate that the average mentoring relationship lasts between two and six years. But almost all of them come to an end at some point.

How do you know when you've reached that point? In all likelihood, you or your protégé will just sense it. But here are two general scenarios to consider. First, when the protégé completes his agenda and learns whatever he came to learn, then it's probably time for him to move on. The relationship may actually continue, but not in terms of mentoring. A second situation is when you feel you have helped him as much as you can. Then it's probably time to "launch" him into the world, to go forward on his own.

Saying Good-bye

Now it is at this point that many mentors drop the ball. Having done a superb job of bringing a young man along and building into his life, they fail to put proper closure on the relationship. In doing so, they miss a great opportunity to seal their work with a permanent, positive impression.

Saying good-bye is rarely easy, but your relationship deserves it. You may have poured countless hours into this man, and he has probably invested a great deal of emotional energy in you. So if possible, why not honor what you have had together by acknowledging and agreeing it is time to wrap things up?

I suggest that you set a time to review your relationship. Talk about some of the highlights of your work together—as well as some of the low lights. Solicit his impressions of what he has learned and how he has grown, and share your own observations along these lines. You might also talk about his future—both how he sees it, and how you see it. Then pray together that God's hand will rest on his life.

One way to ease the termination process is to time it as much as possible around natural, foreseeable milestones, such as a graduation, a transfer, a wedding, or retirement. These rites of passage mark important turning points in life. So if your work with your protégé is nearing closure, and he is coming up to one of these major transitions, it makes sense to time your good-byes so that they coincide with his other changes.

Whatever you do, be sure and tell your departing protégé what the relationship has meant to you, and what you have gained from his life. He deserves that. The relationship may not have been perfect. From your perspective, it may not have seemed particularly close. But the fact that it even existed is significant. Whether the two of you have made the most of it or not, you have shared something for which millions of men today hunger, but few ever experience. That alone is worth celebrating. So give him a hug, shake his hand, and then send him on his way, knowing that a part of you is going out into the world wherever God chooses to take him.

Chapter Eighteen

LEAVING A LEGACY THAT LASTS

Allan Emery of ServiceMaster Industries once was driving Robert Lamont, pastor of the First Presbyterian Church in Pittsburgh, to a speaking engagement near Boston. As they drove along, Allan asked Dr. Lamont to describe his ministry.

"He spoke of his work in such a way that I felt he viewed himself as a spectator to what God had done," Allan recalled. "I suggested that much of what had been accomplished must be because of his gifts and talents."

In response to Allan's comment, Dr. Lamont replied, "When I was a schoolboy, we would occasionally see a turtle on a fencepost and when we did, we knew someone had put him there. He didn't get there by himself. That is how I see my own life. I'm a turtle on a fencepost."

What an intriguing image—a turtle on a fencepost. In many ways it describes the mentoring process. When you see a man achieve great heights, beyond what anyone would have expected, you tend to wonder: Who put him there? Who helped him accomplish his triumphs? In fact, one of my favorite questions to a successful individual is, "Who have been your mentors? Who are the people who account for who and what you have become?"

Quite often, the person instantly lights up in a smile and gives a name or names. He knows immediately what I am talking about. He knows better than anyone that his success derives in large measure from the help of a key individual or two. Such is the power of a mentor.

Caleb As the Protégé

Caleb was a turtle on a fencepost. At age eighty-five he was still eager to go out to battle. "Give me this mountain!" he cried. "The Lord will be with me, and I will drive out the giants in the fortified cities."

That sounds like pretty impressive faith. And it was. Faith to conquer mountains and drive out giants. But the fires of faith rarely ignite by spontaneous combustion. They almost always require a spark from somewhere. What—or who—was Caleb's spark? Conquering mountains and driving out giants can be a daunting task—unless, of course, one happens to be standing on the shoulders of a giant. On whose shoulders was Caleb standing? To use Robert Lamont's metaphor, who put Caleb on the fencepost?

The most likely answer is Moses. If you check the biblical record, you will find that Moses was a mentor to Joshua, who succeeded him. But it seems plausible that Caleb also regarded Moses as something of a mentor. Note that Caleb was one of twelve men selected by Moses to spy out the Promised Land (Numbers 13:1–3, 6). He alone stood with Joshua in supporting Moses when the people wanted to turn back (13:30; 14:6–9). He also was one of the first men named to help Moses divide the land when the nation stood on the brink of Canaan (34:16–19).

Directly or indirectly, Caleb had the benefit of standing on Moses' gigantic shoulders. Not that Caleb's own faith was unimpressive; if anything, it may have surpassed that of Moses. Nevertheless, Caleb's presence in Canaan was largely the result of Moses' faithful leadership. Caleb was poised to drive out giants (with God's help) because Moses had delivered him and the rest of the Israelites from Pharaoh (with God's help).

Today, countless men are trying to scale mountainous strongholds. Like Caleb, they are pitted against giants in their lives. But unlike Caleb, they are often compelled to ask, "Whose broad shoulders can I stand on as I wage the battles to which God calls me?"

My prayer is that God would answer this question by raising up hundreds, thousands, and even tens of thousands of men like Moses, Jethro, Barnabas, and Paul—men of influence, men of wisdom, men of character, men who are *mentors*. That's my prayer to God. My petition to you is: will you be one of them?

I have no idea how many men will read this book. But what could happen if even one out of every ten who do were to commit himself to influencing the life of one other man, of any age, in the kinds of ways I've suggested?

As I write, more than 500,000 men are expected to attend Promise Keepers conferences in 1995. What could happen if one out of ten of these men fulfilled a promise to establish a vital mentoring relationship with one other man?

Beyond Promise Keepers, I think of the millions of men in the body of Christ. What could happen if one out of a hundred of us determined to serve as a mentor to one other man?

I think I can safely say that we would soon have giants of faith in the land, rather than giants to fear.

Four Choices

So again I ask: will you be one of those mentors? By now you know what that involves. You know something of how the process works. But my hunch is that, having read this far, that question generates one of four responses:

1. "I can, and I will."

If that's your response, then I say go to it! Ask God to send you a Timothy, and help to build Christ's life into that man. You will never regret it.

2. "I could"—but you won't.

This, I'm afraid, is the all-too-common reaction to calls for commitment and change. One hundred percent agreement, but zero percent action.

It reminds me of the reporter who was interviewing the renowned psychiatrist Karl Menninger at his clinic in Topeka, Kansas. When the interviewer pressed Menninger on a certain point, the doctor handed him a book he had written on the subject. The reporter politely promised to read it.

"No you won't!" shot back Dr. Menninger in his ever-acerbic manner. "Besides, what would you do about it if you did? Put it down and go on to something else?"

That's my fear with this book. That you will read it, applaud it, and say, "Great! Fantastic! We really need mentoring. Yes sir, everybody ought to have one," and having affirmed that, move on to the next trendy idea.

This is frequently what I observe after preaching in a church. At the end of the service, I'm usually asked to stand at the back for what I call the "glorification of the worm" ceremony—you know, when the people line up to shake the preacher's hand. And they are very sincere. "Oh, Brother Hendricks," they'll say, "what a wonderful sermon. Just like the apostle Paul!"

I've had people come by with tears rolling down their cheeks, saying, "Boy, preacher, you really got to me this time! [Sniffle] Thanks a lot! I really needed that!" They are seemingly broken, really torn up. Yet what do they do? Go home and watch a ball game. There's no fundamental change.

Beware of noble resolutions! John Norcross, a professor of psychology at the University of Scranton in Pennsylvania, estimates that half of all American adults make at least one New Year's resolution. One week later, nearly one quarter have already bailed out. After one month, only 55 percent are still sticking with it, and after six months, it's down to 40 percent.

"If you're nasty enough to call them after two years," Norcross says, "it's about 19 percent."[1]

One out of five. Not bad, in a way. But I wonder how we could up that percentage?

One way is to replace impulsive, emotion-laden promises with realistic, practical plans. For example, who do you know *right now* who might be looking for the guiding presence of an older man? Take out a pencil and write down his name *right now*, to call him about getting together.

Strategic planner Michael Kami uses the term "Monday morning actions" to describe what a person needs to do right away if he intends to make changes. We can talk forever about the need for mentoring and the good it will do, but the real question is: So what are you going to do about it first thing Monday morning?

3. *"I probably ought to, but I'm doing too much already."*

I suspect that this is a legitimate concern for many readers of this book. In all likelihood, you have picked it up because you already know the value of life-on-life relationships. You know it firsthand because you are already involved in touching the lives of others. You're a father trying to find time for your kids. You're a coach for your son's soccer league. You're a scout master for boys at your church. You're a Sunday school teacher for some college kids or young adults. You're a member of a prayer group or a men's Bible study.

In short, you've got a lot on your plate already. So when you read a book like this, you tend to say, "Hendricks, great idea! But there's just no way I can become a mentor. I just can't take on anything more. I know I ought to. I know it's important. But it's just more than I can handle."

May I make a suggestion? Don't look upon mentoring as an addition; look on it as a multiplication. In other words, don't add more to an already packed schedule; instead, accomplish more by applying the principles of mentoring to the relationships you already have.

Mentoring needs to be a mind-set, not just an activity. It's a way of relating to other men, not a task to be checked off a "To Do" list. If you've already got a group of guys that you're working with—fantastic! You don't need to leave them to go find someone else to mentor. You are *already* positioned to influence someone's life in a significant and strategic way. But to do that, you may need to start looking at those relationships as significant and strategic.

Remember, the call to serve as a mentor does not ask you to become someone you are not. It challenges you to be who you are as you interact with other men in your sphere of influence. Sometimes that means "taking on" a protégé who happens to come your way. But just as often, it means building on a relationship that already exists in a way that has significance in the other man's life.

Imagine what could happen if you applied even a handful of the mentoring principles I've mentioned just part of the time, to even a few of your relationships. I'm confident that God would take your five loaves and two fishes and multiply them abundantly, beyond anything that you could ask or think. I say that because I've met men all over the world who have been profoundly influenced by the little things—the word of affirmation, the invitation to a cup of coffee, the pause for a moment of prayer, the timely hand on the shoulder—the seemingly insignificant things that someone did at a key point in their lives. Who could have imagined the results?

4. "Maybe I'll get around to it someday."

Do you know who is most likely to be saying this? Not the men in their thirties, forties, or fifties, but the guys in their sixties, seventies, or eighties. It's the guy who finally has time on his hands—and he intends to enjoy as much of it as possible while he has the opportunity. He's not opposed to the idea of mentoring, you understand. But that's something that ranks right up there with doing his taxes and flossing his teeth on his list of priorities.

If this describes you, let me commend to your instruction the story of King Hezekiah. Hezekiah's reign over Judah was a magnificent peak towering over two dismal chasms that dropped off on either side. His father Ahaz and his son Manasseh were two of the worst kings in all of Judah's history. By contrast, Hezekiah was one of the best. He enacted desperately needed spiritual reforms and carried out extensive improvements to his nation's infrastructure and defenses.

But later in his life, Hezekiah contracted a terminal illness. In fact, the prophet Isaiah told him to "put your house in order, because you will die; you will not recover" (2 Kings 19:1).

Now what would you do in that circumstance? Perhaps the same thing that Hezekiah did: he begged God to spare his life. He reminded Him of all the good things he had done. The Lord had regard for his prayer, and not only healed him, but added fifteen years to his life.

However, the extension turned out to be a mixed blessing. Shortly after his recovery, Hezekiah entertained an entourage of ambassadors from Babylon, but in doing so committed a serious blunder. The Babylonians were still relatively minor players in the geo-politics of the day. At that point in history, Assyria was the superpower that dominated the Middle East. Perhaps Hezekiah was motivated by pride, but he foolishly showed them "all that was in his storehouses—the silver, the gold, the spices and the fine oil—his armory and everything found among his treasures. There was nothing in his palace or in all his kingdom that Hezekiah did not show them" (20:13).

Imagine a president of the United States giving a group of foreign visitors unlimited access to the White House, the Capitol, the Pentagon, the Central Intelligence Agency, the Federal Reserve Bank, the Internal

Revenue Service, Fort Knox, the Strategic Air Command, and every other key nerve center for the nation's defenses and economy. That's essentially what Hezekiah did. How long do you think it would be before a leader like that would be impeached?

Hezekiah faced a different sort of "impeachment" for his foolish mistake. Isaiah told him that someday, the Babylonians would come back and clean his country out. Every single thing that Hezekiah had shown them would be carried off to Babylon. Nothing would be left. Worst of all, many of Hezekiah's descendants would be taken as slaves to serve in the Babylonian court.

There are two lessons to be learned from the later years of this man's life. The first is, don't ask God to prolong your years if you are not using the years you already have. In a way, Hezekiah would have been better off dying fifteen years early. Certainly his country would have. It was during those extra years that he compromised his descendants' future.

I'm afraid a similar thing is happening today. Statistically speaking, men are living longer than ever—an average of about 78 years for white males. But for many, while their days are lengthened, their influence is not. Instead of going out in a blaze of glory, they are dying "inch by inch playing silly little games," as one poet has so aptly described it. Is that the case for you? As you wrap up your life, are you frittering away day after day in the pursuit of silly little games? Or are you preparing your posterity to take over after you're gone?

The second lesson of Hezekiah is, whatever choices you make today will affect your children and their children tomorrow. Do you know what Hezekiah's response was to Isaiah's dire prediction? When the prophet told him his descendants would die in a foreign land, he said, "The word of the Lord you have spoken is good" (20:19).

Good? How in the world could Isaiah's word be construed as good? How could Hezekiah find good in the destruction of everything he had spent his life building? The text explains his reasoning: "Will there not be peace and security in my lifetime?" he thought to himself.

What a sobering parallel to our own times. How many people today are settling for peace and security while the world is hurtling toward unprecedented crises. Just look at the troubles around us—for example, in our cities, in our ever-escalating national debt, and in our environment. In area after area, anyone can see that disaster looms on the horizon.

Yet the tendency is to push off the hard choices and changes into the future, because making them today is just too inconvenient. Peace and security, that's what matters. "Don't bother me now," is the attitude. "Let someone else deal with it. I'm too old. I've already done my part. Yes, I know disaster may be coming. But at least it won't arrive until after I'm dead and gone!"

In this way, some of us are robbing our children's future. In fact, when I look around at the men approaching their senior years today, I have to confess that I see a lot more Hezekiahs than I do Calebs. There are a lot more guys opting for comfort and ease than there are helping the next generation conquer new territory. I say that to our shame; I wish it were otherwise.

When men get old, they start to think about what they will leave behind, and to whom they will give it. They make out a will and designate the beneficiaries. Who will get their money? What will happen to their houses? Who will inherit their personal property—their books, their collections, their tools, their trophies? If they've had a business, who will take it over? Men hire lawyers and spend countless hours putting their affairs in order.

And for good reason. A recent Cornell University study predicts that during the next fifty years, the United States will experience the most massive transfer of wealth in the history of the world—more than $10 trillion—as the Baby Boomers inherit what my generation leaves behind.

What an incredible legacy! And yet, I'm compelled to ask, of what value is this unprecedented windfall if it is not accompanied by a similar transfer of "human capital"? You see, we can button down all the legalities of who inherits our wealth, but we also ought to be asking, who is going to inherit our wisdom?

A Legacy of Wisdom

There is no greater legacy for a man to leave than wisdom. Solomon— who knew a thing or two about wealth and wisdom—wrote in Ecclesiastes that wisdom is unsurpassed as a gift that keeps on giving:

Wisdom, like an inheritance, is a good thing
and benefits those who see the sun.
Wisdom is a shelter
as money is a shelter,
but the advantage of knowledge is this:
that wisdom preserves the life of its possessor. (7:11–12)

Wisdom lasts. That's why Solomon urged young men to "get wisdom. Though it cost all you have, get understanding" (Proverbs 4:7). Friend, there are men out there who would willingly give all they have—indeed, they would forego any material inheritance—if instead they could inherit your wisdom. To deprive them of that is like dying without a will. So I challenge you: Build into another man's life. By doing so, you will pass on a permanent, even an eternal, legacy.

ESTABLISHING A MENTORING PROGRAM IN YOUR CHURCH

After reading this book, you may be wondering what it would take to develop a formal mentoring program in your local church. I heartily encourage you toward that end. But you should know up front that you will be pioneering in territory where few have ventured, with few landmarks to guide you.

I'm bullish on the concept of mentoring in church congregations, because I believe churches generally do better when they grow their leadership, rather than import it. Furthermore, mentoring offers a way for pastors to *exponentially* increase the delivery of spiritual services to their people with *no* increase in the church's budget and only a modest demand on their personal schedule.

Does that sound attractive? Then let me make a few suggestions as you think about implementing the principles and processes of mentoring in your congregation.

It's About Relationships

First, programs for mentoring succeed or fail depending on the extent to which they honor the fundamental law that *mentoring involves a relationship, not a program.* You can put a group of older and younger men in a room, pair them off, and call it "mentoring," but if the relationships go nowhere, genuine mentoring is not taking place.

In other words, you can't force men into mentoring relationships. You shouldn't even try. But what you can do is open the door to the *possibility* of relationships. You may not be able to make the chemistry happen, but you can put the chemicals together under conditions that encourage a reaction. Your program can be a catalyst for getting mentoring relationships started and keeping them fresh and alive.

Getting the Relationships Going

So start by providing opportunities for relational interaction to take place. For example, set up men's breakfasts, men's retreats, outings, work projects, field trips, and other events where men are put together under formal auspices in order to stimulate informal (but valuable) exchanges. And whatever you do, get different generations involved with each other, rather than segregated from one another, as is often the practice.

In planning these venues, give the participants a simple exercise or two to get beneath the exterior just a bit. For instance, in welcoming men to a breakfast, you might announce, "Men, our speaker today will be talking about what it means to be a godly father. While you're talking around the tables, I'd like to ask each of you to tell the others one thing you have valued about your own father, and also one thing you wish your father had done differently." That's a small but significant question that might spark some deeper interaction—especially if you have primed some of the older men to be on the lookout for potential protégés.

A Key to Success: Recruiting Mentors

That brings us to the issue of recruiting mentors. This is probably the key to making a formal (or intentional) program work. I've already described the qualifications and duties of a mentor, so I won't repeat those here. But I urge pastors and church leaders to enlist older men into the mentor's role. They need to be coaxed, or else they'll probably remain on the sidelines.

How do you get a man to serve as a mentor? I recommend approaching him individually, not to make a demand, but to show him an opportunity. Don't just call him up and say, "We're looking for mentors. Would you like to be one?" He'll almost certainly decline. Instead, you will probably have to do some educating, so that he understands what you are talking about. You will likely have to overcome some preconceived notions about the process of mentoring, and some objections that he may offer as to why he is not fit to serve as a mentor. You will probably have to explain that mentoring is not teaching; it is modeling, being there for a younger man, being available to him, and most of all, just being himself around him. You should, of course, stress the benefits—to him, to any protégés with whom he might work, and to the church congregation.

In this regard, you might want to put a copy of this book into his hands. After all, it was written to accomplish the very objective that you are trying to achieve—to recruit men into the mentoring process. So use it for that purpose.

Strengthening Programs, Not Adding Them

Here's one approach to recruiting and training mentors. Invite a group of prospects—whom you have already approached individually—to a meeting, where you lay out the vision for the program, explain what you are asking, point out the benefits, and answer questions. Challenge the men to seriously consider making a commitment to serve as a mentor, and then follow-up individually to learn their decisions.

Next, invite those who agree to become mentors to a training session or retreat to talk about how to find and recruit a protégé, how to make the most of the relationship, and what problems to anticipate. Then send them back into the congregation to see what God will do, what mentoring relationships will form.

One advantage of this approach is that you are not taking men out of already existing programs, which probably cannot afford to lose them; you are helping men become more effective in the programs where they are already serving. Thus your mentoring "program" does not compete with other programs on the church's docket. Instead, it strengthens them by integrating mentoring principles into what is already taking place. Imagine the long-term impact if your congregation's Boy Scout troop, small groups, committees, or task forces were dotted by mentoring relationships!

Expectations

Hyper-inflated expectations will kill a formal mentoring program faster than anything else. Suppose you pair ten men as mentors with ten protégés. Of those relationships, at least three will probably not work out at all. Four or five will be so-so, and maybe two or three will be quite positive, enduring, and perhaps even outstanding. Is that OK? You bet! It's fantastic, because something is better than nothing, and also because you can't always gauge the value of the relationship right away. Sometimes it takes years for the protégé to recognize its benefits. But that delay in no way diminishes the value of the experience.

The point is, keep your expectations realistic. Keep them low and achievable. For example, a simple program might call for the mentor and protégé to check in with each other by phone once a week, and then get together in person once a month. That may not seem like a lot of interaction, but it can be. And isn't it a lot more than is currently taking place?

Mentoring is not about goals, quotas, or achievement badges. It's about inner work and personal growth. Provide a climate for mentoring to happen, but leave the results to God.

What to Call It

One way to lower anxiety is to avoid labeling the program as a "mentoring" program. That will probably be too intimidating for many (see pp. 95–96). Be creative and call it something else, such as Men's Challenge, The 2:2 Program (based on 2 Timothy 2:2), The Brotherhood of Jethro (or Barnabas, after either of those two models of mentoring in the Bible), Reach, Pathfinders, New Horizons, Man to Man, etc.

Support from the Top

Whatever mentoring programs are developed, whether formal or informal, they *must* be supported from the top, or they will neither thrive nor survive. Senior pastors must get behind the program, not just to sign-off on it (permit it), but hopefully to sign onto it (promote it and participate in it). If you are a pastor, I urge you to preach and teach on the nature and value of mentoring. Encourage it from the pulpit. See if you can make mentoring not just a program in your congregation, but a way of life, a way of developing people into the image of Christ.

Resources to Consider

If you are serious about establishing a formal mentoring program in your church or organization, the following books will be helpful. They describe principles and models from churches, the corporate sector, and the public schools:

- Ted Engstrom with Norman B. Rohrer. *The Fine Art of Mentoring.* Brentwood, Tenn.: Wolgemuth & Hyatt, 1989.
- Thomas W. Evans. *Mentors: Making a Difference in Our Public Schools.* Princeton, N.J.: Peterson's Guides, 1992.
- Margo Murray with Marna A. Owen. *Beyond the Myths and Magic of Mentoring: How to Facilitate an Effective Mentoring Program.* San Francisco, Calif.: Jossey-Bass, 1991.
- Linda Phillips-Jones. *The New Mentors and Protégés.* Grass Valley, Calif.: Coalition of Counseling Centers, 1993.
- Michael Zey. *The Mentor Connection.* Homewood, Ill.: Dow Jones-Irwin, 1984.

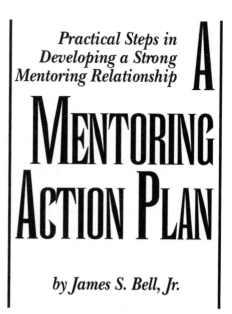

Practical Steps in Developing a Strong Mentoring Relationship

A MENTORING ACTION PLAN

by James S. Bell, Jr.

This book already contains much practical information and advice to put into practice, so why an action plan? If you're a typical reader, you probably want to get an overview of the entire scope of the subject first and then respond. Perhaps you even acted upon some of the suggestions already. But more than likely, you haven't systematically applied everything, chapter by chapter.

Even if you have already found your mentor and/or protégé, you probably have finished the book before sharing the content. This guide can therefore help you in some important ways. First, each question or action point asks you to respond personally and to be accountable based on your peculiar circumstances and needs. Just as no two mentoring relationships are alike, so too the quest itself forms a portrait of you and your eventual mentor. There are no "right" answers, no condemnation for not answering certain questions, and no guaranteed outcomes. Yet, as the Bible says, you will reap what you sow. This can be an effective tool to help achieve the goals of this book if you put in the "sweat equity" required.

Second, like the book, Part 1 of the Action Plan will allow you to do all the groundwork in finding the best mentor(s) possible and getting the relationship underway. Conversely, Part 2 will help you as a mentor to discover your protégé.

Since most of us are called to be both mentor and protégé, we can answer the questions in both parts to establish two relationships. In each chapter, after reviewing "A Key Thought," you can respond to several suggestions in "Mentoring Matters." This leads to a "Point of Action" that will move you along in the mentoring process. Finally, each chapter offers an opportunity to apply the ideas with your mentoring partner; "Relating

Together" is helpful even if you don't have a partner, as it shows you a relationship in action and gives ideas you can use later.

I want to emphasize, however, that all the questions in this entire guide may easily be used within the context of a later established relationship, after you, the reader, have finished the book. Yet if you work through these exercises first, you will perform a courtesy for your mentoring partner. You will have done your research and prepared, giving your partner a strong rationale in choosing him. Rather than merely saying, "Here, read this 270-page book," you can discuss how you answered key questions and draw your partner into the process.

Your new relationship needs some structure, clear communication, goals, etc. The parameters are contained within this guide, and you can learn a lot about each other as your partner learns how you went through the process. You can use this material in your first five, ten, or even twenty meetings to set the stage for further discussions and activities. That depends on the needs and desires of you and your partner.

As you may have already noticed, *As Iron Sharpens Iron* is not a book to file the content in your brain and say you understand more about mentoring. You can't say "been there, done that" if you haven't experienced the doing! So this guide is included to reinforce the points that should have motivated you and give them more concrete definable shape.

Mentoring is not meant to be a course or a technique but an art. It may take surprising and unexpected turns, but whatever happens, it will be profitable. Use this guide not in a legalistic way but as a vehicle to free you, with the help of another man, to be the great man God intends you to be.

Part 1

Chapter 1
Becoming a Marked Man

Key Thought

Men of every age across the entire country are seeking other men with more wisdom and experience to help them face the difficult challenges ahead. Yet too many of us are in a wilderness, trying to cross it ourselves, lacking a mentor to guide us.

Mentoring Matters

1. Think back over the course of your entire life. Apart from your parents, identify those individuals who have had a significant, positive impact on your life. Name as many as you can.

AGE	PERSON	EVENT(S)	OUTCOME
1–10 years old			
10–20 years			
20–30 years			
30–40 years			
40–50 years			
50–60 years			

2. In each case above, describe the possible negative consequences in your life if that person had not influenced you.

3. If you have had no, or very few, mentors in your past, what opportunities or individuals did you miss, and how might those potential mentors have made a difference?

4. Examples are listed from Atlanta, Boston, and Buffalo of those seeking to be mentored. Can you think of at least one friend, family member, or

someone in your community pursuing a mentoring relationship? What are the reasons, and will (or has) it made a difference? Describe it.

Point of Action

Make a phone call or drop a line to as many past mentors as possible. Tell them how their words and actions changed your life. Thank them and allow them to express their thoughts on the past relationship.

Relating Together

Each man should share with the other the critical areas of character development in his past that were influenced by a mentor. How does the present relationship fit the pattern?

Chapter 2
"I Believe in You"

Key Thought

Growth and learning are not just the result of new information but also include personal choices, accountability, and modeled behavior. The latter three can't take place outside the context of a relationship, and mentoring is an effective way to learn and grow.

Mentoring Matters

1. Identify as many of the following attainments in your life that were acquired primarily through behavioral modeling as opposed to mere information: business skills, hobbies, maintenance skills, spiritual disciplines, marriage and parenting, finance, and more.

2. Think back to the example of the seminary student and company president (p. 29). Identify an individual with whom you can "trade" knowledge or skills that would be mutually beneficial. What strengths and weaknesses can you exchange with one another to fill up what is lacking?

3. In the "matrix of influence" it's important to see how our mentors were themselves shaped, aided, and influenced by others. Reviewing the names you listed in your chapter 1 responses, what other individuals and influences were part of the process but played a bit part or supporting role?

4. When a mentor positively affects you, it can in turn be felt by those people and circumstances you encounter. Name a powerful instance where, due to a mentor's influence, others gained because of your growth.

5. In scaling a mountain, men linked together can prevent one man from a dangerous fall. Think of an instance where a mentoring relationship prevented a tragedy in a man's life. Now contemplate the opposite: recall a downfall that may have been prevented by accountability to a wiser man.

Point of Action

Compared to their predecessors of the past, there is a great shortage of leaders today, perhaps due to a shortage of mentors. Approach or read about a successful leader and explore the mentoring connection. What types of character qualities peculiar to leaders would you seek in your ideal mentor?

Relating Together

Begin to share your overall strengths and weaknesses as well as skills and interests. Discuss how you might trade off strengths to compensate for personal weak areas (i.e., a carpentry job for tax form help, etc.)

Chapter 3
Know What You Need

Key Thought

Because of our own blind spots and subjectivity, self-assessment is difficult. We may not see our liabilities and may underestimate our attributes. Yet using the right tools in this area will help later in finding the right mentor.

Mentoring Matters

Though you read this chapter, you probably only addressed the five points of self-assessment in a superficial way. Let's go in greater depth by answering each of the five in relation to career, spiritual life, and family.

1. *What do you want out of life?* List on three separate sheets what you want to accomplish in the three categories above in (a) five years, (b) ten years, (c) twenty years. Make subcategories of knowledge, attitudes, habits, and skills.

2. *What price will you pay?* In each time period above set concrete objectives to attain your goals. Secondly, prioritize with a plan for eliminating obstacles. Count the cost by listing possible sacrifices of lesser priorities.

3. *How can these objectives be carried out?* We fail to plan adequately by failing to ask who, what, where, when, and why. In terms of your prospective mentor nail these down with specific answers.

4. *What is your personal dynamic?* Begin by giving reasons where you fit within the following personality spectrums: introvert/extrovert; high/low energy; relationships/ideas; analytical/intuitive; leader/team player. Explain why you may also be a combination. Again, separate career, family, and spiritual life.

5. *How do you gain knowledge and skill?* Review your life, what you are competent at and enjoy. Isolate three important tasks or activities in

spiritual life, family, and career, and decipher how it "clicked" when you became proficient—written, practiced, tutored. For what tasks was learning the hardest?

Point of Action

Get a better grasp on personal dynamics and its implications for mentoring. Research or observe two members of the same or similar profession. How do their styles differ in carrying out personal tasks? Do certain tasks fit better with particular ways of learning or personality types?

Relating Together

Exchange your personal goals, objectives, and how to attain them. Compare and contrast both your individual paths and your personal style of achievement.

Chapter 4

What Mentors Look For

Key Thought

How do you measure up as a protégé? A mentor is looking for certain qualities that are worth investing in for the future. A good mentor has limited time and many potential protégés. Five qualities that most mentors look for in a potential protégé are (1) being goal-oriented, (2) seeking challenges, (3) taking initiative, (4) showing an eagerness to learn, and (5) accepting personal responsibility.

Mentoring Matters

Evaluate where you are in these five areas that mentors regard as vital:

1. *Goal orientation.* Review the goals you prepared in the last chapter. Are they measurable, attainable, and realistic enough for a mentor to get involved? Spend time establishing, praying, and refining before you try to implement them.

2. *Challenge and responsibility.* Give two examples in your own professional life where you strongly sought (a) the next more difficult task (b) with greater responsibility (c) based on preconceived goals to reach maximum potential. List two occasions where you failed to do the above.

3. *Initiative.* All of us both succeed and fail in being self-starting. Under "Success in Initiative" recall specifics in both cases and relate to the following traits: confidence, deep desire, clear vision, strong will, and perseverance. Under "Failure in Initiative": self-doubt, laziness, passivity, fear, and ignorance.

4. *Eagerness to learn.* Look at the following components related to the mentoring process, and ask yourself how you can improve: (a) becoming more teachable, (b) overcoming the difficult aspects, (c) being curious about the unknown, (d) being willing to explore different avenues, and (e) having a passion to grow in knowledge.

5. *Personal responsibility.* In the long run you have to make it happen. What may impede you from acting upon your mentor's advice or modeling? Analyze whether you have not taken action for any of the following reasons: (a) distractions, (b) lack of commitment, (c) procrastination, (d) shifting responsibility.

Point of Action
You may feel discouraged now and not feel much like mentoring material. Seek out someone who can reinforce your present strengths and potential. See your realization of need as the best first step.

Relating Together
Based on the protégé's self-rating, the mentor should assess these five criteria and make recommendations. If an area is deficient, agree upon a remedy.

Chapter 5

The Marks of a Mentor

Key Thought

As you seek a mentor, remember that he should meet your needs in a give-and-take relationship and be willing to risk his time and expertise for your development. He should possess the character and experience you need to meet your goals for personal growth.

Mentoring Matters

1. Identify three potential mentors by contacting others who know them well. Begin to evaluate what qualities and characteristics you seek in a mentor. Below is a suggested list, just to get you started. You can add other virtues as well. Rank in order of importance, considering your earlier objectives.

___ Faithfulness	___ Self-Confidence	___ Self-Control
___ Honesty	___ Patience	___ Leadership
___ Humility	___ Service	___ Professionalism
___ Godliness	___ Drive	___ Multiple Talents
___ Ambition	___ Practicality	___ Wisdom

2. What kind of relational style do you seek? Describe the balance you desire between speaking and listening, sharing your life versus his.

3. Create a survey regarding prospective mentors by first gathering a list of names. Check with their associates (of all types) regarding their character and proficiencies. Do they see a match with you?

4. As you pursue the list of prospective mentors, gather information on the following:

   (a) Their full network of resources
   (b) Others benefiting from their wisdom
   (c) Their communications skills

(d) Their application of wisdom to your needs
(e) Their openness to sensitive subjects
(f) Their ability to get you to the "next level"

5. Among the skills you seek in a mentor, the most critical probably are modeling, correct diagnosis, and lack of a personal agenda. Through either direct contact or the reports of others, determine the following:

(a) How does the prospective mentor live what he preaches? (Evidence of fruit in his life.)
(b) How well does he discern root issues and apply recommendations for growth in those he influences? (Can he read and develop character?)
(c) Is he ego-centered or attempting to personally gain more from others? (Does he want to receive more than he gives?)

Point of Action
If you have been able to apply the aforementioned to more than one potential mentor, compare your findings. Seek a person whom you respect and knows you well and ask for his advice concerning the results. Do your interpretations match? What future course does he recommend?

Relating Together
In retrospect, review with your chosen mentor why he fits the criteria in this chapter and how your unique attributes will blossom under his direction.

Chapter 6
How to Find a Mentor

Key Thought

Now you need to pray in faith, look around carefully, and approach a mentor about getting together. Try to find someone who meets the criteria of chapter 5, and who has the right "chemistry" and mutual interests.

Mentoring Matters

Let's expand on some of the activities suggested in the chapter to make sure you follow through.

1. Explore the locations where you might find the right mentor—churches, businesses, family, social settings, etc. Don't leave out any potential target areas.

2. In each place above, locate the key contacts that will open doors to the right mentor. Don't eliminate ethical non-Christians.

3. Based on findings from the above research, identify those whom you consider older and more experienced "Pauls" who can mentor you. Evaluate your preferences.

4. Now pinpoint your "Barnabas" men—the soul brother peers with whom you can enter into a mutual mentoring arrangement. Who has the most compatible situation to yours?

5. Finally, you are left with the "Timothys"—the younger men who need your wisdom and guidance. Who would most profit from your unique gifts and experience?

Point of Action

Make an attempt to get together on an informal basis with a Paul, a Barnabas, and a Timothy. Think about the need in your life to be led by an older man, encouraged by a peer, and to help shape a younger man.

Relating Together

Get a better understanding of your own Paul/Timothy relationship. Study the Scriptures together and review the exhortations and examples of Paul to Timothy.

Chapter 7
First Steps

Key Thought

There are many ways, rather than a "right" way, to obtain the services of a mentor. The approach varies along a continuum from friend to stranger. With a mentor whom you don't know, you must attract his interest, win his trust, and actively persuade him to meet your needs.

Mentoring Matters

1. Start with the men you already know fairly well. What levels of trust and appreciation have been established? Based on that, how can you approach each one with a clear idea of what the relationship will accomplish?

2. Think of those you are aware of through personal recommendation or may know distantly. How can you "leverage" your limited knowledge to gain a closer relationship?

3. List those you admire from afar but with whom you have no connection. In this case you will especially need the twenty ideas in the chapter for the first overture. List two or three (if possible) that might work to gain each individual's attention.

4. Every mentor has some problem or need, however small or mundane. Whether it's a car wash or technical information, seek to discover a potential mentor's need and take steps to fill it.

5. Since most men don't view themselves as would-be mentors, plan a "covert" strategy. Begin by using alternative terms that suggest at least a short-term relationship in which you both will concretely benefit.

Point of Action

Of the twenty time-tested approaches listed, determine to put a minimum of three into action among any or all of your three categories of mentors (friend, acquaintance, stranger). Remember, creativity and initiative are the keys to success in these areas. Pray and plan carefully as you make these activities fit your peculiar style and circumstances.

Relating Together

Many of these twenty items may become further activities in your established relationship. Sharing information, evaluating something produced, and joint projects are just a few suggestions. Agree on at least one activity that will enhance both parties and plan a way to get it done.

Chapter 8
Strategies for Growth

Key Thought

Whether your relationship is formal or informal, you need a concrete agenda with realistic expectations. Consider your immediate needs yet relate them to the larger issues in your life. Start by having your mentor evaluate an immediate process or problem in your life.

Mentoring Matters

1. In mapping your agenda you may have some outstanding goals. Yet surface difficulties may point to some deep-rooted liabilities in your character. Start where you are by listing up to three core areas where you need to receive serious help.

2. Now on the positive side: based on your strengths and accomplishments, list three areas where you believe you can make great long-term strides in personal development and achievement.

3. Recall the story of a need for a better prayer life being linked to a lack of discipline. Try to link some smaller felt needs to failure in broader areas. Be open as you think and pray about this, but not overly harsh on yourself.

4. The ultimate goal of mentoring is to make you into a wiser, more mature, more Christlike person. Write a two-page biography of what you imagine yourself to be if this became reality. Create a typical day's thoughts, actions, and words.

5. Some structured mentoring programs were illustrated. Think of some you are personally aware of in businesses, churches, or even families. Can you incorporate any of their principles or goals into your agenda?

Point of Action
Carry out at least one activity related to a problem or process in this chapter. Invite your potential mentor to participate. Prayer and worship should be a mandatory second activity and should precede your choice here.

Relating Together
In formal mentoring programs, a learning contract is often utilized. Though you and your mentor may be more laid back, a clearly defined set of expectations is important. Try to list a half dozen or so of these and discuss their role in your relationship as you go forward.

Chapter 9
Caution: Men at Work!

Key Thought

Through unrealistic or unfulfilled expectations, the mentoring relationship can fall short. The mentor may attempt to be controlling for the advancement of his own agenda; he may even fail in critical areas. The important thing is to take responsibility for our own actions and responses.

Mentoring Matters

1. As you look toward or evaluate an existing relationship, make a list, based on implicit expectations, of what could go wrong. How might the relationship, its benefits, or the mentor himself be potentially disappointing? What obstacles, assumptions, circumstances, weaknesses, etc., might get in the way of your positive goals?

2. Assuming that your mentor will disappoint you, if perhaps only to a small degree at some point in the future, how will you deal with it? Make a list of the ways he could disappoint: missed appointment, not enough input, etc. Now rehearse how to respond in honesty, accountability, and gentleness.

3. Have you ever known someone who could have been a mentor and certainly was a model but had a major fall? How did this shake your confidence in leaders? For each individual you know like this, write out some positive lessons and safeguards you can apply for your own life.

4. We need to counsel each other regardless of our spiritual standing. Even the strongest mentor faces weaknesses and pitfalls. How might you be able to admonish, encourage, direct, or comfort your mentor regarding areas of potential difficulty in his life?

5. Remember the story of the eagles in free-fall at Glen Eyrie? Do you feel pushed beyond your capacity in an area of your life? What steps can you

take to claim responsibility and face squarely the difficulties? How can your mentor help in the process without being too demanding or controlling? Where might you be pushed too hard, and how can you communicate this as well?

Point of Action

As well as seeking recommendations regarding the effectiveness of a given mentor, find out who has actually spent time in a mentoring (or similar) type relationship. Ask them whether they "graduated" and the degree of success in the experience. Were there control problems or insufficiencies? Learn also the positives and keep a record.

Relating Together

As a mentor, be honest with your protégé about your weaknesses. Recount instances where you made mistakes and perhaps didn't even learn from them. Be vulnerable enough to admit that much of your success was not your accomplishments but, rather, God's grace. Allow your protégé to have permission to correct and advise you when necessary.

Chapter 10
Taking Responsibility

Key Thought

There is a growing frustration among men regarding lack of strong growth in Christ. The process of merely acquiring information doesn't substitute for learning by observing and doing. Effective growth occurs only by obedience (practicing what we know or understand).

Mentoring Matters

1. Look back at your life and observe three sets of categories, where you attained (a) knowledge instead of wisdom, (b) achievement instead of character, and (c) profit instead of creativity. How might you have gained

the latter in each case? Look ahead at your mentoring goals, and plan how to attain these three attributes instead of their counterfeits.

2. Christlikeness takes in every aspect of our identity. Is your growth balanced? Ask yourself these (and other) questions in each area:

- *Intellectual:* Am I developing my mind to its full capacity in all areas of interest?
- *Physical:* Is diet, rest, and exercise in order?
- *Social:* Am I pursuing deep, meaningful relationships which are mutually beneficial?
- *Emotional:* Am I reacting at the heart level in a mature fashion?
- *Spiritual:* Am I practicing the spiritual disciplines in a full, balanced way?

3. The authors exhort us to make mentoring a way of life. List multiple mentoring possibilities in other less significant areas you haven't thought about—perhaps hobbies or new ventures. Think about the kind of mentors you will need five, ten, and twenty years from now. The latter is a good exercise for future planning.

4. A major point was made regarding obtaining mentors for your children. List your children, their needs at this stage in life, and the potential mentors from school, church, sports, etc. Begin to approach your kids and these individuals regarding various possibilities. How can your parenting improve with the mentoring dimension brought in?

5. We've talked before about finding a Timothy. This may be frightening because as a protégé you may feel you need a mentor first. Nevertheless, younger brothers can profit from your experience. Sit down with those whom you know may need only the following: (a) someone who listens to their needs and concerns; (b) someone who cares about them; (c) someone who simply tells them stories from your life regarding critical situations; (d) someone who merely supports them in their struggles. If you are willing to do the above, you can truly help a young Timothy.

Point of Action

Review your growth in Christ by recalling significant changes in your walk with Him. Did these events occur from knowledge or obedience, or a combination of the two? Did they come from spiritual disciplines or relationships with others? Choose three principles from Scripture that seem difficult and determine ways (through God's grace) to obey them. Search out someone who has obeyed these principles for help.

Relating Together

Ask your mentor to help you use some of the skills described above to, in turn, mentor your new Timothy. Let him share some of his "secrets" so you can utilize them in your own personal fashion with another younger man.

Part 2

Chapter 11
A Call for Mentors

Key Thought

Part 2 is addressed to mentors themselves. One of the reasons we lack strong leaders is the neglect of the mentoring process, which was behind the great Pauls and Timothys of the New Testament. Yet mentors only have to give of what they possess, which is far more than they realize. As you steer and balance your protégé, he'll do the rest.

Mentoring Matters

1. Let's look at some parallels to Paul/Barnabas/Timothy-type relationships. For peer mentoring, study what Scripture says about Jonathan and David. For an older/younger combination, take a closer look at Jethro-Moses. For a younger/older pair, look into Elisha-Elijah. Can you think of other subtle examples of mentoring in the Bible?

2. Some of the repercussions of divorce for children include insecurity, anger, under-achievement, and low self-esteem. Other root issues of abuse and neglect contribute to similar weaknesses. Think of a young man with gifts but a negative past. How might your mentoring transform these liabilities?

3. Analyze your negative attitudes toward mentoring. (Don't feel condemned by such feelings, as all potential mentors are guilty, at least to a small degree of such attitudes.) Assess the degree and reasons for the following six attitudes that may be present in you: lack of concern, skepticism, indifference, inadequacy, isolation, ignorance. Think and pray about a strategy to eliminate or minimize these road blocks.

4. Here is an effective way to overcome your feelings of inadequacy. Take time to write out in detail what you may have that a younger protégé may

need: experience, knowledge, access, money, resources, friendship, time, uniqueness. Don't be modest, but rather acknowledge God's blessings and go before Him willing to share with those less "fortunate" than you.

5. Though you may not immediately recognize it as such, mentoring in various degrees happens all around you. Identify three instances of one man influencing another. The type and degree may vary.) Perhaps they aren't thought of as mentoring. Don't focus on the famous or grand, but rather the humble and simple acts of service. Could you relate to another in a similar vein?

Point of Action

Do a low-key noncommittal survey of at least three younger men in the areas you operate in: church, work, extended family, or friends. Ask them questions related to whether they or their friends actively seek mentors. Why or why not? For what purposes, etc.?

Relating Together

The mentor should go back and review his initial reactions and observations with the protégé. Talk over the negative attitudes that have been lessened because of your relationship. Probe more deeply the positive assets listed that will benefit the protégé. Try to focus on at least one that hasn't been utilized yet.

Chapter 12
Why Be a Mentor?

Key Thought

Mentoring contains some major benefits for the mentor as well as the protégé. Though a mentor's personal accomplishments may wind down in his latter years, he is rejuvenated by investing in a legacy—the maturity of a younger generation of men with his own imprint.

Mentoring Matters

1. Many mentoring relationships are hinted at in the Bible. Choose one each from the Old Testament and New Testament in which you think the mentor probably gained as much from the relationship as the protégé. Do some background research, if necessary, to substantiate your claim.

2. If you're a mentor over age thirty, to some extent you experience current events and attitudes from an older paradigm or frame of reference. List some of the latest trends or attitudes in which you might gain great insight from a younger man's perspective.

3. You probably view accountability in terms of the judgment of your peers. Imagine a younger man considering not only your advice but also your behavior in terms of a role model. How could this assist your personal growth in a different way than through peer interaction?

4. Make a list of areas in your life where you've achieved peak performance and are moving on. Have you filled these vacancies with new challenges? How would sharing the wisdom of these successes and building up another man actually bring completeness as well as further challenge in your life?

5. You may feel that past choices or weaknesses disqualify you from becoming an effective role model. Analyze the failures and adversity in your life. How can you help a protégé learn from both your mistakes and

victories, warning him of pitfalls and yet seeing the opportunities for growth?

Point of Action

As they hit middle age, some men take unexpected but serious wrong turns. They lack the spiritual and emotional resources to cope with new challenges. Look at your next five years (regardless or your age) and seek the advice of others regarding the difficulties you might face. Ask them also to assess your capabilities to handle them and what steps you might take to discipline and strengthen yourself for times ahead.

Relating Together

Discuss with your protégé the difference between success and significance for both the mentor and the protégé. Privately and then together examine your lives and determine where you have subtly used another's talents in the past for personal gain and where you have given your wisdom and experience to invest in others.

Chapter 13
What a Mentor Does

Key Thought

Young men see in older men the maturity they lack, yet older men may not be aware of this. For this reason a man may have unconsciously mentored others and not even realized it. There are simple gifts such as time, listening, your character, and your faith that will be extremely valuable to the protégé .

Mentoring Matters

1. In the story of the *Odyssey*, Mentor is a male guardian who possesses the gifts of peacekeeping, arbitration, and preserving community values. Do you demonstrate these leadership gifts? How? Also, how might they be used in conflicts your protégé may face?

2. Rate yourself on a scale of 1 to 10 (and explain why) in the following mentor-related roles. Then choose the one most important to you and decide how to improve.

___ Guide (directing others)
___ Exemplar (modeling character)
___ Trainer (shaping a skill)
___ Father figure (nurturing, discipling)
___ Teacher (instructing)
___ Tutor (aid to learning)
___ Counselor (ministering to deep needs)
___ Leader (blazing a trail)

3. Following is a list found in the chapter of very practical endowments to be shared with a protégé. Read the explanations in the text, and for each attribute give one specific way you can contribute.

Information Source   _____

Sounding Board   _____

Wisdom   _____

Confidant   _____

Skills and Behaviors   _____

Plans   _____

Feedback   _____

New Opportunities   _____

Coaching   _____

4. Flip back to the story of Tom and Richie. What seems like common place, low-key interaction turned out to be long-term, significant mentoring. With whom have you built up enough trust and friendship to offer advice in an important decision or spiritual commitment?

5. Though the ten questions on a mentor's suitability found in this chapter

are suggestive, treat them like the Ten Commandments. Read them over each day for a week, jotting down something new each day. After seven days, summarize your commitments, self-evaluation, and goals for growth. Realize that though you may be deficient in some areas, you do qualify and can improve with even a little effort.

Point of Action

It's very important to understand that what matters most is not that you view yourself as a mentor, but whether someone else sees you as such. Summon the courage to ask for an honest assessment by at least two younger men (as well as a couple of peers) who can evaluate your natural mentoring abilities and actions.

Relating Together

The protégé should pick out three of the ten questions of suitability where the mentor rates are above average or superior. The mentor should now settle on three that he wants to build for the future and explain why.

Chapter 14
How to Spot a Protégé

Key Thought

Both you and the protégé you choose stand to benefit by what you have to offer. How do you find the right one? First, ask critical questions about the protégé's background, interests, and commitments. Then ask yourself about your own motivation, contribution, and positive chemistry. Is there a fit?

Mentoring Matters

1. In seeking a protégé, you'll be tempted to employ two extremes: choosing on the spur of the moment or passively waiting. Make a commitment now that your future decision will be based on information carefully gathered and prayed about. The odds of incompatibility will be drastically reduced.

2. Deliberately call to mind some young men who don't fit the mold—that is, exhibit behavior or characteristics that aren't promising. Yet if God builds in "the right stuff" devise a scenario in which these individuals could succeed with direction that fits their peculiarities. Could one of these unusual men be influenced by you?

3. Asking a potential protégé the six personal questions found in the chapter may bring apprehension, to say the least. Turn back and review these six (pp. 171–173). Rehearse each question and how you would ask it in front of a friend or spouse, and request their feedback in order to make adjustments for the "performance" itself.

4. After gathering the data from the future protégé, link it to the next six questions pertaining to how his answers might relate to you. As you review your responses, determine the most critical factor that relates to the protégé, and secondly, the most important consideration for you. How do they mix together?

5. Weight and prioritize all twelve answers to both sets of questions. Create a one-page summary of the findings, and draw three simple conclusions at the bottom of the page.

Point of Action
Make a chart of the four options offered in the chapter's conclusion: (1) The relationship is not for you; (2) Postpone full involvement; (3) Begin, but with certain boundaries; (4) Go full force into the relationship as soon as possible. List what is likely to happen in each instance with a given candidate. Share your one final choice with your spouse, advisor, or peer.

Relating Together
Look at question six in the second set. The mentor should orally recount the protégé's "story" as the mentor perceives it. Devise plot characters and a "happy" ending, based partially upon solid mentoring further down the road.

Chapter 15
You Can Do It!

Key Thought

Men are not involved today in vital relationships where they can grow by sharing joint tasks. Many young men don't have a clear male concept because they haven't related to positive role models.

Mentoring Matters

1. Ask older members of your family how the "extended family/mentoring" concept worked with their parents and grandparents. Can you employ any of these principles with your own children, nieces, nephews, etc.?

2. Discipleship focuses on the commands of Christ. Mentoring expands this to include being a man of God in all areas. Think of three "non-spiritual" activities and how you would connect each to the development of your godliness as a man.

3. Effective praying, both for the right protégé and later with him, is more important than all the other human strategies listed. Search the Scriptures and explore some Christian books on the topic of praying fervently according to God's will.

4. Make a list of all your areas of expertise as well as basic knowledge. How can you use one or more of these areas as an excuse to help a younger man in need? Link these to a real-life situation in your church, workplace, etc. Seek to be mainly a support or facilitator at this point.

5. Now that you're thinking of how to help younger men with legitimate needs, review the list of deficiencies listed in the chapter: (1) prejudice of some type, (2) low self-esteem, (3) limited resources, (4) personal problems, (5) foolish mistakes, (6) minor hard knocks. How might this knowledge help you to be more patient with someone's weaknesses or lack of immediate progress?

Point of Action

Much of this chapter focuses on ways to approach a protégé. Make a commitment to follow through, and set up a meeting with at least one potential protégé. Ideally, this should be a male-oriented activity (to at least some degree) and fun, relaxing, or enjoyable. (This will help you as well, in terms of taking away some of the fear and seriousness.)

Relating Together

It is primarily the evaluation of the protégé as to whether the time spent has been worthwhile. This is a good opportunity to review the benefits of the relationship so far. Ask yourself—and then ask your protégé—whether the person serving as the mentor is at least supporting, if not leading. Then ask whether the protégé is following through on input in order to grow into a more godly man.

Chapter 16
Learning & Growing Together

Key Thought

A learning contract is essentially a statement of purpose with a specific plan for achieving it. This plan includes activities for the protégé relating to his abilities and objectives where he actively participates in the learning process.

Mentoring Matters

1. Create a short-term informal learning contract in which your protégé develops a skill. Besides a good agenda, make sure all the open-ended issues are dealt with, including change, flexibility, end-date, new developments, etc.

2. Ask the protégé to drive the agenda; have him clearly state needs, objectives, results. Now, modify and shape those points based on your experience, as well as realistic expectations.

3. Make an actual assignment from the contract. Go through the process with the protégé of briefing, practicing, execution, and debriefing. In your evaluation determine whether to move on or try again with new insight.

4. Choose at least one option from the following menu: case study, critical incident report, reading list, interview, and field trip. Do an in-depth study of the value, purpose, and benefits of your choice. Assign it to your protégé, once again being specific with parameters, and measure results.

5. Determine ahead of these options how you will deal with both success and failure. Map out the conditions under which you will let the protégé fail and how you will help him remedy his mistakes. Under what conditions will you intervene and protect him? Why?

Point of Action

As a result of your protégé's assignment, do something to encourage and affirm him. If he succeeded in his activity, give him a tangible reward of some sort. If he failed, applaud him for the effort, and, in a positive way, show him how he can improve.

Relating Together

More than likely, the protégé has achieved some growth or success. We often fail to capitalize on success as well as failure. Focus on that accomplishment rather than let it go by. Ask: (1) What can we learn? (2) How can we build? (3) How does it relate to strengths? (4) How does it confirm the value of mentoring?

Chapter 17

Problems & Pitfalls to Avoid

Key Thought
Some conflict is inevitable based on differing time commitments, potential competition, divergent motivations, and changing cycles in growth and learning. Yet if understood, these factors can be used to improve the quality of the mentoring relationship.

Mentoring Matters
1. One way to prepare for some relational conflict is to review your past male friendships. List the factors that caused division and misunderstanding. Which of these were inherent in you and which in your friend?

2. Based on the above assessment, how have you grown and changed so you won't repeat past mistakes? At the same time, what personality types do you think it best to avoid in order to prevent destructive conflict?

3. As you read this chapter you're probably still in the "definition" stage, although you may have assigned an activity to a protégé already. Map out a hypothetical "developmental" stage with all the parameters of time, objectives, achievements, etc. This will aid in both your commitment and expectations.

4. Now consider the "departure" stage. Though you may want to leave the door open for a long-term friendship, a formal recognition of completion is important. What kind of reward, ritual, or rite of passage can be conferred on your protégé for achievement? If you have a hard time with words, try to put in writing for him (projecting, of course) what this kind of relationship means to you. You can always revise later.

5. Envy, jealousy, and pride are very subtle rebels in our sin nature and will block God's flow of grace toward your protégé. Even if you don't directly begrudge his success, you may harbor your own problems with self-esteem, contentment, comparison, etc. Check your heart and repent.

Point of Action
Discuss with your potential (or actual) protégé his success factors, that is, the accomplishments, talents, and ambitions that will help contribute to learning and growth. Adjust your own preconceived agenda of assignments, feedback, etc., to realign to what motivates and activates his achievement.

Relating Together
Low motivation periods are perhaps the biggest threat to full completion of the learning contract. Review together the key reasons (found in the chapter) for this: time, boredom, non-productivity, distractions. Explore where these might be occurring to various degrees. Return to the energizing factors of purpose: abilities, personal satisfaction, and opportunities.

Chapter 18
Leaving a Legacy That Lasts

Key Thought
At this final point, there are varying degrees of commitment to the mentoring process. To ultimately abstain from the vital activity is to deny the next generation of men an inheritance of wisdom—with eternal consequences.

Mentoring Matters
1. Be truly honest with yourself: Which of the four categories of response to mentoring fit you? What will it take to go and do the "I can, I will" response within the next month?

2. How do you generally rate with resolutions and promises? What are the circumstances or character issues that cause you to break commitments? How can it be avoided with your mentoring decision?

3. Consider these two ways of changing your mind-set regarding mentoring: (1) Recognize your ability to influence someone in an existing

relationship in a new strategic way; (2) Realize that in the kingdom of God, Christlike influence is never minor but always significant.

4. List ten ideas in this book that appealed to you. Now commit to implement a percentage (at least 50 percent) of these principles at least one time, in at least one key relationship.

5. In addition to King Hezekiah, search for other incidents in Scripture where godly wisdom was not passed on. What might have changed in that next generation if the men had been given the proper guidance?

Point of Action

Mentoring is often multiplication rather than addition. Go out and apply the mentoring skills you've learned in this book to your existing relationships with men. How would you both be strengthened?

Relating Together

Talk with your protégé about the big picture. Discuss how your mentoring relationship fits into issues like the crisis in leadership, males abdicating their roles, loss of ethics, etc. How can each of you make a positive contribution?

Concluding Questions for Relating Together

1. If you are both convinced of the positive value of mentoring, agree to make a plan to jointly share its benefits with others. Name three good reasons why this is important.

2. Follow up on the above in practical ways: create brief oral and written presentations, be ready to answer questions, make a list of those who might be open and able, and go do it!

3. Bring your message specifically to your local church: (a) demonstrate the spiritual context, (b) talk to the elders about integration with discipleship or men's ministry, (c) be prepared to speak in different venues, i.e., Sunday school, men's group, etc.

4. Discuss and build into your objectives how your mentoring relationship will support your marriage. Though not discussed in the book, mentoring should be geared to improve your relationship with your spouse.

5. Other books on mentoring can serve a very useful purpose. Perform a literature review of other resources on mentoring, especially in the business and church environment.

6. Get involved as a team with a larger body of Christian men, at least on an occasional basis. This could include a conference of a national organization like Promise Keepers or your local Christian men's ministry. They'll get the message of mentoring by your very presence.

Notes

Chapter 2: "I Believe in You"

1. "Helping Dropouts Climb In," *New York Times,* 13 September 1986, 26.

Peer Mentoring

1. Jerry White, "A Friend on All Accounts," *Moody Monthly,* July/August 1991, 52.
2. Fred Hignell III, "Sharing the Paddle," *Moody Monthly,* July/August 1991, 51.
3. White, "A Friend on All Accounts," 52, 54.

Chapter 3: Know What You Need

1. "Letters," *New York,* 2 January 1995, 8.

Chapter 4: What Mentors Look For

1. Douglas Hyde, *Dedication and Leadership* (South Bend, Ind.: Notre Dame Univ. Press, 1966), 62-69.
2. William D. Hendricks, *Exit Interviews: Revealing Stories of Why People Are Leaving the Church* (Chicago: Moody, 1993), 295.

Chapter 10: Taking Responsibility

1. Ted Engstrom, *The Fine Art of Mentoring* (Brentwood, Tenn.: Wolgemuth & Hyatt, 1989), ix-x.
2. Richard Nelson Bolles, *What Color Is Your Parachute?* 1988 edition (Berkeley, Calif.: Ten Speed, 1988), 42-43.

Chapter 11: A Call for Mentors

1. Michael Medved, "Hollywood Vs. Religion," videotape produced by Chatham Hill Foundation, Dallas, Tex., 1994; distributed by Word Inc.
2. Anastasia Toufexis, "The Lasting Wounds of Divorce," *Time,* 6 February 1989, 61.

3. George Barna, *Today's Pastors* (Ventura, Calif.: Regal, 1993), 122.

4. This figure comes from church growth expert Karl George. It is corroborated by a recent study conducted by the Home Mission Board of the Southern Baptist Convention, which found that 80 percent of Southern Baptist churches are declining in membership. Other major denominations report similar findings.

Chapter 13: What a Mentor Does

1. Homer, *The Odyssey,* trans. Robert Fitzgerald (Garden City, N.Y.: Doubleday, 1961), 473-74.

Chapter 15: You Can Do It!

1. Dolphus Weary and William Hendricks, *"I Ain't Comin' Back"* (Wheaton, Ill.: Tyndale House, 1990), 46-47.

Chapter 18: Leaving a Legacy That Lasts

1. Michael Precker, "You say you want a resolution?" *Dallas Morning News,* 30 December, 1994, 1c.

Acknowledgments

Authoring a book is a bit like figure skating: to most observers it has the appearance of being a solo performance, or, as here, the coordinated efforts of a pair. But off the ice, out of the glare of the spotlight, can usually be found numerous figures without whose contributions the skater's routine would never have come together—coaches, choreographers, family, friends, sponsors, equipment suppliers, and a host of others. Our own team of supporters is too large to name in its entirety. But a few people deserve special recognition.

First, of course, are our own mentors, some of whom we have mentioned in the book. We are quick to acknowledge that we are like "turtles on a fencepost," to use Allan Emery's fitting metaphor. We are who we are today largely because of those who invested in us yesterday.

We also want to thank those who have regarded us as guides and mentors, again, some of whom we have mentioned. It's one thing to follow in someone else's footsteps, but it's another thing to forge a path for others. You learn a lot that you might not have recognized if it weren't for someone else watching and emulating you. So thanks to those who have helped us pay attention to our leadership.

John Van Diest, currently the head of Vision House Publishing, could be described as the visionary for this project from a publishing standpoint. A decade ago he encouraged Howard to put down in a book some of the lessons he had learned about mentoring. Even though John's plans for the project never quite materialized, his heart for it never wavered. He helped get the ball rolling so that, when the time and circumstances were right, the material was more or less ready to be delivered.

Bill received invaluable help and inspiration from Pete Hammond of Marketplace in Madison, Wisconsin, and Daryl Heald of the Capital Group in Atlanta, two men whose growing expertise in mentoring relationships is a treasure that ought to be mined for all it is worth.

Another key source of information was John Nieder of the Art of Family Living in Colorado Springs. And Brad Smith, formerly with the Center for Christian Leadership at Dallas Theological Seminary and now with Leadership Network in Tyler, Texas, was the primary source for the list of assessment tools (pp. 177–178).

Special thanks also go to Moody Press for its outstanding support in publishing this book. Greg Thornton, Bill Thrasher, Jim Bell, Jim Vincent, Dave DeWit, Evie Knottnerus, and countless other troops at Moody worked extraordinarily hard—yet with great patience—to bring the project together with seeming lightning speed. Add to this group the many people who reviewed the manuscript and thought enough of it to offer words of endorsement. We deeply appreciate your vote of confidence.

Finally, we are grateful to our families for seeing us through this effort—to Howard's wife Jeanne, and to Bill's wife Nancy and daughters Brittany, Kristin, and Amy. Without their love, patience support, and affirmation, this book would have been neither possible nor desirable.